DISRAELI

DISRAELI

**A PICTURE
OF THE VICTORIAN AGE**

by
ANDRÉ MAUROIS

Translated from the French by
HAMISH MILES
With a New Introduction by
HENRI PEYRE

TIME Reading Program Special Edition
TIME INCORPORATED · NEW YORK

EDITOR *Norman P. Ross*
EXECUTIVE EDITOR *Maitland Edey*
TEXT DIRECTOR *Jerry Korn*
ART DIRECTOR *Edward A. Hamilton*
CHIEF OF RESEARCH *Beatrice T. Dobie*

EDITOR, TIME READING PROGRAM *Max Gissen*
RESEARCHER *Joan Chambers*
DESIGNER *Ladislav Svatos*

PUBLISHER *Rhett Austell*
GENERAL MANAGER *Joseph C. Hazen Jr.*

TIME MAGAZINE
EDITOR *Roy Alexander*
MANAGING EDITOR *Otto Fuerbringer*
PUBLISHER *Bernhard M. Auer*

COVER DESIGN *Louis Di Valentin*

CONTENTS

Editors' Preface   ix

TIME Reading Program Introduction   xv

Part I

I.   TWO GENERATIONS   3
II.   SCHOOLS   9
III.   BRUMMELL AND ST. IGNATIUS   19
IV.   BUSINESS   27
V.   RETREAT   41
VI.   PILGRIMAGE   49
VII.   DOCTRINES   57
VIII.   THE CONQUEST OF LONDON   66
IX.   INDEPENDENT   77
X.   WOMEN   85
XI.   THE BADGE OF A PARTY   93
XII.   M.P.   101

Part II

I.	THE MAIDEN SPEECH	115
II.	WEDDINGS	128
III.	MARY ANNE	140
IV.	THE RIGHT HONOURABLE BARONET	148
V.	YOUNG ENGLAND	161
VI.	THE OAK AND THE REED	170
VII.	LEADER	190
VIII.	OBSTACLES	200
IX.	MR. GLADSTONE'S CRUEL DUTY	210
X.	SHADOWS	219
XI.	THE TOP OF THE GREASY POLE	230

Part III

I.	THE QUEEN	241
II.	MOURNING	252
III.	A CLOUD OF GRANDMOTHERS	264
IV.	THE CHIEF	271
V.	ACTION	281
VI.	ATROCITIES	292
VII.	WAR?	300
VIII.	THE CONGRESS OF BERLIN	312
IX.	AFGHANS, ZULUS, FLOODS	322
X.	THE OUTER WORLD	331
XI.	"HIS FAVOURITE FLOWER"	342

Note and Bibliography	353
Index	359

PUBLISHER'S NOTE

The three verses from Humbert Wolfe's "Humoresque" printed on the half-title page to Part III of this book appear by kind permission of the author and of Messrs. Ernest Benn, Ltd.

ANDRÉ MAUROIS

The name of André Maurois, author of some four dozen books in a writing career that spans almost five decades, today evokes somewhat the same mixed response that Benjamin Disraeli's name did in 1874. That year was a climactic one for Disraeli, erstwhile dandy, occasional novelist, brilliant orator and shrewd tactician in Parliament for 37 years. Rising above his checkered background, he assumed the office of Prime Minister—and promptly met with a startling change in his countrymen's attitude toward him. Maurois describes the phenomenon:

> The adventurer, his genius tolerated by some, his authority contested by others, referred to as "Dizzy" with a familiarity sometimes affectionate, sometimes

scornful, had now become an object of respect. . . . No people are more sensitive than the English to the beauty wherewith time can adorn an object; they love old statesmen, worn and polished in the struggle, as they love old leather and old wood.

And yet, as Maurois adds, "there were many who still associated with his name some confused notion of Oriental mystery."

The same might be said of the biographer. Like Disraeli, Maurois has been "worn and polished" in an enormously successful career; he has emerged as an old statesman of 20th Century letters and as "an object of respect." Yet, even as vague suspicions continued to haunt the English statesman, the French biographer is still viewed askance in certain quarters.

Significantly, Maurois' literary talents have seldom been questioned. He is highly admired for his versatility, and for the intelligence and sensitivity displayed in his wide-ranging works of history, criticism, fiction, satire, biography and autobiography. When *Disraeli* was published in France in 1927, an article in *The Yale Review* said: "M. Maurois' book . . . is wholly a work of art. It is a fancy picture, staged, lighted, and presented with such perfection of wit, style, finesse, and humor that . . . it may take a high place in French literature." The novelist Hugh Walpole found the book "playful without being childish, ironical without being bitter and as creative as a fine novel."

But Maurois' use of his skills, and the ultimate propriety of his biographical approach, have been challenged by several critics. Their basic position is that

Maurois, in attempting to capture the very essence of his subject's personality, goes a step beyond justifiable interpretation and practices artistic self-expression. Ironically, the biographer's interpretive rights had been won originally in a literary revolution which Maurois himself did much to shape.

Through the 19th Century, biography was generally written in the same vein as narrative history; it remained formal, respectful, definitive and safe. The extent of the biographer's task was to marshal all of the evidence, to present it fully and to let the facts speak for themselves. Literary felicity was deemed no virtue. Flights of wit, intuitive flashes of insight, free use of sprightly human sidelights, judicious editing of trivial or pedestrian documentation—all these were frowned on and held in check. Biography languished in a straitjacket.

But a rising undercurrent of romantic protest burst to the surface in 1918 with the publication of *Eminent Victorians* by the English stylist Lytton Strachey. This brilliant book deliberately broke all the old rules. It compressed four important lives—those of Cardinal Manning, Florence Nightingale, the great educator Thomas Arnold and General "Chinese Gordon"—into iconoclastic sketches that crackled with epigram and sardonic wit. Strachey prefaced the collection with a bold pronouncement of artistic principle. In sum, he asserted that a historic figure must be evaluated for himself, not merely as an interesting symptom of his age; it was not only proper but incumbent on the biographer, he said, to interpret and portray his subject as vividly as truth permitted.

Strachey's declaration launched biography as a recognized art form and enlisted a band of young intellectuals as "new" biographers. In the forefront was André Maurois, then 33 years old. Though he later judged Strachey's biographies "a shade nastier than is really fair," Maurois wholeheartedly endorsed Strachey's canon, calling him "the father and master of modern biography."

Maurois went on to make significant contributions to the modern school, testing its precepts in his biographies and elaborating its theories in various lectures and critical studies. But far from being a doctrinaire follower, he arrived at conclusions peculiarly his own, and he tried to bridge the gap between the new life studies and the old, conventional biography. He wrote: "The search for historical truth is the work of the scholar; the search for the expression of a personality is rather the work of the artist; can the two things be done together?" Obviously he believed that they could. But while Maurois scrupulously performed the scholar's work, his sympathies remained unmistakably on the side of the artist.

Of Maurois' five or six major biographies, none shows his ideas at work more graphically than *Disraeli*. Using techniques borrowed from the novelist, he presents Disraeli's life as a developing drama—almost as a plotted story. Lightly he sketches in social and political background as the information becomes relevant to Disraeli's private problems or public career. He does not hesitate to heighten dramatic effects or to play discreetly on sentiment. In glittering analyses of Disraeli's actions and reactions, Maurois creates in the reader the illusion that he is seeing the world through Disraeli's eyes.

Throughout the book, Maurois never fails to produce the concrete detail or anecdote that establishes points of character. To document young Disraeli's foppish excesses, Maurois includes a gilded inventory of one night's finery: "a coat of black velvet, poppy-coloured trousers broidered with gold, a scarlet waistcoat, sparkling rings worn on top of white kid gloves." To reveal the mettle beneath this rare bird's plumage, Maurois quotes Disraeli's scathing rejoinder to a member of Parliament who had slurred him: "I am one who will not be insulted, even by a Yahoo." Disraeli the diplomatist is shown working his suave flattery on Queen Victoria, sharing with that diligent diarist the phrase, "We authors. . . ."

Maurois lavishes special affection on Disraeli's wife Mary Anne. When Disraeli, debt-ridden in mid-career, married a well-to-do older widow, the gentry exchanged knowing glances; but Maurois makes amply clear the warmth and artless humor that endeared Mary Anne to Disraeli. One morning, after the Disraelis had spent the night as guests in a room next door to the famous general Lord Hardinge, Mary Anne exclaimed blithely at breakfast: "Oh, Lord Hardinge, I think I must be the happiest of women! . . . I've been sleeping between the greatest orator and the greatest soldier of the day!" Years later, in Disraeli's frail and somber old age, his devotion to Mary Anne remained touchingly youthful. As the statesman received an honorary doctorate at Oxford, Maurois records that "with his monocle he scanned the ladies' gallery, and, discovering Mary Anne, he threw up to her with his fingers an almost imperceptible kiss."

As the book runs its charming, effortless course, a sketchy impression of the author emerges along with his bold portrait of his subject. Maurois, besides being patently a romantic, is clearly a man of refined sensibilities, tolerant of his characters' weaknesses, urbane and ironic in tone but not supercilious, frank and compassionate yet with a deep natural reticence. Of course these traits ally Maurois closely with his own portrait of Disraeli, but they only suggest the profound similarities that link the two men. Their lives and outlooks are explored in the special Introduction written for this edition by the noted scholar Henri Peyre. Dr. Peyre, who like Maurois was educated in the French humanist tradition, leaves little doubt that Maurois saw himself in Disraeli—and that for once a biographer who saw himself in his subject was seeing right.

—THE EDITORS OF TIME

INTRODUCTION

Henri Peyre is a distinguished scholar of the literature and civilization of his native France. A past president of the Modern Language Association and a recipient of the Legion d'Honneur, he has been a professor at Yale University for almost three decades. He has written a number of studies of French writing, including *The Contemporary French Novel.*

Great biographies are even rarer than great novels. "A well-written Life is almost as rare as a well-spent one," wrote Thomas Carlyle, who was the author of one first-rate biography of Frederick the Great and the subject of another by James Anthony Froude. It may even be that the few writers who have masterfully told of the lives of illustrious men have exercised more influence over generations of readers than novelists have.

In Disraeli, André Maurois encountered the character of an impenitent romantic and an acute realist, of a dreamer and a charmer of ladies who proved also to be a man of action. He was fascinated. Conversely, in André Maurois—one of those brilliant and subtle French intellects who, from Montesquieu to Tocqueville and Gobineau, have excelled at unraveling the complexities of other nations—Disraeli, the extravagant descendant of Venetian Jews who became one of the sturdiest leaders of conservative Britain, found a biographer after his own heart, albeit almost 50 years after his death. *The Life of Disraeli,* first published in France in 1927, stands as one of the masterpieces of its author. It is one of the rare biographies that felicitously blend science and art, accuracy and imagination, objectivity and sympathy.

Although the writer was French and the subject English, they were in certain respects peculiarly suited to each other. André Maurois has told of the early part of his life in a book called *I Remember, I Remember.* Most of his novels and stories also are transpositions of situations, feelings and tensions in his own life. Since an innate reserve prevented him from magnifying his personal problems or from dramatizing conflicts which he had resolved for himself, his novels may be deprived of that intensity which is often gained from those artistic lies that turn out to be truer than truth. More than most creators, in a century which cultivates anguish and wants its heroes to have been pursued by a tragic fate or hunted by their own obsessions, André Maurois has looked upon himself as a happy man. That may have qualified him to understand the people who were long regarded as the only nation in Europe to pursue happiness—the English.

André Maurois is a pseudonym: the writer was born Emile Herzog in 1885. He adopted his pen name during the First World War when, while serving as a liaison officer with the British, he wrote *The Silences of Colonel Bramble;* French officers were not allowed to publish under their own names. The book brought him immediate fame, and he has been known by the pen name ever since.

His family was Jewish; Emile was mildly surprised at first to find that the Roman Catholic faith which was that of the majority of the schoolboys was not his, but tolerance prevailed in those early years of the century, and the boy never felt estranged or bitter. He eventually adopted the faith of the majority of his countrymen, as Disraeli had done in England. Religious issues never tormented him.

The chief influence on his formative years was that of Alain (the pseudonym of Emile Chartier), his teacher of philosophy at the *lycée* of Rouen. All his life he was to remain devoted to that extraordinary teacher, who cast a spell upon his pupils while never attempting to press his views upon them.

Maurois' scholastic achievements were brilliant, and ordinarily would have designated him for a teacher's career, but Alain dissuaded him from that project. He distrusted the young scholar's facility and feared his isolation from the concrete issues of life if he were to choose too soon a career as teacher and writer. Since Maurois' family operated a textile mill, he advised him to gain a knowledge of practical affairs, to learn how to deal with men and with the problems of labor, of efficiency and of administration.

The war interrupted this program and turned Maurois back to a literary career. The young industrialist spent four years in the army between 1914 and 1918. He served with British troops, saw action, squalor and suffering, admired and imitated the humor through which his Colonel Bramble and his even more entertaining Irish Doctor O'Grady made the horrors of the ghastly slaughter bearable. After the phenomenal success of his war books, he scored a triumph with his *Ariel*, a fictionalized life of Shelley which started a French vogue for biographical novels. Maurois has since regretted that book, which offered a half-ironical and superficial portrayal of Shelley the man, ignoring Shelley the poet. But he had read his own inner conflicts in the quixotic liberal dreams of the romantic poet, harshly jolted by real life and by what may be sordid in politics, in love and in the outright disregard of conventions.

None of the other biographies by Maurois was to be as jaunty in tone as his entertaining but hasty narrative of Shelley's life and loves. His *Byron,* his *Lélia,* his *Olympio* (a life of Victor Hugo), his essays on English writers and on American history rest solidly on elaborate research. He became the great master of the art of biography in France. His urbane and acute reflections on biography as an art were given in 1928 as the Clark lectures at Trinity College, Cambridge, later published in France and England the same year, as *Aspects of*

Biography. Maurois' own favorite among his biographies, that of Disraeli, had appeared the year before.

Maurois revealed that he owed the original idea of a book on Disraeli to a comment by the French novelist Maurice Barrès: "The three most interesting men of the Nineteenth Century are Byron, Disraeli and Rossetti." To a continental European, Disraeli offers a strange fascination. The grandson of a Jewish emigré from Italy who had first sought his fortune in Venice and then speculated successfully on the London Stock Exchange, the son of a bookish scholar who spurned commerce and gave up all links with the Synagogue, in accordance with his Voltairean views, and had his children baptized as Protestants, he had far more imagination, far more flamboyance than any other British statesman before Lloyd George and Winston Churchill. The adjective "Oriental" is often affixed to him. Indeed, he dreamt of the Orient as Bonaparte had done; Europe was too paltry a stage for his political fantasies. Since life, fulfilling Oscar Wilde's celebrated paradox, often imitates literature, the British control over Cyprus and the crowning of Queen Victoria as Empress of India, which Disraeli achieved as Prime Minister, were the belated outcome of his lifelong attraction to the East.

There was always something extravagant about Disraeli which has made staid English historians uneasy about that complex personality. They have doubted his sincerity, distrusted the "Oriental" flattery which he lavished on the Queen, the expansive letters which he enjoyed writing to women, his passion for the showy clothes of a dandy, his liking for flowers—and for a flowery style as a writer. The article about him in the 14th edition of the *Encyclopaedia Britannica* remarks that his contemporaries saw him as a "flashy litterateur and opportunist adventurer."

He had been an unhappy speculator in his youth and the debts thus incurred pursued him throughout his career. He was saved from financial embarrassment at one time by the legacy of a sizable sum of money from a woman who admired him. He later married a widow a dozen years older than himself, whose intellectual capacities he had at first treated cavalierly; he proved a devoted and sentimental husband, grateful for the security which his wife brought him and for her unshakable faith in him. "Dizzy married me for my money," she used to remark, "but if he had the chance again he would marry me for love."

At the same time, this Byronic hero—the friend of fashionable dandies, the politician who bolted his party, who took over the platform of his adversaries the Whigs, who shed tears and floods of ink in his fiction over the misery of the working classes in Britain—turned out to be the champion of the Conservatives. In a country where Jews remained excluded from Parliament as late as 1858, he might naturally have attempted to underplay his Semitic affinities. He liked, on the contrary, to recall them. Into the rather stolid and prosaic politics of his Conservative friends he poured romance, nostalgia for the past and visions of a glowing future for the masses whose sturdy nationalist instincts he rightly gauged.

"I am a radical in order to uproot what is bad, a

conservative in order to preserve what is good," he once said. It is a profession of faith which André Maurois— the would-be socialist upon whom fate had thrust the management of an industrial plant—could approve. "To conserve is to maintain and to reform" is another saying of the subtle Disraeli to which Maurois subscribes.

Maurois' narrative is especially brilliant where he deals with the parliamentary debates and the impressive ritual of committees and clubs through which party leaders and members of a cabinet accede to power. Few aspects of British life seem more alien to continental Europeans, and even to Americans, accustomed to very different procedures and often to more acrimonious electoral struggles. Behind the ceremonial of the Court, Maurois lays bare the grave questions of general politics which were at stake, affecting the future of the British Empire and of democracy in Ireland and elsewhere in Europe. But he is a biographer primarily and not a philosopher of history. Behind the broad economic and historical forces, he sees men, feeling, talking, acting according to their prejudices and to their temperaments.

André Maurois stands among a group of Frenchmen (André Chevrillon, André Siegfried, Louis Cazamian, Paul Morand) who, in our century, have explained England to the rest of the world, and even to itself, with the intellectual lucidity on which the French pride themselves—and also with a warmth and affection not often encountered in the judgments of one nation upon another. His life of Disraeli is concise, selective, and expert at utilizing facts without being oppressed by an indigestible accumulation of them. It is lively, quoting from Disraeli's letters and diaries, re-creating his thoughts and his feelings through imaginary, but never artificial, monologues. It is slightly ironical—in contrast with the old-fashioned Victorian biographies, which were reverential, sanctimonious and hypocritical, and which buried the dead man over again with all the gloomy elaborateness of a mortician embalming the corpse.

But Maurois never affects condescension or superiority to the conservative statesman whom he envied. In this he follows the precept formulated in his own *Aspects of Biography:* "The hero is always greater than the biographer."

—HENRI PEYRE

DISRAELI

PART
I

Life is too short to be little.

<small>DISRAELI</small>

I

Two Generations

In the year 1290, on All Saints' Day, King Edward I. expelled the Jews from England. There, up till that date, they had been tolerated. But those were days of the Crusades; in every village, monks were preaching against the Infidels; and the peoples were demanding a Crusade at home. About sixteen thousand Jews left the country. The King insisted on their being allowed to go in peace, without molestation, and his word was obeyed in the main. The sole exception was one master-mariner who disembarked his passengers on a sea-bound sand-bank, bade them "Cry out for Moses!" and raised his anchor. A few dozen Jews were thus drowned, but the mariner was hanged.

Those of the exiled who escaped waves and sailors found an asylum in France. But not for long. In 1306 King Philip the Fair, being pressed for money, decided to confiscate their goods and thrust them back towards Spain. There they experienced two centuries of peace, but after that the faggots were kindled, and it seemed as if this unhappy race, unable to migrate further, was at last about to disappear. But the persecutions were badly regulated. Just when Spain was barring her door to the Jews, the republics of Venice and Amsterdam, and France once more, offered them a welcome. Even in England the Reformation, through the reading of the Bible, was giving rise to a curiosity that was almost sympathetic. The Puritans were assuming Jewish names and searching for the Lost Tribes. In 1649 a petition for the return of the people of Israel was presented by Lord Fairfax. Cromwell showed himself in favour; the decision was confirmed by Charles II. And in this way, towards the close of the seventeenth century, a small community of Portuguese and Spanish Jews was re-established in London. Many of their families, such as the Villa Reals, the Medinas, the Laras, had been ennobled in the time of the Saracen kingdoms; they looked down on the Polish and Lithuanian Jews who were then streaming westwards before the rising of the Cossacks, and refused to admit any such uncouth persons into their synagogue.

In 1748 this Jewish society in London saw the advent of a young Italian, Benjamin Israeli or D'Israeli, who, springing from Cento in Ferrara, had first of all sought

4

his fortune in Venice, and believed that he could succeed better in a newer and more prosperous land. His beginnings were difficult. He speculated, lost, and seemed to be ruined; but having married as his second wife a woman who brought him the blood of the Villa Reals and an appropriate dowry, he entered the Stock Exchange and amassed a very satisfactory fortune.

He was a cheerful and indulgent man, who had laid out in a London suburb a garden in the Italian manner, served his guests with the finest concoctions of macaroni, and after the meal would take up his mandoline and sing a canzonetta. The trace of a Venetian accent thrusting up through the English murmur gave his language a picturesque charm; when he spoke one could catch glimpses, veiled by the yellow fogs of the City, of the gold of St. Mark's and the motley-painted stakes where the gondolas are moored before rose-coloured palaces.

Outside of business, Mr. D'Israeli never mixed with other Jews. Not from designing motives; for he was simple, good-hearted, and above all things fearful of giving offence. But his wife kept them at arm's length. Had she been a Christian, her fortune and beauty would have assured her in London the very finest social standing. It irked her that she was born a Jewess and that through her marriage she had to bear a name which was almost symbolic. In vain did her husband strive to appease her with gifts; she remained mortified, embittered and scornful. To please her (and from natural indifference as well), he never went to the synagogue, but his name was inscribed in the membership of the

Portuguese community, and, ever generous and prudent, he would occasionally make an offering of a few guineas to the God of Israel.

Benjamin and Sarah D'Israeli had an only son, Isaac. He astonished them. They hoped for a great man of business; their son was pale and shy, never went for a walk without a book in his hand, and showed a surprising distaste for every form of action. This indolence roused the sarcastic spirit of Mrs. D'Israeli. The father smoothed out the quarrels by giving presents to mother and son. In his eyes, an unhappy child was a child who wanted a toy. When this son of his ran away from home one day and was found lying stretched on a tomb, he embraced him and gave him a pony.

At the age of thirteen, the youth produced a poem. Despite his benevolence and his optimism, Mr. D'Israeli took fright. He had an engraving of Hogarth's at home representing a poet dying of starvation in a garret. Isaac was packed off by the first boat to a foreign correspondent, and spent four years in Holland and France, under the supervision of a tutor who turned out to be a freethinker and a disciple of the French philosophers. The young D'Israeli returned nourished on Voltaire and full of admiration for Rousseau. When he came back beneath the parental roof at the age of eighteen, with outlandish clothes and long hair, he followed the example of Emile, and threw himself into his mother's arms, shedding profuse tears over her; she tittered, and offered him her cheek with obvious dislike.

For some time Benjamin D'Israeli cherished some small hope, but when he knew the subject of the great poem on which his son was working, to wit, *"Against Commerce, which is the Corruption of Mankind,"* he abandoned the idea of finding him employment in his business, and decided to allow him to live according to his own tastes.

Thereupon Isaac D'Israeli adopted a mode of life which went on unchanged until his dying day. He spent his days in the Reading Room of the British Museum, a delicious spot where, in those days, never more than five or six readers were to be seen. There he covered with notes the sheets of paper with which his pockets were always stuffed. In the beginning the goal of this labour was the writing of a *History of English Literature.* But all at once D'Israeli found himself overwhelmed by a rising tide of paper slips, and resigned himself to the humble but diverting function of a compiler. Under the title of *Curiosities of Literature,* he published a collection of anecdotes which enjoyed great success and decided his career. At the age of thirty-five he married a gentle and simple-hearted woman, belonging like himself to an Italian-Jewish family. He asked nothing more than to love her faithfully provided that she took all domestic concerns from his shoulders, and allowed him to devote his life to reading and taking notes. As it turned out, this arrangement was agreeable to the woman of his choice, and thenceforth the life of Isaac D'Israeli was ordered in accordance with an inflexible programme. After breakfast he went into his library and remained closeted there until luncheon, reading and taking notes. After luncheon, he went to the British Museum, read and took notes. On his way back he stopped at all the booksellers he passed, returned home laden with books, took his tea, and shut himself up until dinner with his purchases of the day, always reading and taking notes. If he went to his club, it was still only to transfer its library on to slips of paper. He loved books as other men love women, or opium, or tobacco; they were as a soothing drug to make him forget life. He was esteemed in the world of letters, where he could count distinguished friends. He was pleasing by virtue of his remarkable gentleness and his total lack of vanity. Byron used to read D'Israeli's little collections with pleasure, finding stories about the lives of great men, about their misfortunes or their egoism, which calmed certain of his own apprehensions. And the name of Byron in its turn was held in veneration in the household. In matters of religion, Isaac D'Israeli was a Voltairean, in matters of politics a Conservative; but any form of government was good in his eyes if it allowed a man of moderate fortune to go on making, without being disturbed, a collection of literary anecdotes.

II

Schools

The eldest son of Isaac D'Israeli, like his grandfather, was named Benjamin. Before him a daughter had been born, Sarah. From infancy the greatest intimacy prevailed between brother and sister. Mr. D'Israeli's rôle as a father was confined to an occasional playful pinching of his son's ear, with all a bookworm's awkwardness. Mrs. D'Israeli, a person by nature easily astonished and confused, listened with respectful alarm to her precocious children's conversation, and tried without success to make their hair curl. They adored her, and told her not a word of what was nearest to their hearts. For their father they had a great admiration, believing him to be a very great writer, and loving his charming features, but they had realized that it was useless to expect him to occupy himself with their concerns. They saw him appear at meal-times, a velvet skull-cup on his grey hair, silent and abstracted. They knew that his sole desire was to get back to his books. When he was detained, his politeness was extreme, but one could feel his exasperation. When he talked with his children, it was not about everyday life, but of his work, of his researches. He was engaged in writing a *Life of Charles Stuart*, and he loved to explain to them that, far from having been a tyrant, the handsome Cavalier King was in reality a martyr. Devotion to the Stuarts and hatred of the Puritans were the sole religion of the household.

Every Sunday the whole family went on foot to visit the D'Israeli grandparents, an interminable and wearisome walk, at the end of which would be found the sour old grandmother, who pinched the children's cheeks, passed acid judgments on their manners, and never offered them a cake. But to make up for that there was the grandfather, who gave them a piece of money, played the mandoline to them, and told them about Italy. Little Ben adored these stories, and especially the ones which happened in Venice. He liked to imagine that city where the houses were a lacework of stone and the roofs were covered with gold. Grandpapa said that the family had lived for a long time in Italy; and further back, in the time of Ferdinand and Isabella, they had had their home in Spain. With Italy was blended the memory of the Turks, with Spain that of the Moors. When Ben thought of his grandpapa's mandoline and macaroni, he also conjured up turbans, vests embroidered with gay colours, lands of luxury and sunshine. Sometimes he lay down beneath a tree in that Italianate garden, and dreamed. He fashioned strange and brilliant scenes, and against their background he would meet beings of perfect beauty, a young English knight whom he rescued from death, a princess to whom he vowed himself. They were all three lost in a forest; night was falling, and his companions were afraid. Then Ben took command, for it was always he who directed, always he who was victorious, in this dreaming of his.

He was sent to school very young, first to a Miss Roper's, then to the charge of the Rev. John Potticany, a respectable household where a clergyman's daughter was "in charge of morals and the linen." There, a surprising fact was revealed to him: he was not of the same religion or the same race as his companions. This was difficult to understand. Yet Ben's house, that red-brick house (Grecian portico, three steps, small railing alongside the pavement), was certainly an English house. His father, with his black velvet skull-cap, his pink and carefully shaven face, his correct and pleasing speech, was an English writer. Ben had learned to read in English books, the songs that had cradled his sleep were English songs, but here, in this school, he was made to feel that he was not like the others. He was a Jew, and his companions, with one exception, were not Jews. How mysterious it was! The Jews, they were the people the Bible speaks of, who crossed the Red Sea, lived in captivity in Babylon, and built the Temple of Jerusalem. Whatever had he to do with them? In the morning, when the whole class knelt in common prayer, Ben and the other little Jew, whose name was Sergius, had to step to one side and remain standing. Once a week a rabbi came to teach them to read Hebrew, an incomprehensible tongue which was written backwards, with characters like the heads of nails. The young D'Israeli knew that these practices held him apart from a mysterious communion, and that in the eyes of his master, and of the other pupils, they had a slightly comical character. This pained him. He was proud. He would have liked to be admired in everything. When they played at horses, he was never willing to be the harnessed one. But the pain came especially from the fact that he did not like Sergius. It was hateful to be thus linked to an inferior being. The boys to whom Ben attached himself had flaxen hair and blue eyes. With them he showed an astonishing patience. There was a boy named Jones, the doctor's son, to whom he used to tell stories of brigands and caverns in the play hour, illustrating them as he went with quick sketches in pencil. When Ben had a new book, young Jones came and sat beside him and they read together. But Jones was still in the middle of the page when Ben, who had run through it at a glance, was already preparing to turn over. He had read so much, and heard so much talk of books from his father, that his vocabulary was immense, and a difficult text did not hold him up. Little Jones sighed, and quickened his pace. Then Benjamin guessed his friend's distress, smiled faintly, and said with the utmost kindness: "I can wait."

In the evening, in their study, Sarah and Ben used often to talk of this strange problem of the Jews and the Christians. Why were they seemingly reproached with an origin that had been none of their choosing, and over which they were powerless? When they asked their father for explanations, Isaac D'Israeli, the Voltairean philosopher, shrugged his shoulders. It was all meaningless. Superstitions. He, for his part, felt no shame in being a Jew. On the contrary, he spoke with pride of the history of his race. But he held it utterly ridiculous to maintain, in an age of reason, practices and beliefs which had been adapted to the needs of a tribe of Arab nomads several thousands of years earlier. Like his own father, and to give him pleasure, he remained inscribed at the synagogue and paid his dues. And to avoid arguments which might have made him lose several hours of reading, he had even given leave for this rabbi to come and teach his son Hebrew. But he believed in no dogma and practised no rite.

In spite of his attitude, and perhaps because of it, he learned one day in 1813 that the London Jews, proud of his literary celebrity, had just nominated him as Warden of their Congregation. His indignation was aroused, and forthwith he wrote them a violent letter:

"A person who has always lived out of the sphere of your observation; of retired habits of life; who can never unite in your public worship, because, as now conducted, it disturbs, instead of exciting, religious emotions, a circumstance of general acknowledgment; who has only tolerated some part of your ritual, willing to concede all he can in these matters which he holds to be indifferent;—such a man, with but a moderate portion of honour and understanding, never can accept the solemn functions of an Elder in your congregation, and involve his life, and distract his pursuits, not in temporary but in permanent duties always repulsive to his feelings."

The consistory condemned the President *malgré lui* to a fine of forty pounds. Isaac D'Israeli refused to pay. He was left in peace for three years, and after that the Jewish community demanded payment of the fine. In the interval the grandfather had died, having retained his sunny serenity, in spite of an odious wife and a disappointing son, to the age of ninety. With him had vanished the only link, and that a frail one, still binding his family to active Judaism. Mr. D'Israeli replied to the consistory, requesting that henceforward his name should be deleted from the list of the faithful. This man, for all his easy-going character, was capable of turning ferocious when his tranquillity was threatened.

Although he had ceased to be a Jew, he had not become a Christian, and in this intermediate state he was quite at ease. One of his friends, however, Sharon Turner the historian, pointed out to him that it would be advantageous to the children if they conformed with the religion of the English majority. To sons especially, if unbaptized, many careers would be closed, since Jews, like Catholics too, were deprived of certain civil rights. Mr. D'Israeli had a great esteem for Turner, who had been the first to explore the Anglo-Saxon manuscripts of the British Museum. Moreover, the handsome and dry grandmother, faithful to her youthful grudges, was pressing him to liberate her grandchildren from a connection which had caused her so much suffering. Isaac D'Israeli let himself be persuaded. Catechisms and prayer-books made their appearance in the house, and one after another the children were led off to St. Andrew's Church, and there baptized.

Benjamin was then thirteen. It was desirable to make his change of religion coincide with a change of school. Where was he to be sent? His father thought of Eton; his mother was afraid he might be unhappy there. It was certain that Eton's welcome to the young Jew so newly converted would not be very reassuring. Ben was ready to tempt fortune, but prudence carried the day in the paternal councils. It happened that Mr. D'Israeli often met in the booksellers' shops with a certain Rev. Dr. Eli Cogan, who bought rare editions and had the name of being the only Nonconformist minister to know Greek. A man who read so much could not be otherwise than perfect; and it was decided that to him Ben should be entrusted.

Dr. Cogan's school was an old ivy-clad house. Round the bare class-rooms lined with oaken benches, hung large pictures which proclaimed: "I am the Way, the Truth, the Life." Three-score and ten pupils, a curious and critical throng, crowded round the newcomer. He was aggressively well-dressed. His costume, too carefully arranged, his dull and olive complexion, and his attractive but foreign features, were all astonishing. His new companions gazed at him with a slightly jeering interest. He faced up to them with boldness and gave back look for look. He was determined to stand four-square and, if need be, to answer scorn with insolence. "They're nothing but boys," he repeated to himself when emotion welled up too strongly, "nothing but boys like myself, and I must be master over them."

The first classes exposed the qualities and defects of his education. The school was very strong in Latin and Greek, much stronger than Ben. But when it came to invention or to writing, several boys discovered that he could open out to them a new world of thoughts and feelings. His sayings and phrases were passed from mouth to mouth. His companions copied out his verses to show them to their sisters or their cousins. A kind of modernist coterie grew up around him. Although he hated violent movement, his temperament yielded to his ambition, and methodically he trained himself to succeed in games and sports. His popularity was great, and he had rapidly acquired a position of supremacy. This intoxicated him. When he went out for a walk alone, he liked now to imagine himself as Prime Minister or the commander of an army. How delightful that must be!

In order to consolidate his power, he organized theatrical performances, in violation of the school rules. He had a passion for the theatre. When his parents had taken him there for the first time, when he had heard those well-made speeches and beheld those astounding adventures, he had been enraptured. At last he was discovering a world of beings after his own heart, of beings who wrought great deeds and spoke like the heroes of his dreams. . . . A troupe of actors was formed. D'Israeli was director, stage-manager, leading actor. The weeks went by; he felt the enjoyment of this new life, and of his power; he was perfectly happy.

So much so that he did not see a storm gathering. Success was giving him joys which he ingenuously supposed were shared by others. He was not quick enough to conceal his scorn for any slow-wittedness. Despite the baptismal water, he still smacked of heresy. The most violent of his enemies were the school monitors, who until the advent of this boy with the black curls, had ruled with undivided authority. This occult power of his, founded upon pleasure, and expanding alongside their own, was irritating to them. They denounced to the Rev. Dr. Cogan the director of the theatrical company and the clandestine rehearsals.

The Rev. Dr. Cogan was most indignant, and came into the class to deliver a discourse on these new and scandalous ways of conduct. "Never in this family, which we here make up," he said, "never have I seen anything comparable. No doubt it is a foreign and seditious mind, one incapable of acquiring the spirit of this school, which has conceived such plans." The opposition gleefully snatched at this phrase. In the succeeding play hour, one group sniggered as it passed beside young D'Israeli. Some one hissed. He turned round and said calmly: "Who hissed?" The biggest of the monitors came forward and said: "We've been led long enough by a foreigner." D'Israeli landed him a blow of his fist straight in the face. A circle was formed round the boxers. D'Israeli was smaller and less strong, but swift and very quick on his feet. He fought with much science, and with ferocious courage. Soon he drew blood from the other, and the school, dumbfounded, saw its legal chief beginning to lose his senses. At last he collapsed. A stupefied silence greeted this fall of a dynasty.

Perhaps the pupils of the Rev. Dr. Cogan would have been less surprised if they had known that for three years the victor had secretly been taking lessons in boxing.

III

Brummell and St. Ignatius

Dr. Cogan requested Mr. Isaac D'Israeli to take away
his son as soon as possible. Ben was restored to home,
to his own room, to the unvarying indulgence of his
own people. Never had a child felt himself more alone,
nor more the master of his life. His father was more
benevolent but less real than ever; his mother, long since
outstripped, admired beatifically from afar. It was only
with Sarah that he could discuss the future.

He was fifteen years old, and facts had proved that
school was dangerous for him; would he find at the University, if he went there, the same prejudices, the same
hatreds? What was to be done? But first of all, what

did he want? With the turmoil of the little schoolboy world, the memories of his intrigues, his triumphs, his miniature wars, had come glimpses, as through scattering clouds, of clear and vivid landscapes; and then he could descry the distant shapes of vast ambition, just as a man drawing near a town will catch sight of the lofty towers soaring above it. Life, it seemed to him, would be intolerable if he were not the greatest among men: not one of the greatest, but quite definitely the greatest. He had his revenge to take, and he felt capable of taking it. But who would explain life to him? Along which road should he turn his steps? Writing? He remarked the impassioned devotion inspired in every heart by a Byron. But so many great poets, even the very greatest, only achieved fame after their death. For posthumous triumph Ben had no taste. He wanted to have the ready coin of his fame: "would you rather have been Homer or Julius Caesar, Shakespeare or Napoleon? No one doubts." As he had two brothers younger than himself, his mother arranged for them little gatherings of children of their own age. And there the future Alexander could be seen walking to and fro, his hands thrust into the pockets of his very tight trousers, pale and melancholy, with a sombre and anxious eye, a Gulliver amidst the Lilliputians.

From the pitiless self-examination to which he gave himself over during the weeks that followed his return, the first conclusion was that he was completely ignorant.

It seemed necessary to reconstruct his genius, starting with the foundations. He mapped out a vast plan of work and allowed himself a year of retirement to rebuild his studies.

Every morning his father would watch him with a tender and sceptical eye, going into the library and coming out with an armful of books. Every evening the diary of his reading was covered with notes: "Friday, June 2nd: Lucian. Terence—the *Adelphi*, which promises to be an interesting play. *Henriade* . . . Virgil, 2nd book of the *Georgics*, which begins with a splendid invocation to Bacchus; it, however, all vanishes in a sleepy lecture on grafting boughs and lopping trees. Prepared Greek . . . Grammar, &c." And another day: "I have a prejudice against Demosthenes, and though his speeches are replete with Virtue, Patriotism and Courage, history tells me that he was a Villain, a Partisan, and a Poltroon!"

Through every room of the house wandered this tall boy in his slippers, carrying piles of dictionaries. In vain did the methodical Mr. D'Israeli beseech him to adopt a fixed place for working: "Pray, my dear boy, keep your papers in order." What displeased the author of *Curiosities of Literature* was to see his son studying with such passion the history of the conspiracies of Venice or that of the great religious orders. Everything that had an air of mystery was attractive to this boy. He was always seeking fresh details on the secret societies, the Vehmgerichte, the Council of Ten, or the Jesuits. He read and re-read the life of St. Ignatius

Loyola and was spellbound by his courage. Ignatius used
to ask himself: What would you do if you became a
saint, to surpass in sanctity both Dominic and Francis?
The question was very like that which Benjamin asked
himself with regard to Demosthenes and Cicero and Pitt.
He liked the precept "Develop yourself: not for enjoyment but for action." And above all he studied the way
in which St. Ignatius had recruited his disciples and
attached them to himself. He was filled with admiration
for the organization of the Catholic Church. Ah! To be
at once the spiritual power and the temporal power. . . .
To be Alberoni or Richelieu. . . . Perfect destinies!

Mr. Isaac D'Israeli was saddened by such remarks.
What! Was this the goal reached by a disciple whom
he had reared on his beloved Voltaire? In the margin
of a tirade of Oedipus against the priests, Benjamin had
written: "This is a speech worthy of a French *Illuminé*;
but in the heroic age *Philosophers* did not exist, and the
good men were contented to obey and consult those institutions which from their youth upward they were
taught to respect." A strange lad this: he soiled books,
and he considered Virgil frivolous. Had the erudite
sceptic engendered an erudite mystic? A strange mystic
too: nothing naïve, nothing spontaneous drew him towards such doctrines. One might have said that reason
made him flee from reason. And this was worrying to
Mr. D'Israeli.

Notwithstanding his horror of all action, he judged
it necessary to intervene. He was anxious to direct his
son to simpler and more practical ends. A friend of his,
Mr. Maples, a solicitor, offered to take Benjamin with

him as his secretary. Maples had a daughter, and the parents had formed plans. But Benjamin shied at the prospect of being buried in lawyer's chambers. "The Bar: pooh! law and bad tricks till we are forty, and then, with the most brilliant success, the prospect of gout and a coronet. Besides, to succeed as an advocate, I must be a great lawyer, and to be a great lawyer, I must give up my chance of being a great man."— "Beware," said Mr. D'Israeli, "of endeavouring to become a great man in a hurry, my dear boy. . . . In this age every one is striving to make an immense fortune, and, what is more terrific, at the same time a speedy one. . . . Oh, my son, it is for you and your companions that I fear." He added that he regretted to see his son forming so exacting an ambition, because his birth and his race closed many avenues to him. But even admitting that Benjamin was right to have desires of a loftier destiny, why should he not begin by watching mankind from the admirable observatory which a solicitor's study provides? There would be nothing to prevent him later on from turning in another direction.

Benjamin was struck by that last argument. It was true that he had no knowledge of men, and that he desired to gain that knowledge. His reading had taught him that many great minds have failed because they have wanted to think alone and disdained the study of the mass of men. It was essential, on the contrary, to mix with the herd, to enter into its feelings, and humour its weaknesses. The myth of Jupiter disguising himself as a beast in order to succeed in his terrestrial enterprises, seemed to him a good symbol. He yielded.

23

A solicitor's office. In the chambers at Frederick's Place, in Old Jewry, he saw a procession of statesmen, bankers, merchants pass by. In the evenings he continued his reading in the paternal library. Sometimes he received an invitation from his chief, and at his house met young women and young girls. He was very pleasing. He had soft, liquid eyes, a chiselled nose, a sensitive mouth, and a skin of extraordinary pallor. In company with women, and in speaking of women, he forced himself to be cynical. It was a complex cynicism, made up of the fear of being duped, of unavowed timidity, of lack of imagination, and of a system. Benjamin had read *Don Juan* and held Byron as his god, and of the poet he knew only that side of the face which he had been willing to display. Brummell was in fashion, with his irritating affectation and his paradoxical insolence. He offered the example of a man of quite humble birth, the grandson of a confectioner, who had checkmated all the snobs of London simply by his own disdainful conceit. The insolence of the Great, that of the Powerful, that of the Pedants, had all been known. But in the dandy was personified a pure insolence, gratuitous and drawing its strength only from itself. Illustrious examples had proved that this method could be successful, and in a world of middle-class lawyers, the youthful D'Israeli wished to make the attempt. He dressed with extravagant refinement, a coat of black velvet, ruffles, and black silk stockings with red clocks; he fixed women with an impertinent eye, answered men over his shoulder, and immediately he thought he could detect the happy results of his attitude. Married women looked at him with smiles which were justifiably envied by men of stature.

Frequently his father took him to dine with the publisher John Murray, where he would meet with well-known writers and listen to conversations which gave him great delight. There he saw Samuel Rogers, and Tom Moore, Byron's friend, who had arrived from Italy where he had met the poet. "Pray, is Lord Byron much altered?" asked Mr. D'Israeli. "Yes, his face has swelled out and he is getting fat; his hair is grey and his countenance has lost that 'spiritual expression' which he so eminently had. His teeth are getting bad; he says if ever he came to England it would be to consult Wayte about them." The young Benjamin listened with all ears, and when he came back at night, made notes of what he had heard.

While observing the others, he was at the same time inspecting himself with a critical eye. He saw that certain of his father's friends found amusement in his precocity, in the liveliness of his repartees, and that others were shocked by his impertinence. By many he was thought to be affected, given to posing, insufferable. As he could not be sincere from fear of being ridiculous, he enlivened his conversation with endless pleasantry, and when he tried to hold back his sarcasms, the memory of the insults he had received at school seemed like an evil demon possessing him. Impudence was preferable to servility. When his excessive aptitude for catching hold of absurdities had made him a dangerous enemy, he reproached himself with the fact and imposed upon himself spiritual exercises in the manner of Loyola. He made a note: "Resolution. To be always sincere and open with Mrs. E———. Never to say anything but what I mean—*point de moquerie*, in which she thinks I excel."

Already the chambers in Frederick's Place were beginning to prove wearisome. The young girl who was intended for him had told him herself: "No . . . you have too much genius for Frederick's Place: it will never do." He was in a hurry to escape. "Think of unrecognized Caesar, with his wasting youth, weeping over the Macedonian's young career! View the obscure Napoleon starving in the streets of Paris! What was St. Helena to the bitterness of such experience? The vision of past glory might illumine even that dark imprisonment; but to be conscious that his supernatural energies might die away without creating their miracles: can the wheel or the rack rival the torture of such a suspicion?"

A holiday trip in Germany precipitated the decision. In company with his father he saw the small Courts of Germany, those brilliant and happy societies, those charming theatres where the Grand Duke himself would conduct the orchestra from his box. They were well received. Military bands played during meals. Old Mr. D'Israeli, with his pink complexion and white hair, was taken for an English general. His son was secretly flattered by the mistake. The world was too beautiful and too varied for any one to spend his youth in turning over the pages of briefs. As they came down the magical waters of the Rhine, under those mysterious hills from which the ivy-clad towers gazed down, he decided that on his return he would turn his back on the whole abracadabra of the law.

IV

Business

During the last months of his career at Frederick's Place, D'Israeli had seen several clients of the firm make rapid fortunes by speculation in South American mines.

The Spanish and Portuguese colonies, Mexico, Bolivia, Peru and Brazil, were then almost all in revolt and were being supported by the English Minister Canning in the name of liberal principles; English financiers were obtaining mining concessions out there; and the English public, rejoicing at being able to serve its doctrines and its pocket at the same time, rushed for stock, which soared wildly. Along with another clerk older than himself, D'Israeli, who believed the rise to be foolhardy, resolved to speculate for a fall. The two young men staked to begin with on a small holding of shares, and then, as they were losing, on a larger. The rise continued, and they found themselves with an adverse balance of about £1000. Impulsively they decided to swing their batteries round and gamble now on the rise.

These operations had brought D'Israeli into touch with John Diston Powles, one of the financiers who controlled the South American stock market. Powles was greatly surprised by the intelligence of this youth of twenty, and showed his interest in him. D'Israeli, for his part, was happy at the chance of penetrating into high finance, an occult power whose mystery had always enchanted him. As a beginning, Powles entrusted him with the compilation and printing of a small booklet on the American mining companies for the use of the general public.

D'Israeli had the profoundest ignorance of mining questions, but the fullest confidence in himself. He obtained his information, wrote in a few days a small and very readable volume, incredibly grave in tone, and induced the publisher Murray, his father's friend, to issue it at the expense of Powles.

Murray in his turn was struck by the self-possession and the persuasive powers of this handsome lad whom he had seen but hardly noticed at his dinners, and in a short time he was surprised to find himself talking with him in great intimacy of the future of his firm. The house of Murray already published an important review, the *Quarterly*, but Murray was wondering if it would not be to his interest to found a daily newspaper on the model of the *Times*. D'Israeli was afire. Murray, a man naturally undecisive and timorous, at once sought to beat a retreat; but he had to deal with a more resolute character than his own. To have a newspaper—this was exactly what the young D'Israeli could most hope for. There lay power, power in an oblique form. Certainly, a great conservative journal must be established. The capital would be made up amongst three: Murray, Powles, and D'Israeli himself. How would the third pay his share? He did not think of that. Money would turn up. What was still needed? An editor? D'Israeli had an idea: Lockhart, the son-in-law of Sir Walter Scott, should be engaged. He lived in Scotland? They would bring him to London. D'Israeli would go and see him, and convince him. Foreign correspondents would be needed? A printing-works? An office? D'Israeli assumed responsibility for everything.

Stormed and overwhelmed, Murray could not offer a long resistance. An agreement was drawn up by which the establishment of a great daily paper was agreed upon, the capital to belong, as regards one half, to Murray, one quarter to Powles, one quarter to D'Israeli. The last-named at once set off for Scotland on his mission. In the stage-coach he read Froissart, felt perfectly happy, and reflected contentedly that "adventures are to the adventurous."

He had prepared the enterprise with infinite pains. The memories of his beloved secret societies had been

of service, and he left with Murray a code which enabled him to write without mentioning names. Sir Walter
Scott would be "the Chevalier," Lockhart, "M," the
Minister Canning would be "X," and Murray himself,
"the Emperor." No sooner arrived in Edinburgh, than
he sent his credentials to Lockhart, who occupied a
small house near Abbotsford, his father-in-law's magnificent property. He was invited to call on the following
day. The writer was dumbfounded when he saw this
child come in, for when he read the name of D'Israeli
he had naturally thought of the father, whom he had
formerly met in London. A chilling and slightly pedan-
tic man, given to mockery, and rather inflated by the
importance of his father-in-law, he took this extreme
youthfulness as if it were an insult, and his welcome
was icy.

D'Israeli felt his courage failing him. But such was
the working of his temperament that the more he was
intimidated, the more detached did he appear. He sat
down with a majestic deliberation which added ten
years to his age, and began with perfect coolness to develop what he called John Murray's project. It was
really that of Benjamin D'Israeli. But he knew that the
opinions of a lad of twenty have small chance of being
listened to: it was for this reason that he used to impro-
vise quotations, attributing to recognized authors ideas
which he had not the nerve to express as his own.

On his lips everything grew immense. In the person
of Powles the partnership was supported by "the whole
of the City," "all the mining interests," "the whole of

America"; Murray was bringing in politicians of the highest importance; in a word, the new journal, which he proposed to call the *Representative*, was "the most considerable enterprise of the day." So strongly did he desire life to be a splendid novel of adventure, that he painted it in rather too lively colours. But in spite of his mistrust, Lockhart was astonished by this fire of genius, and on the following day he presented the young emissary to his father-in-law.

Sir Walter Scott was at this time one of the most illustrious men in the world. Caravans of Americans made the Abbotsford pilgrimage. He treated them with impressive kindliness, and took them to walk in his beautiful grounds, or brought them to fish for salmon in the Tweed, his dogs running at his heels. The house from which he had originally wished to fashion a small country home, had expanded with each successive novel until it had become a copy of a Scottish baronial castle. This style of living was extremely expensive, and Sir Walter's publishers, despite his immense popularity, began to wilt beneath the pressure of contractors' bills. So the young Hebrew who had brought his son-in-law the offer of a magnificent appointment was most cordially welcomed by "the Chevalier." In his fine library, with half a dozen of his dogs clambering over his knees and shoulders, he gave a sympathetic hearing to the explanation of this young man whose romantic ardour was so pleasing. He himself had a taste for business; he approved the project, but insisted on a seat in Parliament for his son-in-law. It was essential that the editor of a great newspaper should be a member of Parliament. Benjamin promised the seat.

He remained for three weeks with the Lockharts, dining with Scott almost every evening. This life suited him to perfection. In the evening Anne Scott would sing Scots ballads to her own accompaniment on the harp, or old Sir Walter himself would tell splendid tales. Every one was enchanted with Benjamin. His father wrote to Murray to the effect that nothing could be urged against Benjamin but his youth, a fault which a few years of experience would be quick to correct; his projects might be vast, but full of good sense, and once at work he was perfectly serious. Murray wrote to Lockhart:

"I left my young friend D'Israeli to make his way with you, confident that, if my estimation of him were correct, you would not be long in finding him out. . . . I may frankly say, that I never met with a young man of greater promise. . . . His knowledge of human nature, and the practical tendency of all his ideas, have often surprised me in a young man who has hardly passed his twentieth year. . . . I can pledge my honour, therefore, with the assurance that he is worthy of any degree of confidence that you might be induced to repose in him— discretion being another of his qualifications. If our great plan should take effect, I am certain that you will find in him a most invaluable, trustworthy friend. . . ."

D'Israeli came back, bringing with him the acceptance of Lockhart, who was to direct both the *Quarterly Review* and the newspaper for £2500 a year. On his return he rented offices and printing-works, engaged as correspondent a German whom he had known at Coblentz, assuring him that this journal would be the focus of information for the whole world, found other correspondents in several European capitals, in South America, in the United States. At last, he believed, everything was going splendidly, and nothing stood in the way of the appearance of the paper, when suddenly there burst upon the triumphant Benjamin's head the most terrific of storms.

He was not familiar with the inner workings of the firm of Murray; he had neglected to have them described to him or to investigate them for himself, and had not in the least imagined that the entry of a man so important as Lockhart was bound to cause some stir there. But John Wilson Croker, an author and politician of talent, Secretary to the Admiralty, and a prominent contributor to the *Quarterly*, but a man of surly temper and malevolent spirit (Macaulay said of Croker that he detested him as much as cold boiled veal), turned up in a fury when he learned of the projects which had been formed behind his back by his publisher with a twenty-year-old whipper-snapper. He made a violent scene with Murray, who laid the blame on D'Israeli and accused him of having revealed by his chattering plans which ought to have remained secret. Almost on the same day there came a crash in American stocks on the Stock Exchange. The first inspiration of the two young clerks had been good, but premature. Now that they had banked on the rise, there came the fall, like a thunderbolt. In a few days the famous Powles was totally ruined; D'Israeli and his friend Evans lost the enormous sum of £7000 sterling.

The hapless D'Israeli thus became incapable of participating, financially at least, in the founding of the newspaper. At the age of twenty he found himself saddled with debts so heavy that he might well wonder how he would ever pay them. Simultaneously he lost his friends, his credit, and his place. He might have been able to remain connected with the enterprise, which would have been only natural seeing that he had been its promoter, but as he was highly displeasing to Croker, and even (which would have greatly surprised him) to Lockhart, who had tolerated him while he thought him useful but considered him a mere adventurer, he was in a few days cut out from this combination which he had formed. He was stupefied. For two months he had been living in an atmosphere of success and eulogy. Murray, Scott, Lockhart, and his father had all treated him as an infant prodigy. He thought he was adored. He was ready enough to think so, the result no doubt of a childhood spent amid a family both affectionate and prone to admire. Abruptly all was forgotten; he seemed to be eyed with wrath and contempt; disaster had succeeded to triumph, and without any transition.

This world was more difficult to handle than he had supposed.

He came home in deep gloom and utterly discouraged; it seemed to him that the very springs of his being were snapped. His father, who in any case was unaware of the most serious aspect of the adventure, the £7000 of debts, assured him that at his age it was absurd to say, as he was saying, that life was a lost game. For several days on end Benjamin was powerless to do anything but brood over his repulse. But after a week of rest and meditation and attempts to understand where he had played his hand wrongly, he was surprised to feel all at once a great desire to write, and more precisely, to write a novel. This first experience of the world, this battle and downfall, made a drama which he suddenly longed to depict, and his desire was to create a hero under whose name he could explain himself to himself.

He was a youth quick to put his ideas into practice, and no less impatient of the conclusion of a book than of political fame. The mask which he adopted was transparent. His hero, Vivian Grey, like himself, was the son of an abstracted man of letters, always shut up with his books. Like himself, he was expelled from a school. Like himself, he was consumed by ardent political ambitions, and paced his room excitedly in his longings to be a great orator. The first article of Vivian Grey's political reasoning was the following: "At this moment, how many a powerful noble wants only wit to be a Minister; and what wants Vivian Grey to attain the same end? That noble's influence. When two persons can so materially assist each other, why are they not brought together?" Deliberately he set out to discover a powerful and stupid nobleman and then to undertake his conquest through flattery. The powerful and stupid nobleman was found, in the person of the Marquis of

Carabas. Vivian succeeded in convincing this latter of the necessity of forming a Carabas party and becoming Prime Minister. Vivian had no doubts regarding success: "For it was one of the first principles of Mr. Vivian Grey that everything was possible. Men did fail in life, to be sure . . . but still all these failures might be traced to a want of physical and mental courage. . . . Now Vivian Grey was conscious that there was at least one person in the world who was no craven either in body or in mind, and so he had long come to the comfortable conclusion, that it was impossible that his career could be anything but the most brilliant." Having thus modelled his hero after his own image, D'Israeli, not without lucid severity, made him run on the rocks, the victim of intrigue and his own blundering, and sent him off, bruised and wounded, to travel in foreign lands in an attempt to forget.

The book was finished in four months, before the author was twenty-one, and unbeknown to his family. The work was far from being devoid of qualities. Everything that D'Israeli had been able to observe for himself, Vivian's youth, his father and the school, was all truthful and living. The tone was sarcastic; a penetrating critic could have detected the influence of Voltaire, and that of Swift. The conversations were made up from those he had heard at Murray's and at Sir Walter Scott's. The parts of original invention were rather childish.

The D'Israelis were neighbours of a certain barrister, Mr. Austen, whose wife, a cultivated, witty and very pretty woman, was an artist, a good musician, and had a taste in literature which was highly esteemed. For a long time she had been interested in Benjamin. When she called on Mrs. D'Israeli, she liked to find this handsome youth who, one day, would be lying on the drawing-room carpet amidst piles of books, and the next, would come down from his room with boxing-gloves still tied over his lace cuffs. She had instantly realized that his frivolity was only an affectation. She had confidence in him, and inspired him with confidence. With her he lowered his defences, taking off mask and breast-plate, was simple and sincere, confessing his fears, his reverses, his desires. He knew that she was honest, and that pleased him. He was afraid of love. Alexander and Caesar did not weep at a woman's knees. The curious thing is that he simultaneously remained sentimental and continued, as in his childish dreams, to seek a mysterious princess to whom he could devote himself. Mrs. Austen brought him the chivalrous emotion of feminine companionship without the obligations of a liaison. Nothing could be better.

He confided to her that he was working on a novel; and when he had finished it, she offered to read his manuscript and, if she thought it successfully carried out, to submit it to her friend Colburn, who was then the most enterprising publisher in London. D'Israeli sent the manuscript to his fair neighbour, and next day received an enthusiastic letter. It was agreed that in order to excite Colburn's curiosity she would submit the novel without the author's name. Only she and D'Israeli would know the secret; and for greater security she copied the whole manuscript in her own hand.

Colburn was a master in the arts of publicity, and immediately saw the possibilities of this anonymous satire. In all the newspapers and all the reviews, short paragraphs announced the forthcoming publication of a society novel from the pen of an author who, for obvious reasons, could not disclose his identity. "An extremely satirical volume," "a collection of portraits of living characters, sufficient to constitute a National Gallery," "a sort of *Don Juan* in prose." With the public prepared by this campaign, the success of *Vivian Grey* was great. Keys were sold giving the names of the living personages who, it was said, had served as models; several eminent men were named as possible authors of the book. It was the sole topic in every drawing-room. D'Israeli and his pretty accomplice were enchanted.

But suddenly, through a subordinate's indiscretion, the secret was revealed. Great was the wrath of the fashionable when they discovered that the unknown author whose talent and knowledge of English society they had been extolling for a month, was a young man of twenty, and did not even belong to the fashionable world. It was generally agreed that it was absurd ever to have had any doubts as to the author's obscure origin, and that this was revealed by the very tone of the work. All those who had imagined they recognized themselves in some ridiculous portrait, now took pleasure in returning the ridicule a hundredfold. The genuine originals were furious. Murray took it into his head that the Marquis of Carabas played a part alongside Vivian Grey which had a close resemblance to his own, and quarrelled brutally with all the D'Israeli family. Those who had been amused by the book had feelings of remorse. One critic remarked that "the class of the author was a little betrayed by his frequent recurrence to topics about which the mere man of fashion knows nothing and cares less." Another denounced "the shameless bluff which had allowed the launching of the book." A third accused the author of having gained a public by the basest and most revolting procedure, and made lengthy fun of the "comic pretentiousness with which the author affects a distinction which he does not possess."

When D'Israeli read this cruel judgment, he let the journal drop and fell into a melancholy reverie. He saw himself as ridiculous, and that was what he dreaded more than anything in the world. Ridiculous. . . . Nothing was left for him now but to die. . . . He tried to laugh. He could only smile, very bitterly. The insolence of these creatures. . . . He closed his eyes and made an effort, beneath the violence of present emotion, to reach a zone of impartial and detached judgment. Was he really, as they claimed, incapable and unworthy of writing? In all sincerity he answered: no! True, his book was mediocre, but literary creation was indispensable for his very life. His childhood's visions, of kings and statesmen, of lovely and appealing women in scenes of light and luxury, were always within him, demanding to come to life. Beside the beauty of such dreams, the sarcasm of fools was beneath contempt. He vowed that in spite of all obstacles he would be an author, and the greatest of authors.

But for a year he had been passing through emotions

that were too extreme, and his nervous strength was giving way. The Austens, seeing that he was greatly cast down, proposed to stage the closing chapters of *Vivian Grey* in real life and to take him to Italy. He accepted with delight.

A month later he was gliding by moonlight on the waters of the Grand Canal; floods of silvery light bathed the Moresco façades; a faint snatch of serenade drifted down through the soft air; the Austrian military band played on the square before St. Mark's; three immense flags floated from the tops of the brightly painted masts. D'Israeli was delighted to find that the floor of his bedroom was of marble, the curtains of crimson satin, the chairs brightly gilt, the ceilings by Tintoretto, and that the hotel itself was the former palace of the Barberini, a family which more than once had provided a Doge for the Republic.

V

Retreat

His travels had calmed his spirit, but the body remained
unhealed. Continual headaches made work almost impossible, and the doctors spoke of an inflammation of
the membranes of the brain. His father had just decided
to leave London and had purchased a large country-
house at Bradenham, amongst the woods of Buckinghamshire. There the young invalid sought his retreat. In this
unfamiliar hall, seated in front of the lofty fireplace,
among the furniture and countless cases of books, he
drew up with his sister Sarah a lucid inventory of the
position.

Twice he had been beaten. The world which he had
wanted to grasp with both hands had slipped through his

41

fingers. He was adding one more phantom "to that king-dom of shadows engendered by fatal precocity." But why? If he accepted defeat, he wanted at least to extract the lesson from defeat.

First of all, he had been affected, haughty, self-centred and vain, in life as in his writings.—Yes, but was that a real offence? "Every man has a right to be conceited until he is successful." Byron was more so than he, and Byron had triumphed.—Yes, but Byron was Byron. In a great poet and in noble blood, arrogance is more easily condoned.—Poor reasoning. The humbler the origins, the more necessary is arrogance. Notwith-standing his rebuff, he clung to his belief that his bold-ness of fancy was of greater worth than the correct per-fection of dull writers and talkers, "gentlemen in stays, as stiff as stones." The only brave attitude was the dandy's, and this was true more than ever in defeat. But one could add to its perfection; a studied nonchalance was of more avail than a brutal affectation. It was a question of shades.

A graver error was that he had wanted to take life by short cuts, to take success by storm. His father had been right in telling him that one could not become a great man in a day. Brilliant as his genius was, he recognized that he had been only a child at the moment when he had wished to act as a chief. Incapable of being at the head of affairs in person, he had had to choose his allies, and he had been mistaken in his choice. He had to learn to know men, and above all to dispense with them. But for that he must abide his time. . . . Patience—that was the first virtue to acquire. In little things it was natural to him, but he had to transform the moments into years. It would be hard. It was necessary. . . . And what next? His tongue had been too free; he had roused the watchfulness of his foes too soon. He had to learn to be discreet, mysterious, impassive; to acquire an exquisite and polished aloofness, a difficult combination, but one which keeps the inquisitive at a distance. Meanwhile, frivolity must perhaps remain as a temporary mask. Read Retz and La Rochefoucauld, who are sound masters in these matters; read and re-read everything about Napoleon. And never confidences, even in intimates.

Passing from the moral to the financial inventory, things were even less resplendent. *Vivian Grey* had brought in £200, but D'Israeli had used the money to repay Murray for the pamphlets on the mines, for which Powles, a ruined man, had not been able to pay. He did not owe this sum, but being penniless he had the elegance to be magnificent. The Stock Exchange debts had been partly squared from the savings of his associate, the clerk Evans, but mainly by loans raised from the moneylenders. The latter dogged his heels whenever he passed through London. He was not afraid of them; on the contrary, he enjoyed visiting them, entering with his youthful features shining with assumed innocence, beginning the conversation with incredible blunders, and then abruptly slipping away from them with some masterly parrying. He was really grateful to his debts for the excitement they brought into a somewhat monotonous life. Moreover, he was determined to pay them off, to the last penny. But how? He had no idea, but he had no doubts of his succeeding. Sarah helped him to retain confidence. In front of her he ventured upon phrases which no other listener could have tolerated with their frank, savage pride, but the impassive Sarah accepted them like articles of faith.

With her, he took pleasure in exploring the beautiful country surrounding their new home. The park of Bradenham delighted him. From the window of his room he could see the great stretches of grass bordered by the unfurling beech-trees. This great mansion, this lordly entrance, satisfied a need within him.

When he came to London, he now saw some of his friends. By correspondence he had made the acquaintance of a young writer of his own age, Edward Lytton Bulwer, who shortly after *Vivian Grey* had made an even more brilliant début with his novel, *Pelham*. Bulwer, like D'Israeli, lived and wrote as a dandy. He had a very beautiful wife, kept up a magnificent style without any money, and entertained his friends in his fine house in Hertford Street.

D'Israeli was asked to luncheon, and came in green velvet trousers, with a canary waistcoat, buckle shoes, and lace cuffs. His appearance at first proved disquieting, but on leaving the table the guests remarked to each other that the wittiest talker at the luncheon-party was the man in the yellow waistcoat. Benjamin had made great advances in social conversation since the days of Murray's dinners. Faithful to his method, he noted the stages: "Do not talk too much at present; do not *try* to talk. But whenever you speak, speak with self-possession.

Speak in a subdued tone, and always look at the person whom you are addressing. Before one can engage in general conversation with any effect, there is a certain acquaintance with trifling but amusing subjects which must be first attained. You will soon pick up sufficient by listening and observing. Never argue. In society nothing must be discussed; give only results. If any person differ from you, bow and turn the conversation. In society never think; always be on the watch, or you will miss many opportunities and say many disagreeable things. Talk to women, talk to women as much as you can. This is the best school. This is the way to gain fluency, because you need not care what you say, and had better not be sensible. They, too, will rally you on many points, and as they are women you will not be offended. Nothing is of so much importance and of so much use to a young man entering life as to be well criticised by women."

In the Bulwer household he also took a few lessons in the life of a married man of letters. Bulwer had been an ardent lover when betrothed; he had become a disagreeable husband who turned angry whenever his wife penetrated the writing stronghold. The charming Mrs. Bulwer was poor and the household lived on the novelist's earnings. He had therefore to produce a great deal and work beyond his strength. Moreover, he was nervous and irritable, especially with his wife. In the evening, to rest himself and to freshen his mind, he needed to see his friends and fellow-writers. He invited them, or he went out. "It is astounding" said Mrs. Bulwer, "it is astounding how authors bore me." Her sole interest was in dogs. She called her husband "Pups"; he called her

"Poodle." Life was not altogether filled by this. Benjamin D'Israeli, a romantic but methodical man, noted that love-marriages can easily endanger love.

For his own part, in the country, he worked. Dividing his time between the woods and his room, he had composed two satirical tales in the manner of Swift or of Lucian, and a fashionable novel, *The Young Duke*. This title had somewhat startled Mr. D'Israeli, who said to Sarah: *"The Young Duke?* But what does Ben know of Dukes?" Sarah had brushed her father aside. The truth was that Ben was totally ignorant of dukes, but he found pleasure in describing receptions of royal splendour, regiments of footmen liveried in scarlet and silver, tables laden with gold-plate, rivers of diamonds on the necks of women, ancestral sapphires and rubies darting their sombre fires, exquisite dishes, carriages laden with oranges and pineapples arriving from the hot-houses of the young Duke, and ortolans, above all the ortolans, for this rare and tiny bird drew a prose poem from Ben: "Oh! doff, then, thy waistcoat of wine-leaves, pretty rover! and show me that bosom more delicious than woman's. What gushes of rapture! What a flavour! How peculiar! Even how sacred! Heaven at once sends both manna and quails. Another little wanderer! Pray follow my example! Allow me. All Paradise opens! Let me die eating ortolans to the sound of soft music!" It was only fitting that a dandy should cultivate his palate. One more conscious frivolity.

Colburn bought *The Young Duke* for £500, which appeased the moneylenders for a time. Its success was not very striking. But Sarah wrote:

"One reading has repaid me for months of suspense, and that is saying everything if you knew how much my heart is wrapt up in your fame. . . . Wherever we go, *The Young Duke* is before us, and its praises for ever resounding. But I know you care nothing for family commendation."

And it was indeed one of Benjamin's recent discoveries, that family glory has small absolute value; but failing anything else, he could put up with it.

Sometimes he went to the Houses of Parliament and listened to the speakers. His judgments were not indulgent: "Mr. Peel . . . improves as a speaker, though like most of the rest, he is fluent without the least style. . . . I have heard Canning. He was a consummate rhetorician; but there seemed to me a dash of commonplace in all that he said. . . . In the Lords, I admire the Duke. . . . There is a gruff, husky sort of a downright Montaignish *naïveté* about him, which is quaint, unusual, and tells. . . . One thing is quite clear,—that a man may speak very well in the House of Commons, and fail very completely in the House of Lords. There are two distinct styles requisite: I intend, in the course of my career, if I have time, to give a specimen of both. In the Lower House, *Don Juan* may perhaps be our model; in the Upper House, *Paradise Lost.*"

Coming out from the galleries, excited and bemused, he sought to imagine what his own eloquence would one day be like, his irresistible arguments, the luminous exposition of detail, and especially the tone, a tone of sarcasm and harshness which would scorch like the simoon, flashes of wit which would gleam suddenly like the stroke of a sword, floods of humour which would drown and dissolve the sticky and pasty speeches of those gentlemen from the backwoods. And at the last would come the irresistible peroration, amid the prolonged applause of every party.

He came to himself once more in a busy street; horses were trotting gaily on the causeway; the passers-by brushed past him, indifferent; to all these Englishmen, D'Israeli would have been no more than the foreign name of an unknown person.

VI

Pilgrimage

At twenty-five, retirement is not a state that can be long supported. A dazzling return into London life would have to be made. But how? After careful reflection, D'Israeli felt convinced that a long voyage abroad ought to precede any attempt, and that for several reasons.

Society in great cities has a short memory. After a few months of absence, no one would think any more of the reverse of the newspaper or the scandal of the novel. Murray himself would be pacified. Lord Byron had set a fashion for the traveller's poem, its episodes linked with the progressive stages of the author. An example to be followed. In it a man stands to profit from the renown of the countries he traverses. Moreover,

49

he felt the need of plunging back into the lands which had seen the origins of his race. It was a hard handicap to be born a Jew, but perhaps it was also a source of strength. In any case it was essential to understand better what the fact meant. He proposed, therefore, not to follow the usual itinerary of the Grand Tour—France, Switzerland, Italy—but to go direct to Spain, where his ancestors had long lived, and then, by way of the Mediterranean, Greece and Turkey, to make the pilgrimage to Jerusalem.

The difficulty was to obtain the consent of his father, who was shocked at the idea of a two years' trip. But the old man was assailed on all sides. Sarah had become engaged to a young Englishman, a friend of her brother's, young William Meredith, and he was anxious to accompany Benjamin, and to make his own Grand Tour before being married. Mr. D'Israeli, who always preferred peace to victory, yielded, and the two young men set off at the end of June 1830. D'Israeli was deeply moved. He loved Bradenham, the old gentleman with his velvet skull-cap, the slightly vain chattering of his mother, the long confidential talks with Sarah, the respectful admiration of his two younger brothers, Ralph and Jem. Why should he leave such an agreeable refuge? How would the wide world receive him, those Englishmen of Gibraltar and Malta, more English than the English of London? He knew his own sensibility and his quick pride. He squared his shoulders. "Adventures to the adventurous."

Arrived at Gibraltar, the first stage, he astonished the young officers there by the variety of his waistcoat buttons and the calculated extravagance of his conversation. He was the first traveller to boast of having a morning cane and an evening cane. At the stroke of noon, punctually, he changed them. All this of course by system, and laughing at himself the while. Spain pleased him, with its white houses and green jalousies, Figaro in every street, Rosina at every balcony. Visiting the Alhambra, he sat on the throne of the Abencerrages with such an air that the old woman custodian asked if he were a descendant of the Moors. "This is my palace," he told her. She believed him.

At Malta, the next stage, a rival loomed up. This was an Englishman, James Clay, who beat the garrison at rackets, Prince Pignatelli at billiards, and the Russian legation at écarté. Obviously a remarkable man, but one could fight with other weapons. "To govern men, you must either excel them in their accomplishments, or despise them. Clay does one, I do the other, and we are both equally popular. Affectation tells here even better than wit. Yesterday at the racket court, sitting in the gallery among strangers, the ball entered, and lightly struck me and fell at my feet. I picked it up, and observing a young rifleman excessively stiff, I humbly requested him to forward its passage into the court, as I really had never thrown a ball in my life. This incident has been the general subject of conversation at all the messes to-day." Mr. D'Israeli shook his head. Why did this son of his, so simple and natural at home, become such a coxcomb in public? Indeed, Benjamin made himself so odious at Malta that the officers' mess gave up inviting "that damned bumptious Jew boy." He

did not care a rap, and went to pay a great round of
visits in an embroidered Andalusian jacket, white trousers, and a sash of all the colours of the rainbow. Half
the population followed him and business was held up
for the whole day. He dared to present himself in this
costume at the governor's, a cold and distant man, who
burst out laughing and took a fancy to him. The gravest
of Englishmen are fond of extravagance, from fear of
that ennui which is so powerful in their nature.

He left Malta in the garb of a Greek pirate, with
blood-red shirt, silver buttons as large as shillings, a
sash stuffed with pistols and daggers, a red cap, red
slippers, wide sky-blue trousers heavily trimmed with
embroidery and ribbons. The famous James Clay accompanied him, a fresh conquest. They took along with
them as valet, Tita, formerly Lord Byron's gondolier,
an admirable Venetian, who had stabbed two or three
persons, and used to prevail upon pretty maidens on the
poet's behalf. After Byron's death he had fought for the
Greeks at the head of a regiment of Albanians, and then
for no very clear reason had been stranded at Malta,
in destitution.

D'Israeli was enraptured with the Turks, took to wearing a turban, smoked a pipe six feet long, and spent his
days outstretched on a divan. These habits of idleness
and luxury were in harmony with an indolent and mel-
ancholic side of his nature which Western activity had
kept concealed, but had not completely suppressed.
Mehmed Pasha told him that he was not a true Englishman because he was capable of walking so softly. He
liked the movement of the Eastern street, the varied

types and costumes, the flash of colours, the call of the muezzin, the barbaric drum announcing the approach of the caravan, the solemn and decorative camels followed by the frieze of Arabs. With such a background, ambition was lulled. The world appeared suddenly in an aspect more profound and more unreal. It was as if one had been living in a fairy tale or in one of the Thousand and One Nights.

His impressions became grave and austere when, having passed through Syria, he turned his steps towards Jerusalem. His mood attuned itself without difficulty to those burning and arid landscapes. He fell in with some nomad tribes, whose sheikhs made him welcome and opened their tents to him. Their noble simplicity, the finished perfection of their manners, their inborn courtesy, all enchanted him. He found a lively pleasure in imagining that three thousand, six thousand years earlier, his ancestors had been just such lords of the desert. What English family could point to such a past of civilization?

He crossed a desolate plateau. No wells, no green thing, no birds. Here and there an olive thrust its twisted silhouette against the blazing blue of the sky. Suddenly he found himself on the edge of a gloomy ravine, and saw on the summit of the opposite ridge a stony and austere city, surrounded by crenelated walls which at intervals were overtopped by towers. The landscape was one of terrible harshness, the city was Jerusalem, the eminence on which the young traveller stood was called the Mount of Olives.

At Jerusalem he passed the most moving week of his

life. His exaltation was supreme. He went to kneel in the
Holy Sepulchre. He liked to think of Christ as of a young
Hebrew prince. He did not understand how a Jew could
not be a Christian; in his eyes that was to stop half-way
and to renounce the glory of the race, which was that
it had given the world a God. Before the tombs of the
kings of Israel he stood lost in dream. As a mere boy
he had been irresistibly attracted by the story of that
young Jew, David Alroy, who about the thirteenth century had wished to emancipate his people from the
Turkish yoke. In those days the Jews, although a subject
race, used still to elect a chief, who bore the melancholy
title of the Prince of the Captivity. Of these princes
Alroy had been one. And he, Benjamin D'Israeli, son
of this same people, could not he likewise be a Prince
of the Captivity? There, in that narrow court hollowed
out in the rock, before those half-open tombs, he determined to write the story of Alroy, and began it the very
next day.

After leaving Palestine, he rejoined his future brother-
in-law, Meredith, in Egypt, where he had preceded him.
He had just arrived there, however, when the young man
caught smallpox, and died within a few days. The picture of Sarah's grief cast a cloud over the return journey. On board ship he shut himself up and worked. He
brought back the drafts for two books; one was *Alroy*,
his Jewish romance, the other, *Contarini Fleming*, like
Vivian Grey, the story of a young man. *Vivian Grey* had
expressed the political ambitions of its author, *Contarini
Fleming* was a portrait of the young poet that D'Israeli
sometimes longed to become. He was pleased enough

with it. "I shall always consider this book," he wrote, "as the perfection of English prose and as a *chef-d'œuvre*."

A *chef-d'œuvre* it was not. Like *Vivian Grey*, the book opened brilliantly, but then lost itself in the sands. Obsessed by his own adventure, D'Israeli collapsed in his novels at the same point as in his life. But Contarini, like himself, did not lose confidence: "I believe in that Destiny before which the ancients bowed. Modern philosophy, with its superficial discoveries, has infused into the heart of man a spirit of scepticism, but I think that ere long science will again become imaginative, and that as we become more profound we may become also more credulous. Destiny is our will, and our will is our nature. The son who inherits the organization of the father will be doomed to the same fortunes as his sire. All is mystery; but he is a slave who will not struggle to penetrate the dark veil."

Such was the picture of the world which D'Israeli brought back from his travels in the East. He had seen the immense confusion of peoples, and their multiplicity of interests. He had understood how difficult it is to know fully, to foresee, to pass judgment. All is mystery. But he believed also that, notwithstanding the shock of the waves, a strong hand can hold the rudder firm, and that Benjamin D'Israeli, after a rough passage, would steer his vessel to the longed-for shore, provided that he were firm and bold.

He arrived at Bradenham in October. Already the beeches in the park were losing their leaves. Mr. D'Israeli had aged; his eyesight, worn out by excessive reading, was failing; his fine dreaming eyes seemed to be dulled. Sarah was in deep gloom, and told her brother that she would never marry, but devote her life to him. The presence of the amazing Tita lightened his home-coming a little. D'Israeli, who had brought him back, was much embarrassed by his charge. But his father was not the man to leave in want the gondolier of Lord Byron. He engaged him for some ill-defined duties, and the tall Venetian with his long moustachios, who had moistened the lips of the dying poet and caught his last words—"Augusta . . . Ada . . ."—now calmly estab-lished himself, with all the good nature of the Southern giant, beneath the half-lights of an English sky.

VII

Doctrines

"A funnel, and not the effigy of Queen Victoria, should have been the minted token of her reign."

OSBERT SITWELL.

During the whole of his journey, Disraeli (he had decided to abandon the prefix as having a foreign air) had reflected much on life, on his past experiences, on the future. The longer he meditated, the more he came to feel that the career of a statesman was the only form of success that could give him true happiness. Formerly when he wondered which path to follow, he added: "To write? To act?" Now he knew that literary fame would not satisfy this desire: "Poetry is the safety-valve of my passions, but I wish to act what I write." So there could be no further hesitation about the road to be pursued: he must enter Parliament. This was a difficult undertaking. The electoral system, designed in days gone by for the accommodation of an aristocracy, allowed a young man of good family to become a member of Parliament on the day of his majority. But it seemed to be constructed with the special object of discouraging irregular beginnings like those of Benjamin Disraeli. In the present month of October 1831, the problem set for this impatient young man was in the following terms.

First, a distinction had to be drawn between the county members and the borough members. The former were elected by the freeholders, proprietors of land bringing in at least forty shillings, in one single voting-place for each county. Not only had the candidate to buy, as everywhere, the votes of the electors, but he had also to convey them, feed them, and lodge them. He must be ready also to intimidate hostile electors by having armed bands at hand to warn them off from the hustings, where the voting took place in public. All this was very expensive. In 1827 the election costs for the two Yorkshire seats had exceeded £50,000. A Disraeli, rich only in his debts, could not afford the honour of becoming a county member. These seats almost all belonged to wealthy landlords, who thus derived the right of wearing spurs in the House. An elegance both cavalier-like and desirable, but alas, inaccessible; it could no longer be thought of.

To become a member for a borough was little easier for a beginner without the right connections. Not all of the boroughs in the country were represented. Those which were had been chosen in the most arbitrary fashion. In Tudor times the Crown had granted representation to towns which it knew to be loyal. Under the Stuarts this prerogative had been abolished, with the result that the list had suddenly been closed. In this way there were great towns of recent prosperity which remained unrepresented, while on the other hand towns which barely existed, the so-called rotten boroughs, still kept their representatives. There were boroughs in which the proprietors of certain houses were the sole electors; by buying up these houses the landlord of the place could be sure of every vote. In others they were the "pot-wallopers," that is to say, those who could boil their own pot on their hearth. Elsewhere they were the mayor and corporation, fifteen or twenty electors at most. In Edinburgh, a very large city, there were thirty-one electors. Sheridan, a candidate for the borough of Stafford, noted in his expenses: "248 electors at £5, 5s.=£1,302." The rich nabob who had just amassed a fortune in the Indies, battled guinea for guinea against the great local landlord. "Can anyone," said Lord Lansdowne, "blame a coppersmith who has seven children and is offered £600 for his vote?" Certain solicitors made a practice of banding the electors together into a syndicate and then going to London to sell the seat to the party that bid highest. These so-called "open" boroughs were open only to money. As for the closed boroughs, they were those where the seat belonged without the possibility of contest to the fief, and the proprietor disposed of it in favour of a son or a nephew. The great Whig and Tory families also preserved a few "pocket boroughs" for the intelligent young men of the party whose start in politics it was felt proper to facilitate.

Finally, the Ministry had at their disposal a certain

number of constituencies where property belonging to the Government alone conferred the right of voting, and some others where they themselves bought the electors by means of jobs or favours. Adding these, which were styled Treasury boroughs, to those of the great Tory landlords, it was found that at every general election two-thirds of the House of Commons were nominated by the Ministry without opposition. It was not surprising that the Tory party had been in power for forty years, and it was hard to imagine how it could possibly be overthrown.

Nevertheless, since 1815, the country had been discontented. The peace, which had thrown England open to Continental trade, had brought with it an industrial crisis, had ruined manufacturers, and lowered wages. Protective duties upon corn, maintained by a Tory Government that represented the small country landlords, were held responsible by the people of the towns for the high cost of living. The electoral system in particular was blamed for all the nation's ills. The Whigs had been dexterous enough to make these criticisms the planks of their electoral platform and to take the head of a movement for a wider franchise. It might have been urged in retort that they had found the rotten boroughs and the pocket boroughs excellent institutions so long as their party had profited by them; but the fashion was all for electoral Reform; it was to cure all ills. "All young ladies," said Sydney Smith, "all young ladies will imagine, as soon as the Bill passed, that they will be instantly married. Schoolboys believe that gerunds and supines will be abolished, and that currant tarts must come down in price; the corporal and the sergeant are sure of double pay; bad poets will expect a demand for their epics."

At the very time of Disraeli's return from his travels, the Reform agitation had reached the pitch of rioting. It was easy to foresee that the Government would be forced to grant an election. This was the moment to conquer a seat. But how? And where? There was indeed the borough of Wycombe, close to Bradenham, where the family could count on friends and on tradespeople. But Wycombe was a pocket borough of their neighbour, Lord Carrington, who would not be much in his favour; and in any case, under what political label ought he to present himself there?

In the course of his youthful reading, Disraeli had made a prolonged study of the two great parties which were disputing power. It was at the time of the Revolution of 1688, when the Stuarts had been expelled, that the enemies of the throne, great noblemen jealous of the Crown, or Scottish Puritans hostile to the established Church, had been ironically dubbed the "Whigs," an abbreviation of "whigamores," the name given to a group of rebel peasants in the West of Scotland. So the name signified the rebels, the enemies of the King. The King's partisans, for their part, had received from their Puritan adversaries the nickname of "Tories," one given to certain footpads in Ireland, to indicate that they were merely papists as contemptible as the Irish. As often happens, these nicknames had been taken up with pride and become war-cries.

The real dividing lines between these factions had disappeared with the Stuart dynasty. But parties survive the causes they serve. In certain great families, sprung from rebel ancestors, a Whig tradition had persisted, a tradition of independence, opposition to the Crown, alliance with the dissenting religious sects, and often also of sincere liberalism. At the same time the great mass of small village squires and gentlemen farmers remained Tory, conservative, loyal to the King and the established Church.

The French Revolution, and then the Napoleonic wars, by closely linking the ideas of liberalism and the guillotine in the English popular mind, had put the Tory party in power for a very long period. Until 1815 the Whigs had been reduced to nullity. The peace having brought in its train the spirit of criticism, the industrial crisis, and discontent, the Reform party had grown up. Until 1830 the popularity of the Whigs had slowly and steadily gathered force. With the French Revolution of July, it had become irresistible. The Duke of Wellington, the chief of the Tory party, and since Waterloo the best-loved man in England, had seen the London mob hurl stones at his house. A popular legend had it that the old soldier was in league with Polignac and accused him of wishing to carry out a *coup d'état*. In London and at Birmingham the tricolour flag had been unfurled. In the country the farm-labourers had set fire to the threshing-

mills of the squires. Ten thousand workmen had besieged
St. James's Palace. The English bishops who had voted
against Reform in the House of Lords were booed in
the streets and did not dare to show themselves again.
Little Lord John Russell, leader of the Reform party of
the Whigs, was the idol of the people. A saying of his
was quoted with admiration: "When I am asked if such
or such a nation is fit to be free, I ask in return, is any
man fit to be a despot?" When he went along the roads,
whole villages would line up to cheer him.

In short, after full and careful analysis, it appeared
that a candidate's best interest in 1831 lay in joining
the Whigs. But the D'Israeli family was Tory. History
showed the Tories as the partisans of those Stuarts so
dear to the heart of Mr. Isaac D'Israeli. He had always
taught his son that the Whigs were merely an oligarchy
in revolt against a martyr-king. Moreover, the young
Disraeli refused to show fitting enthusiasm for the liberal sentiments of the Whigs. He thought that the new
electoral law had been carefully constructed so as to
bring to the poll a whole class of tradesmen and manufacturers, cold and calculating men, the natural supporters of the Whigs, against the Tory farmers, and not in
the least for the sake of hearkening to the authentic voice
of the people. He had no taste for this alliance of the
cynicism of great landlords and the greed of great
spinners.

The fashionable doctrine amongst the Whigs and their
allies was utilitarianism, born of a kind of anti-romantic
reaction of the middle-classes. The invention of the

steam-engine and industrial machinery, the astounding development of English railways and mines, had inspired in them a passionate belief in material progress. The new science of political economy had taught them that the relations between men are not moral relations or duties, but are decreed by laws no less exact and inevitable than the law of gravity or the movement of the stars. The law of supply and demand was their gospel, the locomotive their fetish, and Manchester their Holy City.

Disraeli, the painter of great parks and flowering gardens and glittering mansions, detested this reek of coal. Political economy bored him; he could not believe that men, men of flesh with mobile faces, his heroes, Retz, Napoleon, Loyola, were condemned to combine like so many crooked atoms in order to produce the cheapest possible calico in the richest possible world.

Moreover, would the Whigs have welcomed him? Their liberalism did not extend to the choice of their friends, and the love of liberty was for them the monopoly of a clan. One could if necessary become a Tory, but one had to be born a Whig. The kingdom governed by the Whigs, thought Disraeli, saturated with his Venetian reading, would be the King transformed to a Doge and hedged in by a Council of Ten.

Ought he then to offer himself to the Tories? But this would be to adopt, in his twenties, a set of superannuated notions, to range himself under leaders who were booed by the crowd at the street-corners, to accept the burden of the faults of the past fifty years, to condemn himself to refuse all reform, however reasonable. Was it not better to follow Bulwer's example and join the Radicals, and then, outflanking the Whigs, make ready to fight the latter with their own weapons? Whig? Tory? Radical? A difficult choice indeed! The simplest way would have been to obtain a borough from some benevolent landlord. That was not impossible. But it was essential to be well known to those who had such seats in their gift, and, before all else, to gain entry to the political world. And in the England of 1831 this world of politics was indistinguishable from the world of fashion. The entrance to Parliament lay through the drawing-rooms. It was there that one had to win favour. One had to dine with the Duke of Wellington, with Sir Robert Peel, the Tory chiefs; with Lord Melbourne, Lord John Russell, the great Whigs; with Lord Durham, the great Radical. Round a table, where the crystal threw back the soft gleam of the lights, where beautiful women mingled their smiles with the parleying—there was the fitting place to meet with those who held power in their dispensation.

So, a touch of the frivolous still, to acquire the right to gravity.

VIII

The Conquest of London

*"It turned out that I had a very fine leg,
which I never knew before."*

LETTER OF DISRAELI.

Absence had worked the expected effects. London knew
nothing of Disraeli the Younger beyond that he was a
writer of talent, a very handsome lad, who dressed with
an amazing extravagance, and had returned from the
East with a wealth of stories which it was diverting to
hear. It required only one invitation to set in gear all
those that mattered. It came quite as a matter of course
from Edward Bulwer.

Bulwer, no less ambitious than Disraeli and better
endowed than he by birth, had advanced considerably
ahead of his friend during the past two years. At the
time when they had published, one his *Vivian Grey*, the
other his *Pelham,* it could only be supposed that they
were setting off along much the same lines. But Bulwer

had husbanded his youthful fame better than Disraeli. In April 1831 he had had himself nominated a member of Parliament and sat among the advanced Radicals; his books had conquered a public; he was editor of an important review.

This imposing façade concealed grave domestic difficulties. Such fruitful prizes could only have been won by relentless toil, to which all else, and Mrs. Bulwer in particular, had been sacrificed. Poor Poodle came to feel that she had lost her Pups for ever. When she saw him alone (which was seldom) she complained. In society, the couple appeared to be as one.

A few weeks after his return, Disraeli received a letter from Bulwer:

"MY DEAR DISRAELI,—If I am not among the very first, let me, at least, be not the last, to congratulate you on your safe return. I only heard of it yesterday. . . . 'Mr. Disraeli, sir, is come to town,—young Mr. Disraeli! Won't he give us a nice light article about his travels?' "

A few weeks later Disraeli rented a bachelor's flat in Duke Street. Sarah knew that her brother was wretched the moment he was deprived of flowers, and sent him from Bradenham a few pots of geraniums, which were lovingly tended. Straight away he dined at the Bulwers'. The house and the table were absurdly and magnificently lavish. Mrs. Bulwer, prettier and more elegant than ever, had on her knee a dog "not larger than a bird of paradise, and at least as brilliant." Champagne was poured out in cup-shaped glasses; Disraeli had never seen this, and it struck him as a detail of admirable refinement. The company was worthy of the setting: great names, great beauties, great talents. Especially did he eye the ravishing Mrs. Norton, one of Sheridan's granddaughters, and Count Alfred D'Orsay, who had lately arrived in London and won the position, unprecedented for a Frenchman, of grand master of the dandies.

Many of the ladies requested that the author of *Vivian Grey* and *The Young Duke* should be presented to them. A certain Mrs. Wyndham Lewis, wife of a member of Parliament, was very insistent.

"I was introduced 'by particular desire,' " he wrote to his sister, "to Mrs. Wyndham Lewis, a pretty little woman, a flirt, and a rattle; indeed gifted with a volubility I should think unequalled, and of which I can convey no idea. She told me that she liked 'silent, melancholy men.' I answered 'that I had no doubt of it.' "

He reaped an invitation from Mrs. Norton. He had pleased her; he had spoken little, but with brilliance, and she had need of conversationalists. The English at that period had the trick of replacing the essential verb of every sentence with a gesture. This young man with his few and perfect periods was cutting into that fashion of inarticulacy.

He went to Caroline Norton's in a coat of black velvet, poppy-coloured trousers broidered with gold, a

scarlet waistcoat, sparkling rings worn on top of white kid gloves.

The Nortons occupied a flat in Storey's Gate so small that one large sofa filled the whole of the drawing-room. White muslin curtains were crossed over the windows, before a flower-covered balcony. It was from this same balcony that Caroline Norton used to greet her old friend Lord Melbourne as he passed every morning on his way to Parliament. Norton, said rumour, tolerated this sentimental friendship because he found it profitable.

The tiny drawing-room was filled with a tightly packed crowd of politicians and celebrated men of letters, and positively illuminated by the extraordinary beauty of the Sheridans. In one arm-chair sat the mother, of whom it was said that she remained more beautiful than any woman in the world except her three daughters. These were the mistress of the house (Mrs. Norton), Mrs. Blackwood, and, loveliest of the three, Georgina (Lady Seymour), beside whom even her sisters paled. Mrs. Norton had black hair, which she coiled in tresses round her head, the features of a Greek beauty, and an adorable way of blushing. If some phrase in the conversation touched her, a pinkish tint would suddenly mingle with her slightly olive hue, linger for an instant—and vanish. Her eyes and lips flashed such colour that she seemed to be made of precious stones: diamonds and rubies and sapphires. Lady Seymour, with her pale and limpid complexion, was quite different, and her softly lit eyes looked like fountains in the light of the moon. When any one commented to Mrs. Norton on the emotion left by such a galaxy of beauty, she would look round her tiny drawing-room and her dazzling family with a complacent smile, and say: "Yes, we are rather good-looking people."

Mrs. Norton's conversation was an enchantment to Disraeli. She had an exquisite way of telling free stories, modestly lowering those eyelids of hers fringed with their long thick lashes. "Yesterday I dined with the Nortons," he wrote to Sarah. "It was her eldest brother's birthday, who, she says, is 'the only respectable one of the family, and that is because he had a liver complaint.' The only lady beside Mrs. Norton, her sister Mrs. Blackwood, was very handsome and very Sheridanic. She told me she was nothing. 'You see Georgy's the beauty, and Carrie's the wit, and I ought to be the good one, but then I am not.' I must say I liked her exceedingly; besides she knows all my works by heart, and spouts whole pages of *V. G.* and *C. F.* and the *Y. D.*"

The three Sheridanic Graces were soon to play a charming rôle in the life of the young author. All three were very free-and-easy; Mrs. Norton, delighted to leave an intolerable husband, liked to have Disraeli as her escort for the theatre or a ball. He found it agreeable to show himself in her company.

London in those days had a Watteau-like charm: dinners, balls, river-parties. Disraeli shared in everything. He was amusing, he brought pretty women, he was fresh from foreign travel. He was sought after: "I make my way easily in the highest set, where there is no envy, malice, &c., and where they like to admire and be amused. . . ." The table of "Dizzy" (as Mayfair had nicknamed him) was strewn with noble invitations, which he accepted with pleasure. In this brilliant, witty, and cordial world, he felt himself more at his ease and more in his proper sphere than amongst the middle-class people of his childhood. The free and fearless grace of these young women and young noblemen cast a spell over him. In their midst he met with the friends of his dreams, the fair-haired youths, lithe and splendid Englishmen, and with Englishwomen of high birth, the loveliest. He relished the luxury of the houses, the beauty of the flowers, the splendour of the women. On the surface at least, his dry pride was dissolved. He took confidence. He lived in a fever of joy. "I wish that your organization," his father wrote to him, "allowed you to write calmer letters." But Ben was quite incapable of writing a calm letter. The beauty of life was intoxicating him.

His deep interest in history led him to seek out old people. One of his closest women friends was the aged Lady Cork, who still, in spite of her eighty-seven years, entertained guests every evening. She was the prettiest and most diverting of dowagers. The heroes and heroines of her youth, of her maturity, and then of her old age, favourites, soldiers, poets, had all vanished. She had seen revolutions in every country of the world; she remembered Brighton when it was a fishing harbour, and Manchester as a village. But she still remained unaltered, alert and gay, thirsting for amusement and novelty. Finding both wit and curiosity in this young man, she accorded him her protection, a powerful one, in the social world.

"A good story!" he wrote to Sarah. "On Monday, I think, Lady Sykes was at Lady Cork's, and Lord Carrington paid her a visit.

"LADY C. Do you know young Disraeli?

"LORD C. Hem! Why? Eh?

"LADY C. Why, he is your neighbour, isn't he, eh?

"LORD C. His father is.

"LADY C. I know that. His father is one of my dearest friends. I dote on the Disraelis.

"LORD C. The young man is an extraordinary sort of person. The father I like; he is very quiet and respectable.

"LADY C. Why do you think the young man extraordinary? I should not think that *you* could taste him.

"LORD C. He is a great agitator. Not that he troubles us much *now*. He is never amongst us now. I believe he has gone abroad again.

"LADY C. (*literatim*). You old fool! Why, he sent me this book this morning. You need not look at it; you can't understand it. It is the finest book ever written. Gone abroad, indeed! Why, he is the best *ton* in London! There is not a party that goes down without him. The Duchess of Hamilton says there is nothing like. Lady Lonsdale would give her head and shoulders for him. He would not dine at your house if you were to ask him. He does not care for people because they are lords; he must have fashion, or beauty, or wit, or something; and you are a very good sort of person, but you are nothing more.

"The old Lord took it very good-humouredly, and laughed. Lady Cork has read every line of the new book. I don't doubt the sincerity of her admiration, for she has laid out 17s. in crimson velvet, and her maid is binding it. . . ."

A story for Sarah, no doubt; it would be rash to believe every word of it; when Benjamin's success was in question, the family tolerated a rather garishly coloured picture, and he himself realized that Sarah, as she read it, shared in Ben's imaginative powers.

In the evening the whole of the English aristocracy assembled at Almack's, a kind of private dance-club, under the patronage of the most exclusive of great ladies and governed by the strictest rules. One could enter its precincts only in breeches and silk stockings. Once the Duke of Wellington had tried to enter differently attired, but the doorkeeper had stepped forward and said: "Your Grace cannot be admitted in trousers." Whereupon the Duke, as a disciplined soldier, had gone off with not a word of complaint. Disraeli became a regular attender at Almack's. Many marriages were arranged there, and dazzling alliances were proposed to him: "By the bye, would you like Lady Z. for a sister-in-law, very clever, £25,000 and domestic? As for 'love,' all my friends who have married for love and beauty either beat their wives or live apart from them. This is literally the case. I may commit many follies in life, but I never intend to marry for 'love,' which I am sure is a guarantee of infelicity."

Feminine favour brought in its wake, but more slowly, the men. By some he had been invited to political luncheons, and this was his foremost desire. One evening, at Lord Eliot's, he found himself seated beside Sir Robert Peel, the great chief of the Tory party. The whole table seemed to be sorely intimidated. With hungry curiosity Disraeli scrutinized this stern and powerful personage on whom, from his adolescence, destiny had lavished everything which Disraeli, for his part, was coveting.

The son of a great manufacturer, owner of one of the seven largest fortunes in England, Peel had as a child been brought up to become Prime Minister. At five years old, he was hoisted on to tables and made to repeat his speeches. He had come down from Oxford with a "double first" in classics and mathematics, a rare achievement. At twenty-one, his father had bought a seat for him in Parliament. At twenty-three he had been a secretary of state. For some time he had been reproached for his ingratitude towards Canning, whom he had fought sternly to the death after having been his friend, but the political world had forgotten, and now at forty-three he had acquired an unbelievable prestige, even amongst his adversaries. He was the very symbol of English honesty and solidity. It was found good that he was tall in stature and had features of Roman firmness; it was accepted that he should be haughty and chilling.

Disraeli caught unawares the nervous movements of a susceptibility which was almost morbid, but only natural in a man accustomed to power, and realized that the Minister must be difficult to live with. But on that evening Peel had decided to make himself agreeable; he treated the young writer with slightly condescending familiarity, and joked with appropriate dignity; he was far from imagining that this insignificant neighbour was taking the measure of a great man.

Sometimes Disraeli would reflect: "But is it really essential to enter Parliament? This life of pleasure, idleness, literary work, is altogether delightful. At bottom, I am indolent, like all men of high imagination. . . . I wish to be idle and enjoy myself, muse over the stormy past and smile at the placid present. Alas! I struggle from Pride. Yes! It is Pride that now prompts me, not Ambition. They shall not say I have failed."

One day, on expressing these feelings to Bulwer, his friend turned towards him, took his arm, and said with every sign of sincerity: "It is true, my dear fellow, it is true. We are sacrificing our youth, the time of pleasure, the light season of enjoyment—but we are bound to go on, we are *bound*. How our enemies would triumph were we to retire from the stage!"

Yes, without a doubt, the game must go on. But sometimes, when some evening party had been charming, when London at night gleamed dimly in the fog as he came out from some ball, when a pretty woman had lingered as she pressed his hand in farewell, he would tell himself that ambition was a vain folly, that this frivolity he had feigned so long was his true nature, and was wisdom too, that it would be delightful to live on for ever at the feet of the three Sheridan sisters, a fond and indolent page.

IX

Independent

*"Good-bye, my dear lord. You have shewn
me the finest spectacle these Islands can
afford—a great nobleman living at home
among his own people."*

DISRAELI.

In June 1832, the bill for electoral Reform was passed
by the Lords. Up to the last moment they had hoped to
be able to block it. They had even heroically overturned
the Whig Cabinet, but no sooner did the Duke of Wellington try to form a Ministry than the country rose. The
tocsin was rung from the church towers. Everywhere
work was at a standstill. Lord Stanley, the most brilliant
of the young Whigs, had leaped upon a table and proclaimed: "If the Lords resist, His Majesty can put coronets on the heads of a whole company of his Guards."
The walls were placarded with posters calling upon
Englishmen to withdraw their money from the Bank.

The Bank of England was the only national institution

more respected than the Duke. The insurrection of depositors had beaten that of the peers. His Grace could do nothing but give the order: "My lords, right about turn! March!" The Reform party had carried the field; the elections which were to be held under the new mode of franchise could only seal its triumph; the overwhelming of the Tories was a certainty.

It may be imagined with what interest a Disraeli had followed these grave events; in a time of such commotion, the moment seemed to have come for securing a seat for himself in Parliament. As soon as the Reform Bill was passed, he set off for Wycombe, the borough near his father's property, and began to visit the electors. The constituency belonged to the Whigs, but Disraeli meant to stand as a Radical. In his innermost heart he liked the Tories better and better, finding that the old party of the landlords rooted in their fields and of gentlemen farmers had a picturesque greatness which none other could equal. With a few of these he had made alliances. In his own county of Bucks, he was on good terms with the Duke of Buckingham, and more particularly with his son, Lord Chandos, both of them great landlords after his own heart and generous to the point of folly. The old Duke had ruined himself by the extravagance of his entertainment of the French royal family, and for economy's sake had been living for two years on board his yacht. These were traits that seemed designed for Disraeli's pleasing.

Furthermore, every time that he found himself in a gathering of country gentlemen, he felt delighted. "Magnificent asses," he would say. And he said it with no trace of contempt; on the contrary, with envy. He admired their strength and their calm, but he did not dare to lean upon them. The formula was outworn; the nation would have none of it; what was to be done? He turned up, on the contrary, fortified with letters of recommendation from advanced men like Joseph Hume and the dreaded Irishman, Daniel O'Connell, letters which Bulwer had procured for him. Bulwer had even made great efforts to secure that no candidate should be put up against his friend, but he had failed; the great Whigs did not care for this eccentric and sonorous young man, better known for his waistcoats than for his love of Reform. By the Tory side he was made tolerably welcome in the county, first because the party, having no chance of winning the seat for itself, preferred to see it held by an independent, and further because the Tory sentiments of old Isaac D'Israeli were well known. Benjamin's opponents declared that he was nothing but a Tory in disguise; to which he retorted that the closest thing to a Tory in disguise was a Whig in power.

The local election happened to be put forward a few weeks on account of an unexpected resignation, with the result that it was still held under the conditions of the old electoral law. This being so, the borough could muster only about thirty electors. The Ministry offered the official candidature to Colonel Grey, the son of the Prime Minister: "The Treasury," wrote Disraeli to Mrs. Austen, "sent down Colonel Grey with a hired mob and a band. Never was such a failure. After parading the town with his paid voices, he made a stammering speech of ten minutes from his phaeton. All Wycombe was assembled. Feeling it was the crisis, I jumped up on the portico of the Red Lion and gave it them for an hour and a quarter. I can give you no idea of the effect. I made them all mad. A great many absolutely *cried*. I never made as many friends in my life or converted as many enemies. All the women are on my side and wear my colours, pink and white. Do the same."

When the good people of Wycombe had seen the apparition on the porch of the Red Lion of this pale young man with black ringlets and lace cuffs, carrying a gold-headed cane, and carefully arranging his curls before beginning to speak, they had expected some puerile oration. But a voice of astonishing power had suddenly flooded the High Street with sarcastic eloquence, had attacked the Whigs with bitterness and vehemence, and Wycombe had yielded to an uneasy enthusiasm. As for Disraeli, he was intoxicated at the first taste of this new pleasure, of feeling himself master of a public, of becoming his own listener, of marvelling at the strong and harmonious phrases dictated to the orator by the god within him. "When the poll is declared," he concluded, pointing to the tail of the large lion which adorns the porch of the hotel, "my opponent will be *there*: and I" —he pointed to its head—"and I shall be here!" Never had Wycombe seen its old lion thus jewel-like in the setting of such startling words.

On polling-day Disraeli made one more speech. He did not wear, he said, the badge of any party; the Tories had supported him, but the people had supported him first. He sought the amelioration of the lot of the poor (a rare formula in electoral declarations at a time when the poor had no votes). And he was sprung, moreover, from the people, and had in his veins neither Tudor nor Plantagenet blood.

Then, one after another, the thirty-two electors of Wycombe climbed upon the hustings; they announced their votes publicly and the result was proclaimed. The timid and stuttering colonel had twenty votes, the brilliant orator of the Red Lion, twelve. He was not at the beast's head.

He climbed on the platform once again, and said: "Good! The Whigs have cast me off, and they shall repent it." But he was sad and disappointed.

When October came, the general election with the extended franchise was proclaimed, and Disraeli returned to Wycombe. This time again he offered himself as an independent candidate. "I care not for party. I stand here without party. . . . Englishmen, rid yourselves of all that political jargon and factious slang of Whig and Tory —two names with one meaning, used only to delude you—and unite in forming a great national party which can alone save the country from impending destruction."

The Conservatives, on the advice of his friend Lord Chandos, accorded him as on the first occasion a benevolent neutrality. They were reproached for this support by a Radical candidate. "I am a Conservative," he said, "to preserve all that is good in our constitution, a Radical to remove all that is bad." He declared himself happy to see that, in this constituency at least, the Tories were reverting to the great tradition of the party, which formerly, under men like Bolingbroke, had been a popular party. Attempts were made to drag demagogic declarations from him touching the Corn Laws, but he maintained an attitude of reasonableness: "If we have recourse to any sudden alteration of the present system, we may say farewell to the county of Bucks, farewell to the beautiful Chilterns. . . . You will ask is bread, then, always to be dear? By no means, but it is surely better to have dear bread than to have no bread at all." But all this sound sense passed unrewarded: Grey, 140 votes, Disraeli, 119. All over England the Whigs won a prodigious triumph, and came back with a majority that bade fair to keep them in power for many a long day. Having lost this opportunity, Disraeli would no doubt have to wait a long time for another.

Soon after, when the new Parliament had met, he went to hear his friend Bulwer, who had been re-elected. In the evening he wrote to Sarah:

"Bulwer spoke, but he is physically disqualified for an orator; and, in spite of all his exertions, never can succeed. . . . Macaulay admirable; but between ourselves, I could floor them all. This *entre nous;* I was never more confident of anything than that I could carry everything before me in that House. The time will come. . . ."

In his diary he noted: "The world calls me *conceited.* The world is in error. I trace all the blunders of my life to sacrificing my own opinion to that of others. When I was considered very conceited indeed I was nervous and had self-confidence only by fits. I intend in future to act entirely from my own impulse. I have an unerring instinct—I can read characters at a glance; few men can deceive me. My mind is a continental mind. It is a revolutionary mind. I am only truly great in action. If ever I am placed in a truly eminent position I shall prove this. I could rule the House of Commons, although there would be a great prejudice against me at first."

Just as he had felt the desire to write a novel after the reverse of the newspaper, so after two political reverses he felt desirous of writing a poem. He had gone into retreat at Bradenham, where he lived closeted in his room, or walked in solitude under the beeches of the park meditating a great theme. It was a subject he had first turned over in his mind during his travels in the East as he gazed upon the plains of Troy: "Homer . . ." he had murmured, "and why should not poems yet be written as great as Homer's?" To Disraeli that meant: "Why should not *I* write . . . ?" It was only a question of finding the subject for the modern epic.

Napoleon seemed to him the obvious one. At the beginning of the poem the genius of Feudalism and the genius of Democracy would make their appearance before the Deity. Each would eloquently defend its title to the governance of mankind, for if Disraeli admired feudalism in the past, he believed democracy to be inevitable in the future. The first canto, then, was a dialogue between Disraeli and Disraeli; the difficulty was to make God choose. But the Almighty prudently declared that a man of supernatural stature had just been born and that the party chosen by this genius would triumph. This man was Napoleon, and the Italian campaign was to form the subject of the second canto: "What do you think of it?" he wrote to Mrs. Austen. "The conception seems to me sublime."

When the first canto had been completed, he went to read it to her one evening. A few friends had assembled, and they found the scene irresistibly comic. This tall young man leaning against the mantelpiece, toying with his curls, glancing complacently at the rosettes of red ribbon adorning his pumps, and proclaiming himself the Dante and Homer of his time, excited such merriment as could hardly be checked. Soon the first two cantos were published; their public welcome was cold; Disraeli had never felt very strongly about being a Homer; the poem was beginning to weary him; he flung it in a corner and thought no more about it.

X

Women

To the disappointed man of ambition the world offers
sure and sweet revenge; frequently, if he be amiable,
it treats him better than a great conqueror or a minister.
In the eyes of women, the very fact of an unplaced
man's idleness is a merit, as it places him at their service. To this delicious bondage Disraeli gladly submitted. He was happy to be restored to the incomparable
sisters, his three lovely Sheridans. His circle of fair
women widened. Ladies who were neighbours at Bradenham, sisters likewise, Lady Chesterfield and Mrs.
Anson, took him to the most splendid fancy-dress ball.
Lady Chesterfield went as a Sultana, and Mrs. Austen
as a Greek, her long loosened hair falling to her

knees. The Marchioness of Londonderry, as Cleopatra, sparkling with diamonds and emeralds, requested Disraeli to be presented to her. In this splendid house blazing with lights, he was happy for a moment, floating gently on a living sea of precious stones and lovely faces.

He had a mistress; he loved her and composed a love story in her honour, *Henrietta Temple,* quickly succeeded by a novel on the life of Byron and Shelley, *Venetia.* The real Henrietta was married, but free in her ways. She belonged to the brilliant little circle beloved by Disraeli, so that it was easy for them to gather round themselves the best company in London.

Every day they were bidden to some river-party, to a garden-party in the flower-clad groves worthy of Veronese, to some delightful supper after the Opera. Sometimes he rode to hounds, mounted on a perfect Arab mare which belonged to his mistress, taking every jump and winning the esteem of the most exacting horsemen. He had no taste for this sport, but refused to let himself be checked by any obstacle; that was part of his system.

Bulwer had introduced him in a new house, that of Lady Blessington. Disraeli had already heard many tales of its hostess's life. Margaret, Lady Blessington, was the daughter of a small Irish magistrate, who had forced her at the age of fifteen to marry a madman for the sake of money. Lord Blessington, a great landlord and man of property, an eccentric, a widower, and the father of two daughters rich to the tune of £30,000 a year, had discovered this young beauty hidden away; he offered to bring her to England, obtain her a divorce,

and make her his wife. Lord and Lady Blessington had
set off for Italy accompanied by a young Frenchman,
Count D'Orsay, a model of beauty, brilliance and culture. No one doubted but that he was Lady Blessington's
lover, and no doubt he really was. Lord Blessington had
conceived an incredible affection for Alfred D'Orsay,
and had made a will leaving him the greater part of his
wealth, conditionally upon his marrying one of the
testator's daughters, at choice. The daughters thus formally and bindingly bequeathed were then eleven and
twelve years of age. Four years later, in 1827, Count
D'Orsay, true to his signature, had married the second,
Lady Harriet, a pale slip of a girl of fifteen, who was
taken away from school for the marriage. The world
added that Alfred D'Orsay had given his word to Lady
Blessington never to make Lady Harriet his wife in the
full sense of the word, and that this arrangement had
been respected. Then Lord Blessington had died suddenly. D'Orsay and his young virgin wife had returned
to England to enter upon the inheritance, accompanied
by Lady Blessington. The schoolgirl had grown up, and
become very pretty, and soon, suffering under the polite
scorn of her husband and the presence of her step-
mother, she had left the house in Seymour Place, never
to return.

Such was the tale accepted by London, but Bulwer,
as he brought Disraeli to Lady Blessington's, added
lights and shades to the portrait: "Lady Blessington was
essentially sympathetic, and admired with enthusiasm.
She had all the Irish cordiality of manner, and a
peculiar grace of her own. She was benevolent, kindly

and generous to a rare degree. She understood her critical position and never tried to force herself on female society. She commanded the best male society, and her house was agreeable. Whatever her faults, she was undeserving of much that scandal had laid to her charge.

"She had been accused of making up the marriage of D'Orsay and her daughter-in-law, Lady Harriet. There was no foundation for this story. She was against it. Lord Blessington had enforced it, and Lady Harriet herself pleaded her affection for D'Orsay, when he tried to evade Lord Blessington's importunity. To all appearance the affection between her and D'Orsay was that of a mother for a spoilt child. I feel a strong conviction that, at least after D'Orsay's marriage, there was never any criminal connection between them. Nor, indeed, any love of that kind, especially on her part. She was confessedly of a very cold temperament, though most affectionate to her friends, and most true to them. She was middle-aged when I first knew her, and much of her early beauty was then gone. But she had a singularly sweet and gracious face, and a wonderful symmetry of form, till she grew too stout."

Disraeli was enchanted by the house. One passed through a drawing-room in gold and ruby, filled with beautiful amber vases which had belonged to the Empress Josephine, to enter the long, narrow library with its white walls on which mirrors alternated with panels of bound books. Through the tall window at the end could be seen the trees of Hyde Park. Round the room were sofas, ottomans, tables of enamel covered with bibelots, and in a yellow satin fauteuil, Lady Blessington, dressed in a gown of blue satin, cut extremely low. Disraeli admired her beautiful shoulders, the full and firm curves of the bosom; he liked the hair drawn tightly back from a centre parting, the turquoise clasp on the brow. With her first words he was conquered.

When he came to know better the charming couple that she and D'Orsay made, with their reciprocal attentions and the almost childlike gaiety they seemed both to extract from the little pleasantries which formed, as it were, the household tradition, he forgot for ever Lady Harriet, the old nobleman, and the rest of the dark story, and found whole-hearted enjoyment in the friendship of two delightful creatures. On her side, Lady Blessington found him full of genius, eloquence and ingenuousness, in fact very like his Vivian Grey. As she was not received by any woman, she entertained every evening, and Disraeli acquired the habit of coming almost daily. Often he was silent, simply enjoying the pleasure of being in this drawing-room he was so fond of, standing at the window and gazing out over the gravel paths of Hyde Park. The last rays of the sun gleamed on the gilded flowers of his waistcoat. He held a white cane in his hand. His pockets were laden with gold chains. When a topic interested him, he would move over to the talkers and grow animated, and then the ease of his speech and the force of his sarcasm were astonishing. When he talked he was like a racehorse a few lengths from the winning-post. Every muscle was called into play, and into every sentence he infused an extraordinary energy of expression. He possessed the art of bringing into apposition words so far apart that their proximity gave them a fierce and disturbing power. It was a pleasure to listen to him, but a slightly tense pleasure. Towards midnight, after the House had risen, Bulwer arrived, and the dialogues of the two friends were dazzling.

But Disraeli liked still better to see Lady Blessington alone. She had become his confidante and a counsellor in his amorous adventures. He told her everything, how he had loved Henrietta, how he had had her received at Bradenham by his parents, simple-hearted people who had seen no harm in it, how he had felt remorse for that, how she had got him deeper than ever into debt by her zest for parties and suppers, how this liaison was threatening to compromise his career, and also how ambition in his heart was a stronger sentiment than love. Later he had told her of the breaking of his liaison. She understood everything. He talked to her of Bradenham, of old Mr. D'Israeli, of his mother. He disclosed to her the impatient sadness lying concealed beneath his wit and light-heartedness. In this easy-going freedom he was charming. Just as he was deemed artificial and cynical by those who knew him slightly, so he was found to be natural and soft-hearted by a true friend like Lady Blessington. He asked her advice, childish sometimes; he had her explain men to him; he inquired of her about the latest French books and took counsel regarding his reading: "What of Balzac? Is he better than Sue and George Sand-Dudevant? And are these inferior to Hugo?" He even confessed to her his shyness and the weakness of his nerves: "Indeed, I know not how it is, but I am never well, save in action, and then I feel immortal. I am ashamed of being 'nervous.' Dyspepsia always makes me wish for a civil war. . . . I am dying for action, and rust like a Damascus sabre in the sheath of a poltroon."

Sometimes in the drawing-room of his feminine acquaintance, he would meet the politicians in power. For a moment he raised his dandy's mask and spoke with fire of affairs of State. Ah, how he envied them, occupying those posts where words are turned to action! One evening at Caroline Norton's, he was presented to Lord Melbourne, the great Whig Minister, who continued to come there regularly, stretched himself with nonchalant air upon the divan, spoke little but listened with pleasure. Melbourne was allured by the originality of this young man's ideas and the boldness of his eloquence. Abruptly, with his surly good nature, he offered to help him: "Well now, tell me, what do you want to be?"—"I want to be Prime Minister." Melbourne shrugged his shoulders and sighed. "No, no," he said very seriously. "No chance of that in our time. It is all arranged and settled. . . . The next Prime Minister will be Stanley, who is like a young eagle over the heads of all his rivals. . . . No, go into politics, you will be right; you have ability and enterprise, and with patience I dare say you will do very well. But you must put all these foolish ideas out of your head."

"Out of your head"—easy words for a Lord Melbourne, who had known everything and tasted everything; but this young Disraeli wished to live, and could not conceive of life without glory. In his hearing the three lovely Sheridans were arguing with spirit on the sovereign good. "What is the most desirable life?" And serious of a sudden, young Dizzy, from the depths of his divan, answered with fire: "A continued grand procession from manhood to the tomb."

XI

The Badge of a Party

"I prefer the liberties we now enjoy to the liberalism they profess, and find something better than the Rights of Man in the Rights of Englishmen."

DISRAELI.

At the elections of 1833 the victory of the Whig party had been so startling that they might have been supposed to have half a century of power in front of them. But the sense of security will destroy everything, even coalitions which appear invincible.

Among the victorious liberals, if there were some genuinely reformist spirits like Lord John Russell, or bolder still like Lord Durham, there were also men who were conservatives without knowing it, like that Lord Stanley in whom Lord Melbourne described the future Prime Minister. Before long a split became inevitable; Stanley and his friends left the party, and the Tory scale jumped up with a bound.

The amusing thing was, that the Tory ranks were likewise fighting under a leader who kept a constant eye on his opponents' side, and seemed to prefer the approbation of the latter to that of his own partisans. Sir Robert Peel's ambition was to dominate all parties—the sole ambition left to a man who has dominated his own. Under his direction the Tory party had taken the new name of "Conservative," and he meant this word as opposed to "reactionary." Thus a conservative Liberal like Stanley and a liberal Conservative like Peel approximated to such a degree that it was no longer easy to distinguish between them. And of the two no doubt, the more liberal was the Conservative.

Such changes of position were bound to make the personal political evolution of a Disraeli distinctly easier. This return to the fearless and popular traditions of the old-time Tories was exactly what he had desired from the beginning of his career. He saw clearly that eventually he would have to join hands with one of the existing groups. He had tried to fight as a freelance; he had been beaten, and beaten again.

In a country possessed of an old parliamentary tradition, and especially in a country which, like England, has a respect for loyalty and a contempt for systems, it is all but impossible to slip in between the parties. From within a party, it is possible to prepare to hive off; new ideas can be imposed only under an accepted label. The moment had arrived for Disraeli to make his choice, and make his submission.

If he still hesitated to offer his services to the Conservative party, this was simply a question of personalities. For Disraeli, the lover of a flashing figure and a picturesque character, the cold Sir Robert Peel was hardly attractive. The Duke, it is true, was more picturesque, with that brusque straightforwardness of his, but the Duke had retired from the scene. The insult at the moment of the Reform had been too much; he did not like to compromise himself with the populace. He had chosen the more agreeable part of being the old national hero. Young men in the clubs would get him to tell the stories of his campaigns. "At Salamanca I was kneeling behind a low wall when I saw the left wing of the French giving. 'By God!' said I, 'that will do. . . . I'll attack them at once.' " When he passed along the streets on horseback, the crowd raised their hats to him. He was satisfied, and was fully decided to take no further hand in battles that brought no glory.

About this time Disraeli dined one evening beside Lord Lyndhurst, the Tory Lord Chancellor. Lyndhurst's father, the story ran, had said to him one day: "Jack, you'll be a boy all your life through!" It was a true prophecy. At sixty, the Lord Chancellor retained a taste for the imaginative in human affairs, was more amused than outraged by the weaknesses of his fellows, and used to learn poems by heart in order to train his memory. His wide indulgence was shocking to sober spirits; it was a delight to Disraeli. Here at last was some one who talked to him of politics and parties as he thought of them himself, not as a religion, but as an art.

He never tired of hearing the tale of all the great events of the century, and especially of those small and precious details which bring history back to life, of learning for instance that on the eve of Canning's death the sky was blue but the wind cool, that Canning had wanted to dine out, that Lyndhurst had seen him shiver. The Lord Chancellor had admitted this young Disraeli to his friendship, and given him his advice. One day he asked him to dine with a very young Under-Secretary of State named William Gladstone, and gave wise lessons to both of them: "Never defend yourself before a popular assembly, except by retorting the attack; the hearers, in the pleasure which the assault gives them, will forget the previous charge." A serious man, this young Gladstone, of the Peel type; he could not be very pleasing in Disraeli's eyes, or in Lyndhurst's either, and the dinner was rather dreary, but they were served with a swan, very white, very tender, and well stuffed with truffles, and that in itself was good company.

Thanks to Lyndhurst, Disraeli began to penetrate behind the scenes of the political world. For still a little while longer he coquetted with Lord Durham and his Radicals. The two extreme parties were both seeking a constituency for him. He let things take their course. But these incompatible flirtations were known in London and made a bad impression: "From Durham to Wellington . . . ," people said, "devil take it! This Disraeli must be a very impartial spirit." "Altogether the type of friend one expects of a Lyndhurst," added the peevish Greville.

A fresh reverse at the poll succeeded in curing him. Three hard lessons sufficed. Independence stood condemned. Disraeli had himself elected to the Carlton Club, the heart of the Conservative camp, and decided to present himself henceforward as a Tory candidate. At last he wore the badge of a party.

A man's variances are always explicable enough to himself, and Disraeli, although he had been a Radical and had turned Conservative, prided himself in all good faith on his consistency. To an outside observer, the continuity was less evident. When the exigencies of the political campaign led the new-made Tory to attack O'Connell, from whom he had formerly solicited a letter of recommendation, the Irish tribune burst into a tremendous fury. At a meeting in Dublin a few days later, he spoke of this attack, and of his letter, concluding amid laughter and applause: "The Jews were once the chosen people of God. There were miscreants among them, however, and it must have certainly been from one of them that Disraeli descended. He possesses just the qualities of the impenitent thief who died on the Cross, whose name, I verily believe, must have been Disraeli. For aught I know, the present Disraeli is descended from him, and with the impression that he is, I now forgive the heir-at-law of the blasphemous thief who died upon the Cross."

Every newspaper in London reproduced this vivid harangue, which afforded amusement to many people whom Disraeli irritated. For his part, sentiments forgotten since his childhood surged up in him when he

read these insulting phrases. Ah, how he would have
liked to thrash this man as he had thrashed the insulting schoolboy in days gone by! He hastened to
D'Orsay's and asked him to arrange a meeting. But
O'Connell had already killed a man in a duel, and had
taken a vow never to fight again. Disraeli threw a challenge to the son, Morgan O'Connell, who replied that he
avenged insults offered to his father, but could not
accept responsibility for all that his father said. Whereupon Disraeli wrote a violent letter to O'Connell:

"MR. O'CONNELL,—Although you have long placed
yourself out of the pale of civilisation, still I am one
who will not be insulted, even by a Yahoo, without
chastising it."

He passed harsh judgment on the double refusal to
fight of the father and son, and concluded:

"We shall meet at Philippi; and rest assured that,
confident in a good cause, and in some energies which
have been not altogether unproved, I will seize the first
opportunity of inflicting upon you a castigation which
will make you remember and repent the insults that
you have lavished upon

"BENJAMIN DISRAELI."

After this letter he recovered his calm and his self-
contentment. He donned his most dazzling costume, his
most richly broidered waistcoat, appeared at the Opera,
and was widely complimented on his courage.

Sarah and old Isaac wrote that they did not care for this unpalatable hubbub around their name, and expressed disapproval of so much ferocity. Benjamin checked them: "There is but one opinion among *all* parties—viz. that I have *squabashed* them. . . . It is very easy for you to criticise, but I do not regret the letter. Critics you must always meet. W. told me the last letter was the finest thing in the English language. . . . One does not like the Yahoo as coarse, others think it worthy of Swift, and so on. . . . The general effect is the thing, and that is, that all men agree I have shown pluck."

It was true. His friends, and society too, disapproved of the rather low form of O'Connell's attack, and did hold that Disraeli had shown courage. But society does not make up public opinion. In England the opinion that counts is that of tradesmen behind their counters, of clergymen in their villages, of that immense, suspicious, unimaginative mass which composes the English nation. And for this mass the picture that was beginning to take shape, through the newspaper accounts, of this young author-politician was one of a kind most distasteful to the English spirit. It was that of a noisy, showy fellow, devoid of political faith, ludicrous and insolent. No doubt O'Connell had been brutal, "but Mr. Disraeli," as the *Spectator*, for example, remarked, "chose to commence a war of abuse with the greatest master of abuse; and then finding himself worsted, pretends that he is an injured person. He reminds us of the puppy yelping under the pain of a kick from some strong-limbed horse, at whose heels he had been snapping and snarling for miles."

This offensive portrait was still only a weak and ill-defined shadow, but, associated with an almost unknown name, how dangerous such an image can be! It is the "character," a fictitious being, but no less real than the true man. Once it is formed, all the facts that fit in with it are seized upon by public opinion, all the others ignored. The young Disraeli would have been greatly surprised if he had met himself as an Englishman in the City might have imagined him at that time. He would have kept the creature at arm's length, with horror and scorn; he would not have doubted that he had just met the most redoubtable enemy he would henceforth have to fight.

XII

M. P.

The season of balls came round again. Once more Mrs. Anson, with flowing hair, was the loveliest of slaves, and Mrs. Norton a marvellous Greek; once more Benjamin Disraeli was the brilliant and frivolous dandy, whose silhouette, hung with gold chains, stood sharply out against Lady Blessington's windows. But how weary sometimes he was of this mask; how tiring it was to be Disraeli! His silences became longer and more frequent, heavy too with gloomy meditation which he suddenly broke off with a burst of sarcasm. The years were mounting up; thirty-two: that is old—for a page.

Only through his friendship with Lord Lyndhurst was

he brought remotely into touch with real power. This cynical and charming old man consulted him as an equal. They united in deploring the oblique direction which Peel was giving to the party. Under his orders the Conservative party was an army without a faith, because the chief himself was not a believer. In practice, Peel found himself brought to the defence of the country's traditional institutions, the monarchy, the House of Lords, the Anglican Church; in theory, he was tempted to think that they were indefensible. The Conservative party was rich; it counted among its adherents the owners of forests, of country mansions, of factories; it had neither genius nor doctrine. Peel spoke frequently of conservatism, but he had no idea of what he wanted to conserve.

On the other hand, the more Disraeli reflected on the political life of England, the more did it seem necessary in his eyes to face things squarely and courageously. For him, to be a Conservative was not just to uphold with an apologetic smile a constitution held to be out of date; it was a proud and romantic attitude, the only intelligent one, the only one which loyally took into account the authentic England, those villages grouped round the manor-house, that vigorous, obstinate breed of small squires, that aristocracy at once so venerable and so assimilative, nay, history itself. "This respect for precedent, this clinging to prescription, this reverence for antiquity, which are so often ridiculed by conceited and superficial minds, appear to me to have their origin in a profound knowledge of human nature." What was needed was to set up, against the theoretic doctrines of the liberals and utilitarians, a doctrine of realism.

To him the whole issue of modern politics was between an historic school and a philosophic school; he chose history. A country is not an abstract being whose rights can be deduced by a plain mental process. A nation is a work of art, and a work wrought by time. It has a temperament like that of an individual. The greatness of England in particular is sprung, not from its natural resources, which are mediocre, but from its institutions. The rights of Englishmen are older by five full centuries than the Rights of Man.

Such was the customary turn of the young doctrinaire's ideas. In 1835 he published his *Vindication of the English Constitution in a Letter to a Noble and Learned Lord, by Disraeli the Younger*, a work of political philosophy, and its perfection of form and matureness of thought were recognized by the best judges. The existence of a House of Lords might seem absurd to minds which did not admit of representation without election; Disraeli showed that the greater danger was that of election without representation. It was possible for an oligarchy of professional politicians to secure their own election, and rule the country without being the reflection of its will. The House of Lords, on the other hand, represented real powers. It represented the Church in the person of the Lord Bishops, the Law in that of the Lord Chancellor, the counties in the Lords Lieutenant, the land in its hereditary proprietors. As for the House of Commons, he desired, on the contrary, that it should be much more widely recruited than had been secured by the very limited Whig reforms of 1832. It seemed to him that the duty of a Conservative leader was to have the courage to defend the past in so far as it was living and likely to live, but also to sweep the party clean of prejudices and outworn principles, and above all to guide it boldly in the direction of a generous policy, inspired by love of the ordinary, common people and capable of conquering them.

The book had a great success. "They'll have to find a seat in Parliament for this young man," grumbled the Duke. Peel wrote a letter that was almost amiable. As for that old Tory Isaac D'Israeli, he was delighted: "You have now a positive *name* and a *being* in the great political world, which you had not ten days ago. You never wanted for genius, but it was apt in its fullness to run over. You have rejected the curt and flashy diction which betrayed continual effort. All now flows in one continuous stream of thought and expression—at once masculine and graceful." It would be infamous, wrote Lyndhurst, if Disraeli were not now placed in a position which might give the party the full benefit of his talents, his activity, his untiring zeal.

From now onwards the fruit was ripe; it could not be long in falling. And what is more, it was high time. Creditors were yelping louder than ever. Bailiffs were sometimes seen wandering to the very doors of Bradenham. Four appearances as candidate, an extravagant mistress, an expensive dandyism, had tripled Disraeli's debts. He willingly lent his friends money borrowed for their benefit, which they never returned. Only once, in a very stiff corner, he reminded D'Orsay of a debt, and received the answer: "I swear before God that I have not sixpence at my banker now." It was perfectly true.

King William IV. died on the evening of the anniversary of Waterloo. He was succeeded by a girl Queen, eighteen years old. At eleven o'clock the next morning Victoria called her first Council. Disraeli went to Kensington Palace with Lord Lyndhurst, who was going to pledge fealty to his Sovereign. On his return, Lyndhurst, deeply moved, described to Disraeli this assembly of all that was most illustrious in England, the sea of white plumes and stars and uniforms, the doors suddenly flung open, a silence deep as that of a forest, and the young girl advancing to her throne in the midst of this crowd of prelates, statesmen and generals. Disraeli was spellbound by the recital. There he saw united all the things he loved: the pomp of ceremony, a glittering gravity, the chivalrous homage to a woman of all the strength of England. How he would have loved, he also, to kneel before his Queen, to kiss that youthful hand. But he was nobody, and the years were passing.

The accession of a new Sovereign brought with it the dissolution of Parliament and a General Election. This time Disraeli, well backed by Lyndhurst, received numerous offers of safe constituencies. Among others Wyndham Lewis, the husband of the flirtatious little chatterbox he had formerly met at Bulwer's, asked him if he would like to be his fellow-member for Maidstone, a constituency with two seats where the Conservatives were bound to win. It was to Mrs. Wyndham that he owed the offer. For a long time he regarded her as very tiresome. Once at the Rothschilds', the lady of the house had said to him: "Mr. Disraeli, will you take Mrs. Wyndham Lewis in to dinner?" "Oh, anything rather than that insufferable woman!" he had replied. "However . . . great is Allah!" And sticking his thumbs, as he liked to do, in the armholes of his waistcoat, he had marched off to the torture.

But after a few meetings he had changed his mind. She had neither wit nor culture, but she talked about affairs with good sense. Her judgments on politicians were not foolish. More than once he had found her advice sound. And in the end he allowed himself to become quite a frequent guest at dinner in the Wyndham Lewis's large London house overlooking Hyde Park. It was obvious that Mrs. Wyndham was interested in him. She admired him and was able to be of service to him, a blend which women savour in friendship, and he paid his court to her, half-serious, half-humourous, which pleased the fancy of this rather ripe beauty.

During the campaign she played the part of his electoral godmother. Disraeli wrote her affable letters, telling her of his pleasure in seeing their two names side by side on the placards. He had completely forgotten his first antipathy. Nobody, not even Sarah, was more adept in praising him than this lady.

"Mark what I prophesy," she wrote: "Mr. Disraeli will in a very few years be one of the greatest men of his day. His great talents, backed by his friends Lord Lyndhurst and Lord Chandos, with Wyndham's power to keep him in Parliament, will insure his success. They call him my Parliamentary *protégé*."

Her good opinion of the candidate was shared by at least one man, and that was the candidate himself. "When I meet you again as my constituents," he said to the electors of Maidstone, "not a person will look upon me without some degree of satisfaction, and perhaps some degree of pride."

Voting took place on July 27th. Lewis and Disraeli were elected. Thus the latter obtained almost without a struggle, and within a few days, the seat which he had so long desired. Life was strange. Always beaten at Wycombe, where he thought himself known and well esteemed, he was suddenly victorious at Maidstone, which he had never seen until a week before. What roundabout path had chance taken to bring him to the goal? It was to the material solicitude of a talkative little woman that he owed his seat. His meeting with Mrs. Wyndham herself he owed to the friendship of Bulwer. That friendship had sprung from *Vivian Grey*. *Vivian Grey* would never have been written had it not been for the collapse of Murray's newspaper and the South American speculations. Those speculations had been entered upon by virtue of his time in the chambers at Frederick's Place. To those chambers he had been sent because the persecutions at Dr. Cogan's school had shown his father the impossibility of a University education.

Thus, step by step, running right back into childhood, he traced an unbroken chain of circumstances in which an unlucky event was the cause of fortunate events, and the latter in their turn the causes of disasters and reverses. How hard it was, in this perfect but obscure ordering, to find a rule or a law! How mysterious it all was! It brought him to the point of regarding existence as a continuous miracle. And yet through all this darkling forest, there ran a gleaming Ariadne's thread—the will of Benjamin Disraeli. On the methods and results of his acts he might have been deceived; he had almost always been mistaken. But never had he lost either a clear view of the goal or the firm resolve to attain it. Perhaps that sufficed. . . . Certainly that sufficed, as here he was with his foot in the stirrup. Benjamin Disraeli, M.P. . . . a fine title and a fine adventure. In a few months an assembly prone to admiration would be listening to perfect periods, to muscular phrases, to the astounding conjunctions of rare adjectives and vigorous nouns. A few years, and the Right Honourable Benjamin Disraeli would be at the head of the Colonial Office or the Exchequer of this great Empire. And after that. . . .

To Sarah Disraeli.

"MAIDSTONE, *July* 27, 1837. 11 *o'cl.*

"DEAREST,—Lewis 707, Disraeli 616, Colonel Thompson 412. The constituency nearly exhausted. In haste, DIZZY."

To Mrs. Wyndham Lewis.

"BRADENHAM, *July* 30*th*, 1837.

"We all here wish very much that Mr. Wyndham and yourself would come and pay us a visit among our beechen groves. We have nothing to offer you but simple pleasures, a sylvan scene and an affectionate heart. . . . I suppose my colleague is in Glamorganshire. My kind regards are his and yours.

"DIS."

Mrs. Wyndham Lewis to Major Evans
(*her brother-in-law*).

"I have been paying a visit to Mr. Disraeli's family. They reside near High Wycombe—a large family house, most of the rooms 30 and 40 feet long, and plenty of servants, horses, dogs, and a library full of the rarest books. But how shall I describe his father; the most lovable, perfect old gentleman I ever met with? A sort of modern Dominie Sampson—and his manners are so high-bred and natural. Miss Disraeli is handsome and talented, and two brothers. Our political pet, the eldest, commonly called Dizzy, you will see a great deal of; you know Wyndham brought him in for Maidstone with himself."

Disraeli to Mrs. Edward Lytton Bulwer.

"It is odd that my electioneering struggle should terminate in being M.P. for Maidstone. We are the children of the gods, and are never more the slaves of circumstances than when we deem ourselves their masters. What may next happen in the dazzling farce of life the Fates only know."

D'Orsay to Disraeli.

"You will not make love! You will not intrigue! You have your seat; do not risk anything! If you meet with a widow, then marry!"

At Bradenham he spent the three months that passed between the election and the meeting of Parliament; he felt the need of meditating on the past and preparing himself for the future. Alone, or sometimes with Sarah, he took long walks through that delightful countryside. The season was mild and sunny, the air perfumed with flowers, humming with the murmur of bees, quickened by the fluttering of white butterflies. Often, after long following of some narrow winding footpath, he would suddenly see before him a wide stretch of turf in the sunlight, a group of cedars, an old manor-house covered with ivy or Virginia creeper. It was for such sights that he admired England as he did. In each of those houses there was some sturdy ruddy-cheeked gentleman, a clear-eyed son, handsome daughters, mysterious and virginal. There lay the springs whence London drew its strength; thence came the men who upheld the Empire for its Queen. It was this grandeur and this beauty in one that would have to be understood if he was to be worthy to govern this country, and Benjamin Disraeli, wandering amidst the trees and flowers, reflected that, perhaps because he belonged to an older and more harassed race, he loved these English rather more than they were capable of loving themselves.

But what a struggle it would be to tear himself away from this refuge! Alone with his parents and his sister, he felt himself all-powerful; he had the right to be himself; say what he might, he would be admired; no paltry spirit, no jealous rival, would be spying on him. From his schooldays he had retained a feeling of apprehensiveness at the idea of a new session beginning. A new term meant a battle to be fought, a part to be played, and danger. He was highly strung, and his body asked to be spared; he brought it up to the fence with jabbing spurs, but not without anxiety and weariness. This time especially, in this vigil over his parliamentary arms, he wondered what this new school and his redoubtable comrades would be like. What seas would he have to brave on emerging from so tranquil a haven?

PART II

. . . Whether a man become a king or a beggar, there will always be the same eye, dark or grey, the same mouth, prudent or rash, the same hand; between this persistence of nature in each of us, and the endless variations of circumstance, our history passes as it were through the rollers of a printing-press, continually receiving the twofold impression. . . .

. . And thus, although nature can in no way be altered, any more than curly hair can be straightened, it is none the less possible to put one's trust in nature. Better still, it is because nature cannot be altered that one's trust can be put in it. Reach down to that and you are touching bedrock. And the power of a Caesar or an Alexander came no doubt chiefly from the fact that they had a liking for differences, and never laid blame on the pear-tree for not bearing plums.

ALAIN

I

The Maiden Speech

At Bradenham it was possible to believe that all England was agog with the entrance of Benjamin Disraeli to Parliament. In London conversation centred rather on the young Queen, her ease of bearing, her intelligence, the affection which she seemed to feel for her Prime Minister, Melbourne. Many people too, coming back from holidays, were talking of their first railway journey; they had experienced a certain sense of danger, but soon put it out of their heads.

Immediately Disraeli found his Wyndham Lewis "colleagues" again. Mrs. Wyndham Lewis, proud of her protégé, took him to the theatre to see Kean, in a well-

heated box. He went to receive Lord Lyndhurst's congratulations, and to compliment him in his return, for
this sturdy old man had just married a young girl and
his sole topic was of having a son. Then Wyndham
Lewis showed him the Houses of Parliament.

As the old Palace of Westminster had been partly
burnt down, the Lords and Commons were sitting in
temporary halls. There they were rather crowded, but
Disraeli managed to make sure of a seat for himself
just behind his chief, Sir Robert Peel. The latter was
cordial and invited the new member to join him at a
small dinner-party at the Carlton on the following
Thursday. "A House of Commons dinner purely. By
that time we shall know something of the temper of the
House." That "we" was very acceptable. Wyndham
Lewis, when he came home, said to his wife: "Peel took
Disraeli by the hand in the most cordial fashion."

From the first divisions it was plain that Lord Melbourne's Whig Ministry, with the support of the Irish,
was going to retain power. For a fortnight Disraeli remained a silent spectator of the debates. He had a great
desire to speak, but was terribly intimidated. He saw
himself set about with great men. Opposite him, on the
ministerial bench, in front of the official red box, was
the Whig leader, Lord John Russell, very small in his
black frock-coat of old-fashioned cut, his face half hidden beneath a hat with an enormous brim, and with a
stricken air, Lord John, the perfect symbol of his party,
who advanced the most daring ideas in the most archaic
style, and uttered the word "democracy" with an aristocratic drawl. Near him was Lord Palmerston, the For-

eign Secretary, with his dyed and carefully brushed
side-whiskers, Palmerston of whom Granville said that
he looked like some old retired croupier from Baden,
and whom the Whigs deemed vulgar, because he had not
that ceremonious respect for the Crown which the Whigs
had always shown, even when they were dethroning
kings. Nearer to him, standing out against the massive
table which separated the Ministers from the Opposition, Disraeli could see from behind the imposing figure
of Sir Robert Peel, and in profile, the brilliant Lord
Stanley, with his fine curved nose, his sensitive mouth,
his curled and slightly unruly hair, Stanley the indolent, the disdainful, the intelligent, dressed with a carefully considered negligence that was full of lessons for
Dizzy. Over by the entrance, amongst the Radicals, was
his friend Bulwer; and in the midst of the Irish band,
his formidable foe, Daniel O'Connell.

He was troubled also by the contrast in this assembly
between the majesty of its ritual and its carelessness for
appearances. Nobody listened; members chattered during the speeches and moved endlessly in and out; but
the Speaker was in robes and wig, the ushers brought
in and removed the mace, and a fellow-member was
referred to only by the appellation of "the honourable
gentleman." All these small details delighted a neophyte
who had so long observed them from without. He was
certain that on the day when he would rise to speak, he
would commit no blunder, would address himself solely
to the Speaker, following the accepted fiction of the
place, would call every barrister-member "the honourable and learned gentleman," every officer-member

"the honourable and gallant gentleman," Sir Robert
Peel, "the right honourable baronet," and Lord John,
"the noble Lord opposite." Already in his thoughts, his
phrases were cast in the parliamentary mould. If he
became a Minister, how grandly he would strike his fist
on that scarlet box! At the close of a loudly acclaimed
speech, with what an air of negligence would he drop
into his seat on the Treasury bench, wiping his lips with
handkerchief of fine cambric! But now that he had
measured at closer quarters the powerful inertia of this
great body, a certain anxiety was mingled with his
impatience.

In establishing the powers of the House, a discussion
had opened on a subscription opened by a Mr. Spottiswoode to furnish Protestant candidates with the funds
necessary to fight the Catholics in Ireland. This subscription had been extremely distasteful, not only to
the Irish, but also to the Liberals, who held it to be contrary to the liberty of the electors. O'Connell had just
spoken on the subject with vehemence when Disraeli
rose in his place. It had been arranged that Lord Stanley
should reply on behalf of the Conservatives, but Disraeli
had gone up and asked for his place as spokesman, and
Stanley, surprised but indifferent, had granted it.

Irish and Liberals both looked with curiosity at the
new orator who now rose opposite them. Many of them
had heard it said that he was a charlatan, an old Radical
turned Conservative, a novel-writer, a pompous orator.
It was known that he had had a violent quarrel with

O'Connell, and a strong detachment of the latter's friends had grouped together as soon as Disraeli rose. On the Conservative benches, the country gentlemen examined with some disquietude this decidedly un-English face. The curls vexed them, and the costume. Disraeli wore a bottle-green coat, a white waistcoat covered with gold chains ("Why so many chains, Dizzy?" Bulwer had said to him. "Are you practising to become Lord Mayor, or what?"), and a great black cravat accentuated the pallor of his complexion. It was a grave moment and he was playing a great part. He had to show to the Liberals what manner of man they had lost in him, to the Conservatives, that a future leader was in their midst, to O'Connell, that the day of expiation was at hand. He had several reasons for confidence; his speech had been elaborately prepared, and contained several phrases of sure effectiveness; and the tradition of Parliament was such that these beginners' speeches were greeted with kindliness. "The best maiden speech since Pitt's" was the remark generally passed to the orator. Young Gladstone, for example, whom Disraeli now found again on the benches of the Commons, had delivered his five years before amid general sympathy: "Spoke my first time for fifty minutes," he had noted in his diary. "The House heard me very kindly and my friends were satisfied. Tea afterwards at the Carlton." But Gladstone came from Eton and Oxford; he had a handsome English face, with firm and familiar features, dark-coloured clothes, and a grave manner.

Disraeli's voice was a trifle forced; its effect, one of unpleasing astonishment. Disraeli tried to show that the

Irish, and O'Connell in particular, had themselves profited by very similar subscriptions. "This majestic mendicancy . . ." he said. The House had a horror of long words and there was a titter of laughter. "I do not affect to be insensible to the difficulty of my position. (*Renewed laughter.*) I am sure I shall receive the indulgence of honourable gentlemen—(*Laughter and 'Question!'*); but I can assure them that if they do not wish to hear me, I, without a murmur, will sit down. (*Applause and laughter.*)" After a moment of comparative calm, another slightly startling association of words roused the storm. From the Irish group came hisses, scraping of feet, and cat-calls. Disraeli kept calm. "I wish I really could induce the House to give me five minutes more. (*Roars of laughter.*) I stand here to-night, sir, not formally, but in some degree virtually, the representative of a considerable number of members of Parliament. (*Loud and general laughter.*) Now, why smile? (*Continued laughter.*) Why envy me? (*Loud laughter.*) Why should I not have a tale to unfold to-night? (*Roars of laughter.*)"

From that moment onwards the uproar became such that only a few phrases could be heard.

"About that time, sir, when the bell of our cathedral announced the death of the monarch——(*'Oh, oh!' and much laughter.*) . . . If honourable members think it is fair to interrupt me, I will submit. (*Great laughter.*) I would not act so towards any one, that is all I can say. (*Laughter and cries of 'Go on!'*) But I beg simply to ask——(*'Oh!' and loud laughter.*) Nothing is so easy as to laugh. (*Roars of laughter.*) We remember the amatory eclogue—(*Roars of laughter*)—the old loves and the new loves that took place between the noble Lord, the Tityrus of the Treasury Bench, and the learned Daphne of Liskeard—(*Loud laughter and 'Question!'*). . . . When we remember at the same time that with emancipated Ireland and enslaved England, on the one hand a triumphant nation, on the other a groaning people, and notwithstanding the noble Lord, secure on the pedestal of power, may wield in one hand the keys of St. Peter, and——(*Here the hon. Member was interrupted with such loud and incessant laughter that it was impossible to know whether he closed his sentence or not.*) Now, Mr. Speaker, we see the philosophical prejudices of man. (*Laughter and cheers.*) I respect cheers, even when they come from the lips of political opponents. (*Renewed laughter.*) I think, sir— (*'Hear, hear!' and 'Question, question!'*)—I am not at all surprised, sir, at the reception I have received. (*Continued laughter.*) I have begun several things many times—(*Laughter*)—and I have often succeeded at last —(*Fresh cries of 'Question!'*)—although many had predicted that I must fail, as they had done before me. (*'Question, question!'*)"

And then, in formidable tones, staring indignantly at his interruptors, raising his hands and opening his mouth as wide as he could, he cried out in a voice which was almost terrifying and suddenly dominated the clamour: "Ay, sir, and though I sit down now, the time will come when you will hear me."

He was silent. His adversaries were still laughing; his friends gazed at him, saddened and surprised. During the whole of his ordeal, one man had supported him with great firmness—the right honourable baronet, Sir Robert Peel. Sir Robert was not in the habit of showing noisy approval of the orators of his party; he listened to them in an almost hostile silence. But on this occasion he turned round several times to the young orator, saying "Hear, hear!" in a loud voice. When he turned towards the Chamber he could not contain a slight smile.

Lord Stanley had risen, and scornfully, without saying one single word on the incredible reception of which one of his colleagues had just been the victim, had resumed the question seriously. He was listened to with respect. Silent and sombre, Disraeli leaned his head on his hand. Once again a defeat, once again hell. Never, since he had followed the debates of the Commons, had he known of so degrading a scene. Was the life of the Cogan school going to begin again for him now in Parliament? Would he still have to fight and hate, when he desired so much to love and be loved? Why was everything more difficult for him than for others? But why, in his first speech, had he challenged O'Connell and his band? It would be hard now to swim against the stream. Would it even be possible at all? He had lost all standing in the eyes of this assembly. He reflected with bitterness on the idea he had conjured up of this début. He had imagined a House overwhelmed by his phrases, charmed by his images, delighted by his sarcasms; prolonged applause; a complete and immediate success. . . . And these insulting guffaws. . . . Defeat. . . . O for the haven of the Bradenham woods!

A division forced him to rise. He had not heard the debate. The excellent Lord Chandos came up to him with congratulations. He replied that there was no cause here for congratulations, and murmured: "It is a reverse. . . ." "No such thing!" said Chandos, "you are quite wrong. I have just seen Peel and I asked him, 'Now tell me exactly what you think of Disraeli.' Peel replied, 'Some of my party were disappointed and talk of failure. I say *just the reverse*. He did all that he could do under the circumstances. I say anything but failure; he must make his way.' "

In the lobby the Liberal Attorney-General stopped him and asked with cordiality: "Now, Mr. Disraeli, can you tell me how you finished one sentence in your speech, we are anxious to know: 'In one hand the keys of St. Peter and in the other——'?"

" 'In the other the cap of liberty,' Sir John."

The other smiled and said: "A good picture!"

"Yes," replied Disraeli, with a touch of bitterness, "but your friends will not allow me to finish my pictures."

"But I assure you," said the Attorney-General, "there was the liveliest desire to hear you from us. It was a party at the bar, over whom we have no control; but you have nothing to be afraid of."

What was this? On others, then, the impression of an irreparable collapse had not been so unmistakable as on himself? Like many highly-strung men, Disraeli picked up confidence again as quickly as he lost heart. Already the cloud of despair was lifting. Writing to Sarah on the following day, he circumscribed the extent of the disaster: "As I wish to give you an *exact* idea of what occurred, I state at once that my *début* was a *failure,* so far that I could not succeed in gaining an opportunity of saying what I intended; but the failure was not occasioned by my breaking down or any incompetency on my part, but from the physical powers of my adversaries. I can give you no idea how bitter, how factious, how unfair they were. I fought through all with undaunted pluck and unruffled temper, made occasionally good isolated hits when there was silence, and finished with spirit when I found a formal display was ineffectual." He signed it: "Yours, D.—in very good spirits."

On the same day, entering the Athenæum, Bulwer saw old Sheil, the famous Irish member and O'Connell's lieutenant, surrounded by a group of young Radicals who were rejoicing in the Disraeli incident. Bulwer went over to them and remained silent. Suddenly Sheil threw down his newspaper and said in his shrill voice: "Now, gentlemen, I have heard all you have to say, and, what is more, I heard this same speech of Mr. Disraeli, and I tell you this: if ever the spirit of oratory was in a man, it is in that man. Nothing can prevent him from being one of the first speakers in the House of Commons. Ay! I know something about that place, I think, and I tell you what besides: that if there had not been this interruption, Mr. Disraeli might have been a failure; I don't call this a failure, it is a crash. My *début* was a failure, because I was heard, but my reception was supercilious, his indignant. A *début* should be dull. The House will not allow a man to be a wit and an orator, unless they have the credit of finding it out. There it is."

This little oration, coming from an opponent, left a shock of astonishment. The young men dispersed, rather embarrassed. Bulwer went up to Sheil and said: "Disraeli is dining with me this evening. Would you like to meet him?"

"In spite of my gout," said Sheil, "I long to know him. I long to tell him what I think."

Sheil was charming at dinner. He took Disraeli aside and explained to him that this noisy reception had been a great opportunity for him. "For," said he, "if you had been listened to, what would have been the result? You would have done what I did; you would have made the best speech that you ever would have made: it would have been received frigidly, and you would have despaired of yourself. I did. As it is, you have shown to the House that you have a fine organ, an unlimited command of language, courage, temper, and readiness. Now get rid of your genius for a session. Speak often, for you must not show yourself cowed, but speak shortly. Be very quiet, try to be dull, only argue and reason imperfectly, for if you reason with precision, they will think you are trying to be witty. Astonish them by speaking on subjects of detail. Quote figures, dates, calculations. And in a short time the House will sigh for the wit and eloquence which they all know are in you. They will encourage you to pour them forth, and then you will have the ear of the House and be a favourite."

A speech so intelligent, and showing so deep an understanding of the English, flooded the future with light for Disraeli. Nobody was more capable than he of understanding and following such counsel. He liked to fashion himself with his own hands like a work of art. He was always ready to touch up the picture. Once more he had fallen into the mistake wherewith his father had so often reproached him, that of being in a hurry, of wanting to be famous at one stroke. But he would know how to advance slowly.

A week later he rose in the midst of a discussion on authors' rights. Almost every one was inclined to give him a favourable welcome. Tories and Liberals were of one mind, that this man had been unfairly treated. That was distasteful to them. They were sportsmen; they preferred that an orator, like the game, should have his chance. A sense of shame lingered in their minds from that brutal afternoon. They were inclined to support this odd young man if he dared to make another trial. They would even put up with the excessive brilliance of his phrases and with his unheard-of images. But to the general surprise, he uttered nothing but what was commonplace and obvious, on a subject with which he was thoroughly familiar, and sat down amid general approval. The author of the project replied that he would carefully bear in mind the excellent remarks of the honourable member for Maidstone, himself one of the most remarkable ornaments of modern literature. Sir Robert Peel was strong in his approval, "Hear, hear!" and many members went up and congratulated Disraeli. An old Tory colonel came up to him and said, after some amiable growling: "Well, you have got in your saddle again; now you may ride away." To Sarah he wrote:

"Next time I rise in the House, I shall sit down amidst loud cheers."

Far from having been of disservice to him, this sorry beginning had given him the prestige of a victim. Within three weeks he had acquired, in this extremely difficult assembly, a kind of popularity. He was courageous; he spoke well; he seemed to have an exact knowledge of the subjects he dealt with. "Why not?" thought the English gentlemen.

II

Weddings

From January, Disraeli's success in the House was certain. He had passed through that period of waiting and tiresome gravity which had been prescribed by Sheil, and now, as the latter had foretold, they wanted him to be brilliant. His brother Jem, who came to listen at one sitting, was able to go back and tell them at Bradenham how, as soon as Ben rose, all the members came flocking back to their places, and how a marvellous silence had fallen for him to speak. Old Isaac listened to this story with a full heart, and Sarah murmured: "God bless you, dear one!" She had always known, had Sarah, that her brother was a great man.

Politics had obliged Disraeli to cut down his share

in social life. In any case, life had altered for many of his friends. The Bulwer *ménage*, brilliant and precarious, had been shattered. Bulwer had taken his wife to Italy to attempt a strengthening of their union, but at Naples he had conceived a subject for a novel, set himself to write *The Last Days of Pompeii*, and had neglected Rosina just as in London. Poor Poodle, deserted in this foreign town, deprived even of her cherished dogs, had allowed herself to receive the attentions of an Italian prince. Bulwer emerged from his dream to vexation at this reality, and after two or three painful episodes they had had to separate. Rosina Bulwer, poor and embittered, now only saw her husband's friends to complain of him. Bulwer felt remorse, and was unhappy. Disraeli found grounds here to confirm his distrust of love marriages.

The beautiful Caroline Norton too had lost her gaiety. Her odious husband, after profiting from Lord Melbourne's friendship for his wife, had suddenly brought an action against them both with a plea for adultery. She had been able to prove that scores of times he himself had driven her to the Minister's door. The jury had found against Norton, but he none the less abandoned his wife and kept the custody of the children, whom the law of England did not allow Mrs. Norton to claim. She beseeched her friends, Bulwer and Disraeli, to have the law modified. In the little flat at Storey's Gate, the flowery balcony and the muslin curtains now heard nothing but plaints and prayers. People did not go there so often.

Disraeli still went sometimes to Lady Blessington's, on evenings when the House did not sit. But there too the scene was overcast. D'Orsay had lived in such style, and played for such heavy stakes, that money was running short. Creditors were to be met with at the door. The only house which remained tranquil and hospitable was that of the Wyndham Lewises. Mrs. Wyndham Lewis had neither the grace nor the wit of the Sheridan sisters, but perhaps a young member of Parliament, ambitious and susceptible, had more need of affection than of grace, and to Disraeli this was a precious friendship.

One morning about six months after his entering Parliament, he had news of the sudden death of his colleague. He hastened to his widow, whom he found greatly overwhelmed.

Disraeli to Mrs. Wyndham Lewis.

"It is natural, after such severe trials as you have recently experienced, and such petty vexations as you are now forced to encounter, that you should give way to feelings of loneliness and sorrow. It is natural and inevitable; but you must not *indulge* such sentiments, and you must endeavour not to brood over the past. The future for you may yet be full of happiness and hope. . . . As for myself, I can truly say, that the severe afflictions which you have undergone, and the excellent, and to me unexpected, qualities with which you have met them, the talent, firmness and sweet temper, will always make me your faithful friend, and as far as my advice and assistance and society can contribute to your welfare or solace you under these severe trials, you may count upon them."

He continued, in fact, to visit her faithfully. Rosina Bulwer, a friend of the family, followed with perturbation and mistrust these visits of a familiar of her husband's. Mary Anne had confessed to her that Disraeli bore her an affection which was more than friendly. Rosina, who had learned to distrust men of letters, advised the greatest prudence. At the time of the Queen's coronation, each member of Parliament received a commemorative gold medal. It was to Mrs. Wyndham Lewis, and not to Sarah, that Disraeli presented his.

The closing formulas of their letters grew more inflamed. From "ever your affectionate friend" he had passed to "Farewell! I am happy if you are." It was significant that he was beginning to share between her and Sarah those openly exultant recitals of his successes. Before her also the mask was lowered, the buckler laid aside. "Every paper in London, Radical, Whig, or Tory, has spoken of my speech in the highest terms of panegyric." "Lord Chandos gives a great banquet to the Duke of Wellington, Lord Lyndhurst, Lord and Lady Londonderry, Lord and Lady Jersey, Sir Robert and Lady Peel, Sir James and Lady Graham, and Lord Stanley. You will be rather surprised, I think—at least I am—that I should be invited to it, but Chandos is a good friend, and greatly triumphs in my success in the House." "The Londonderrys gave the most magnificent banquet at Holdernesse House conceivable. Nothing could be more *recherché*. There were only 150 asked, and all sat down. Fanny was faithful, and asked me, and I figure in the *Morning Post* accordingly. . . . I think it was the kindest thing possible of Fanny asking me, as it was not to be expected in any way." The descriptions of rooms full of orange-trees, tables covered with marvellous glass, smoked salmon, caviare and *foie gras*, were sent at the same time to Sarah and to Mrs. Wyndham Lewis. She was beginning to be one of the family.

Was he thinking of marriage? He had not forgotten Count D'Orsay's advice: "If you meet a widow. . . ." But he was not blind to the possible objections. He was thirty-three, she was forty-five. She was far from holding a status in fashionable society as brilliant as his own; the hostesses who quarrelled for Disraeli were not enthusiasts for Mary Anne. A fortune? Wyndham Lewis had left his wife a life-interest in the Grosvenor Gate house, and an income of about £4000. It was enough to live on and to entertain worthily, but it was not a great fortune; there was no spare capital to allow of Disraeli's debts being paid off; moreover, it was not an alienable fortune, and as Mrs. Wyndham was the elder of the two, there was a grave risk of Disraeli finding himself forced, in the mid-course of his life, to give up his house and his mode of living. Moreover; Mary Anne was far from being a cultivated woman. Society found her rather ridiculous; it was said that she had never been able to remember which came first, the Greeks or the Romans. After a conversation about Swift, she asked for his address to invite him to dinner. Other women found her stupid and frivolous; she talked a great deal, and with alarming exuberance; her frankness reached the pitch of tactlessness. In matters of furniture or clothes her taste was freakish and detestable. A young writer and a future Minister of the Crown could surely find a more brilliant wife.

But Disraeli judged otherwise. Contrary to fashionable opinion, he did not think her stupid. True, she was ignorant, but what did that matter? He had seen her in action during several elections; she understood men; she had a sound judgment; she did what she had to do well and thoroughly; she would be a useful companion. Her frivolous talk amused Disraeli and relaxed him. He had had only too many brilliant friends amongst women, and he had no mind to find himself obliged to withstand an assault of wit in his own home. Mary Anne admired him; he felt that she lived only for him. In his moments of depression, which were frequent, he had need of consolation. He had suffered more severely from his thorny beginnings than his somewhat cold manner allowed one to suppose. To find another Sarah, a Sarah who was a wife as well as a sister, had long been his desire. There are some men who feel the need of keeping their independence for the sake of romantic adventures; Disraeli had made trial of passionate love, only to find at once that it was in conflict with ambition. To him the refuge of a lasting tenderness was far more tempting.

He had always been impulsive. As soon as he felt persuaded that Mary Anne was a desirable wife, he told her so. His declaration was not ill received. She had the highest esteem for his talents and the fullest confidence in his future; but circumspect and calm, she was anxious to give herself time for reflections, and asked him for a year in which to study his character.

Parliament was in recess. Bradenham was tranquil and flowering. Disraeli was in love. He set himself to write a tragedy. Day by day he kept Mary Anne abreast of the work and of his love. "My progress has been great and brilliant; you know I am not easily satisfied with my efforts, and not in the habit of speaking of my writings with much complacency. You may therefore credit there is some foundation when I tell you, that I think my present work will far exceed your expectations. . . . I envy the gentlemen about you, but I am not jealous. When the eagle leaves you the vultures return. There! that is sublime.—There is hardly a flower to be found, but I have sent you a few sweet-peas."

Four days later: "I write in good health and in good spirits. I prosper in my work. I am satisfied with what I have done. I look upon my creation and see that it is good. Health, my clear brain, and your fond love;—and I feel that I can conquer the world."

Six days later: "I cannot reconcile Love and separation. My ideas of love are the perpetual enjoyment of the society of the sweet being to whom I am devoted, the sharing of every thought and even every fancy, of every charm and every care. . . . I wish to be with you, to live with you, never to be away from you—I care not where, in heaven or on earth, or in the waters under the earth."

But soon the answers to Disraeli's letters became fewer and colder. A strange and prolonged silence disturbed him as to Mary Anne's feelings. What was happening? She had asked for a year to study his character. Could it be that the final judgment had been unfavourable? He asked for an interview, which he obtained, and a rather painful conversation passed between them. Mrs. Wyndham Lewis was surrounded by friends who disapproved of this match. Young Disraeli was known to be heavily in debt. How could it be supposed that he loved a woman thirteen years older than himself? No doubt he had paid her his court only to ward off the money-lenders with the news of this marriage. Rosina Bulwer had been talking much of Dizzy's great love for Mary Anne's four thousand a year. This was the finishing touch to the portrait of this handsome and unscrupulous adventurer; he had flattered every party in order to obtain a seat; he was ending by marrying an old woman in order to have a house and a revenue. These rumours had reached Mary Anne herself, and had given her pause. She was an orderly woman and kept her accounts with care. She loved, but she did not wish to be duped, and said so rather harshly. After leaving her house, he wrote to her:

". . . By heavens, as far as worldly interests are concerned, your alliance could not benefit me. All that society can offer is at my command; it is not the apparent possession of a jointure that ever elevates position. I can live, as I live, without disgrace, until the inevitable progress of events gives me that independence which is

all I require. I have entered into these ungracious details because you reproached me with my interested
views. No; I would not condescend to be the minion of
a princess; and not all the gold of Ophir should ever
lead me to the altar. Far different are the qualities which
I require in the sweet participator of my existence.
My nature demands that my life should be perpetual
love. . . .

"Farewell. I will not affect to wish you happiness, for
it is not in your nature to obtain it. For a few years you
may flutter in some frivolous circle. But the time will
come when you will sigh for any heart that could be
fond, and despair of one that can be faithful. There
will be the penal hour of retribution; then you will think
of me with remorse, admiration and despair; then you
will recall to your memory the passionate heart that you
have forfeited, and the genius you have betrayed."

Mrs. Wyndham Lewis to Disraeli.

"For God's sake come to me. I am ill and almost
distracted. I will answer all you wish. I never desired
you to leave the house, or implied or thought a word
about money. . . . I have not been a widow a year. I
often feel the apparent impropriety of my present position. . . . I am devoted to you."

On August 28th, 1839, they were married at St.
George's, Hanover Square. In her account book Mary
Anne entered a note: "Gloves 2/6. In hand, £300. Mar-
ried 28. 8. 1839. Dear Dizzy became my husband."

A few days before, he had written to her:

"I feel that there never was an instance where a basis of more entire and permanent felicity offered itself to two human beings. I look forward to the day of our union as that epoch in my life which will seal my career: for whatever occurs afterwards will, I am sure, never shake my soul, as I shall always love the refuge of your sweet heart in sorrow or disappointment, and your quick and accurate sense to guide me in prosperity and triumph."

This indeed was exactly what he expected of the marriage.

During that same year another member of Parliament was married, younger but no less brilliant, that same William Gladstone with whom Disraeli had dined at Lyndhurst's on the occasion when the truffled swan had been served. It was a very different marriage, and it is not without interest to make brief mention of its circumstances. Gladstone had met his betrothed during a journey in Italy; she was the daughter of Lady Glynne and was travelling with her mother, her sister, and their attendants, in a large family-coach. In Florence, a young man with regular and powerful features had greeted them. "Who is that?" Catherine Glynne had asked. "Do you not know him? That is young Gladstone, the man who, according to what every one is saying, is certain to be Prime Minister of England."

The young statesman on holiday had immediately formed an intimacy with this handsome and pious girl. He had had a long conversation with her in Santa Maria Maggiore; they spoke of the contrast between the parsimony of the English in the ornament of their churches and the luxury of their private life. "Do you think," she asked him, "that we can be justified in indulging ourselves in all these luxuries?" In his diary he noted: "I loved her for this question. How sweet a thing it is to reflect that her heart and will are entirely in the hands of God. May he, in this, as in all things, be with her." He had asked her hand when they found themselves alone together in the Coliseum, beneath the Roman moonlight. She had hesitated, but he had seen her again in England, and strolling with her in a garden near a river, he had told her the story of his soul, and how he had wished to become a clergyman, how his father had opposed it, how he had resigned himself to politics, realizing that a statesman can consecrate his power to the glory of the Church. This moved her, and she consented to become his wife.

"We shall accept for our rule of life," he had thereupon told her, "that line of Dante: *In la sua volontade è nostra pace.*" And they had been married in a village all decked with flowers by the respectful cottagers, who threw down their humble rugs along the path which the procession was to take. About five o'clock that same afternoon they had read the Bible together. "This daily practice will, I trust, last as long as our joint lives."

Mrs. Gladstone had brought a touch of whimsy into the austere life of her husband. He was all method and punctuality; she had natural good sense and humour. He classified everything; she lost everything. She teased him, saying it was good for him to have an untidy wife because it made him more human. He for his part had taught her to analyse her sentiments, to watch over her soul, and to keep a diary. There, for instance, one could read: "Engaged a cook after a long conversation on religious matters, chiefly between her and William."

She was charming, Catherine Gladstone.

III

Mary Anne

A married man, a fine house in Park Lane; dinner to
his colleagues, with forty covers set; rather fewer chains,
a little less lace—Disraeli had greatly altered in a few
months. Mary Anne might have a thousand faults in the
eyes of others; she was the very wife who had been lacking to this proud and sensitive man. She made him live
in a paradise of slightly comical adoration, but its security was soothing after long and painful vexations.

Some time after their marriage, she outlined a twofold portrait of the couple they were:

Very calm.	Very effervescent.
Manners grave and almost sad.	Gay and happy-looking when speaking.
Never irritable.	Very irritable.
Bad-humoured.	Good-humoured.
Warm in love, but cold in friendship.	Cold in love, but warm in friendship.
Very patient.	No patience.
Very studious.	Very idle.
Often says what he does not think.	Never says anything she does not think.
It is impossible to find out who he likes or dislikes from his manner.	Her manner is quite different, and to those she likes she shows her feelings.
No vanity.	Much vanity.
Conceited.	No conceit.
No self-love.	Much self-love.
He is seldom amused.	Everything amuses her.
He is a genius.	She is a dunce.
He is to be depended on to a certain degree.	She is not to be depended on.
His whole soul is devoted to politics and ambition.	She has no ambition and hates politics.

"I am as ugly and stupid as Mrs. Disraeli," the bitter and jealous Rosina Bulwer would sometimes say; having lost her husband, she took it ill that somebody else had managed to find another. But the parallel portraiture gave proof of infinitely more wit than Rosina would grant to Mrs. Disraeli. She alone up till then had understood the profound melancholy hidden beneath the Disraelian irony, the contrast between the light and mocking manner of the former dandy, and the dark, violent emotions seething beneath that frail crust.

She accompanied him everywhere. At Bradenham the family adored her; she brought good humour into a house invaded by old age. Mr. D'Israeli was going blind, a hard lot for a man to whom reading was the whole end of life. Sarah, taking notes for him all day long, enabled him to continue his labours. Mary Anne and her sister-in-law communed together in admiration for Dis.

Frequently the Disraeli couple would spend a few days in the country, in noble houses where Mrs. Disraeli's naïve remarks enjoyed a great success. To some ladies who were discussing the beauty of certain Greek statues, she replied: "Oh, but you ought to see my Dizzy in his bath!" To another lady: "I find your house is packed with improper pictures. There's a horrible one in our room. Dizzy says it is Venus and Adonis. I had to stay awake half the night to keep him from looking at it." One morning, when the pair had spent the night in the room next to that of Lord Hardinge, she said to the latter at breakfast: "Oh, Lord Hardinge, I think I must be the happiest of women! When I woke up this morning, I said to myself: 'How lucky I am! I've been sleeping between the greatest orator and the greatest soldier of the day!'" There was much laughter; but the laughter had to be prudent and only when the husband had his back turned. Although more alive to the ridiculous than any one, Disraeli defended his wife with ferocious loyalty. He never uttered a word of reproach to her.

One day, staying with Bulwer, who was then living on the Thames, the couple were taken out in a boat by

Prince Louis Napoleon, pretender to the Imperial throne of France, and an exile high in fashionable favour in London. He ran them aground in the middle of the river, in quite a dangerous position. Mary Anne in her indignation treated Napoleon as a bad waterman and not at all as a future Emperor. "You ought never to undertake things you cannot accomplish! You're always too adventurous!" The Prince laughed heartily, and Disraeli, silent and very sombre, was amused.

When a member of Parliament is successful, his only thought is for a Ministry; and Dizzy had every ground to hope for it soon. Liberalism had foundered. The people had been told that the Reform would bring an end to all their woes; the people had forced the Reform on the Lords, and the woes were worse than ever. Everywhere machinery was driving out the artisan; the hand-weavers were dying of hunger; the number of paupers was mounting. The masses, suffering from unemployment, accused the political regime. They were now told that the Reform had been too narrow, that it had confined itself to replacing the Lords of Acres by the Lords of Cotton and the Counter, that universal suffrage alone would at last ensure the happiness of the poor. A whole party had been formed to demand the People's Charter. Terrible men these Chartists were: they demanded not only universal suffrage, but a secret ballot, payment of members, equality of constituencies. Many of the well-to-do took fright. Others thought: "Nothing will happen, because in this country nothing ever does happen." The one sort petitioned Ministers to take action against the Chartists, the other to take it against the manufacturers. The Liberal Ministry found itself in the tightest of corners. Placed in power by a coalition of the doctrinaires, the great manufacturers and the traditional Whigs, it could do nothing for the working-classes without causing discontent among its own allies. For the relief of poverty its sole idea had been the new Poor Law, which established the Workhouse, where the indigent had to be nourished, but kept confined and subjected to the sternest regulations. These prisons, where a wife was parted from her husband, where a father could hardly ever embrace his children, had instantly become the object of deep popular loathing. Dickens, in *Oliver Twist,* had drawn a picture of them both horrible and true. The people hated them so much that many poor wretches preferred a hovel with neither fire nor furniture, and poverty absolutely refused to seek shelter in this Bastille of the poor.

In contrast, the Tory party profited by the unpopularity of its adversaries. For Peel, the son of a manufacturer, and a supporter of the Poor Law Bill, the situation was difficult to exploit in Parliament. But a Disraeli could imagine no combination of circumstances more favourable to his ideas. That regret for the past which is felt by the unfortunate, that sadness at having seen the substitution of a hard administrative charity for the friendly aid of parish or manor-house, was nothing else, transformed into naïve sentiment, than that popular conservatism which he had always preached. Whence came the evil, according to his view? From the advent to power of parvenus who cast off on to the shoulders of the central government, contrary to all English tradition, the duties which were those of their class.

When the Chartists came to present their petition to Parliament, signed with twelve hundred thousand names, and when the two great parties refused to take it into consideration, when Lord John Russell, that father of the Reform, prosecuted by law the Chartists, those sons of the Reform, Disraeli was almost alone in speaking publicly in their favour. He was far from sharing their belief in the healing properties of universal suffrage; he believed that for a social ill there can only be a social remedy, but he declared his sympathy in their misery, his astonishment at seeing them attacked by a Lord John Russell who had set them the example. "The time will come," he said bitterly, "when the Chartists will discover that in a country so aristocratic as England even treason, to be successful, must be patrician. They will discover that great truth, and when they find some desperate noble to lead them, they may perhaps achieve greater results. Where Wat Tyler failed, Henry Bolingbroke changed a dynasty, and although Jack Straw was hanged, a Lord John Straw may become a Secretary of State."

"A remarkable speech," it was said. "I wonder what he wants?"

"I think he must be going to turn Radical."

"Why, the whole speech was against Radicalism."

"Ah, then he is going to turn Whig, I suppose."

"He is ultra anti-Whig."

"Then what the deuce is he?"

"Not a Conservative, certainly."

"Then I suppose he is crotchety."

"What does he mean by 'obtaining the results of the Charter without the intervention of its machinery'?"

"I took him to mean that, if you wished for a time to retain your political power, you could only effect your purpose by securing for the people greater social felicity."

"Well, that's sheer Radicalism. Pretending that the people can be better off than they are, is Radicalism and nothing else."

The Liberals felt themselves threatened, and tried a counter-attack. The Tories had found a scapegoat in large-scale industry, and a bogey in the Poor Law. The Whigs meditated reprisals against the great agriculturists, and against the protective Corn Duties. Four bad harvests had just sent prices up. Why should it not be supposed that unemployment came from the high cost of living? By a Free Trade policy they would please both workers and great employers. True, the farmers would be left dissatisfied, but as they were almost all Conservatives, that was of no electoral importance. Disraeli formerly upheld the Protectionist doctrine. Who would profit by the suppression of the duties? The poor? No, the manufacturers, for wages would fall with the cost of living. And why should agricultural England be sacrificed to industrial England? Why should they risk discouraging and ruining the farmers? The Free Traders said: "We shall import our foodstuffs, we shall become the workshop of the world." But who could see into the future? Suppose the world changed, suppose it became one great workshop everywhere, who would feed England then?

The Whigs wavered: their weakness still had vigour in it, but their defeat was certain. The Duke refused power. He became very taciturn; he was still seen in the drawing-rooms, where he was received like a sovereign, but he traversed them without saying a word, and his only answer to a remark was "Ha!" So it would be a Peel Ministry, then, and the party's most brilliant orator would of course be included. When this was mentioned to Mrs. Dizzy, she used to blush like a young girl.

IV

The Right Honourable Baronet

On August 30th, 1841, Sir Robert Peel went to Windsor to kiss hands. In the time of her light-hearted beginnings, the Queen had disliked this grave and shy-mannered man, so different from the charming Lord Melbourne who made her live like a sovereign of the eighteenth century. But now she had married the handsome Prince Albert of Saxe-Coburg, and Albert, austere in his own character, liked Sir Robert and esteemed him. Everything that Albert liked was admirable, and this time the Queen welcomed the Tory leader with confidence.

For several days unofficial lists of Ministers had been in circulation. They all contained the name of Disraeli, but Peel had not yet summoned him.

Soon he learned that his friend Lyndhurst was Lord Chancellor; Lord Stanley had the Colonies, the Duke of Buckingham, the Privy Seal, young Gladstone, the Board of Trade. One by one all the posts were being filled. At the Carlton nothing could be seen but groups of politicians exchanging their congratulations. Only Disraeli had received no message from the Premier. Was Sir Robert going to abandon one of his best lieutenants? It seemed impossible, but if by ill chance it were so, what a deception, what a disaster! Once in power, the Conservatives would stay there a long time. To be excluded now would mean exclusion for the life of one legislature, perhaps of two. All the patient work of four years was crumbling. Already he thought he could read in the glances at the Club an amused irony, and conversations would stop short on his approach. At the end of the week, in despair, he decided to write to Peel:

"DEAR SIR ROBERT,—I have shrunk from obtruding myself upon you at this moment, and should have continued to do so if there were any one on whom I could rely to express my feelings.

"I am not going to trouble you with claims similar to those with which you must be wearied. I will not say that I have fought since 1834 four contests for your party, that I have expended great sums, have exerted my intelligence to the utmost for the propagation of your policy, and have that position in life which can command a costly seat.

"But there is one peculiarity in my case on which I cannot be silent. I have had to struggle against a storm

of political hate and malice which few men ever experienced, from the moment, at the instigation of a member
of your Cabinet, I enrolled myself under your banner,
and I have been sustained under these trials by the conviction that the day would come when the foremost man
of this country would publicly testify that he had some
respect for my ability and my character.

"I confess to be unrecognised at this moment by you
appears to me to be overwhelming, and I appeal to your
own heart—to that justice and to that magnanimity
which I feel are your characteristics—to save me from
an intolerable humiliation.

"Believe me, dear Sir Robert,
"Your faithful servant,
"B. DISRAELI."

On the previous night Mrs. Disraeli, unable to endure
any longer her Dizzy's sadness, had herself written to
the Prime Minister without her husband's knowledge:

"DEAR SIR ROBERT,—I beg you not to be angry with
me for my intrusion, but I am overwhelmed with anxiety. My husband's political career is for ever crushed,
if you do not appreciate him. . . . Do not destroy all his
hopes, and make him feel his life has been a mistake.

"May I venture to name my own humble but enthusiastic exertions in time gone by for the party, or
rather for your own splendid self? They will tell you
at Maidstone that more than £40,000 was spent
through my influence only.

"Be pleased not to answer this, as I do not wish any human being to know that I have written to you this humble petition.

"I am now, as ever, dear Sir Robert,
"Your most faithful servant,
"MARY ANNE DISRAELI."

To Disraeli Peel replied in a dry letter, making special insistence on an unimportant phrase in the former's letter: "from the moment, at the instigation of a member of your Cabinet, I enrolled myself under your banner." He drew his attention rather acidly to the fact that no member of his Cabinet had been charged with any such mission. (Disraeli had never mentioned any mission; he had only meant that he had attached himself to the Conservative party through the influence of Lyndhurst, a member of the Peel Ministry.) Peel added that he had a bare sufficiency of posts at his disposal for those who had already served under him, and that he thought that the insufficiency of the means at his disposal would be understood by men whose collaboration he would have been proud to have and whose qualities he did not dispute.

The truth was that Peel would have liked to give Disraeli a post; but he was surrounded by colleagues who would have none of "that adventurer." Croker for instance, that Croker more detestable than cold veal, who had been the eye-witness and the cause of Disraeli's defeat at the time of the establishment of the newspaper, and Lord Stanley, who, haughty and familiar, had declared that "if that scoundrel were taken in, he would not remain himself."

But Peel had not managed to defend Disraeli with much ardour. The pair were too widely different. Round his own parliamentary cradle Peel had assembled Fortune and Morality and Respect; round Dizzy's belated baptism there flitted no doubt the pale phantoms of Debt, with Cynicism and Fancy by their side. The Peels were famed for their good taste. Their London house was charming, with its flowered balconies overlooking the river, and its admirable collection of Dutch masters. "One dines remarkably well at your house," French visitors would say to them. Lady Peel was beautiful and kind; her portrait by Lawrence, modelled on the "Straw Hat" of Rubens, was held by many connoisseurs to be the painter's best picture. Everything connected with Peel evoked ideas of Flemish solidity and virtuous beauty. Everything connected with Dizzy seemed gimcrack. On Lady Peel diamonds gleamed with dark fires; on Mrs. Disraeli the finest stones looked as if they were glass. Mary Anne's house at Grosvenor Gate was decorated with a bad taste that screamed aloud. His furniture was dreadful, her gowns ridiculous. Small details: but they added to the Minister's mistrust. Moreover, he found the doctrine no less displeasing than the man. By his birth Peel was much nearer to the factory than to the manor or the cottage, much more of a Puritan than a Cavalier. In fact, he was essentially a member of the middle-classes on a grand scale. In his heart and mind he was in his opponents' camp. He was attracted by the reasonings of the economists, by their honest aspect, and by Bright's large boots, much more than by the irony of a too brilliant orator. Gladstone was a man after his own heart, like him "Oxford on the surface, and Liverpool below," like him, a parliamentarian at twenty-one and an Under-Secretary of State at twenty-five, Gladstone, who said a prayer before he rose to speak, and could envelop the simplest question with long, obscure sentences. Disraeli abased himself to the point of soliciting office; Gladstone, when offered a Ministry, wondered anxiously whether the Cabinet's religious policy would permit him to accept. It was a great relief to an honest and timid soul like Peel's to find ambition thus wrapped around with appropriate sentiments. When Gladstone at last accepted, Peel clasped the young Minister's hands firmly and said to him: "God bless you!" How could he possibly have treated the cynic Disraeli in that way? Stanley was right; the fellow was impossible.

The Ministry once formed, Parliament met; Disraeli went to the House full of apprehensions; his position was difficult. In opposition the party had been happy to make use of him; but henceforward the unhappy Conservative without a post would be left a solitary creature. Proposals would be defended by the Ministers themselves. Nothing was now expected of him but his vote, a painful lot for an original mind. His enemies were amused at his mishap; his bearing was spied upon with malicious curiosity. They waited for him to turn against

the leader who had abandoned him; many false coun-
sellors egged him on to that; the Radicals made him
advances.

He realized the danger. Against Peel he was animated
by sentiments of great force. The refusal of a post was
quite proper, but the tone of the refusal had been ill-
judged. When Disraeli looked at the ministerial bench
and saw the smug faces of the mediocrities who had
spurned him, he had a furious desire to jump the traces,
but he kept a firm rein on his over-keen spirit. Now
more than ever, he had need of patience. This was the
opinion of Mary Anne likewise, who was admirably
tender during these hard times.

To its surprise, the House saw Disraeli punctually in
attendance, voting for the Government with perfect good
grace. Peel, in his anxiety to please the Free Traders,
abolished the customs tariff on more than seven hundred
articles, and replaced the revenue thus lost to the Budget
with a curious novelty, the Income Tax. The Protectionist Disraeli did not quail. He confined himself to a great
speech on a technical and uncontroversial subject, the
consular representatives, an accurate discourse full of
figures and instances, but so interesting that for three
hours he held in motionless silence a House which had
at first been restive. Seeing him passed over by Peel,
there were many who had doubted his talents. His return
to the stage was startling, and all the more remarkable
as the subject offered him so little assistance.

Amongst the most ardent in their congratulations was
a group of young men just lately down from Cambridge,

returned to Parliament by the recent elections. This modern eloquence of his, with its freedom from stereotyped phrases, had delighted them. "It is exactly as if you were talking at the Carlton or at your own table," said young Smythe to him. "The voice not at all forced, the elocution distinct; a trifle nonchalant, and always with a tincture of sarcasm." They were charming, this young Smythe, with his friend Lord John Manners and all the little circle surrounding them. Belonging to ancient and illustrious families, they were owners of dream-castles perched high in the hill-top mists, or deep hidden amid the trees of great parks. They had been brought up at Eton and Cambridge, where they had formed noble friendships and united in constructing a political doctrine based on the revival of the old institutions, and on the reconciliation of the people with an aristocracy conscious of its powers. It was the purest Dizzy.

The industrialism which had successfully seduced the men of riper years was no religion for youth. The young have a perpetual need of fervour which was disappointed by the calico religion. "Buy in the lowest market and sell in the highest"—this seemed to them an unsatisfactory gospel. The anti-romanticism of 1820 was succeeded by a romantic reaction. These young Englishmen had serious thoughts of a resuscitation of Chivalry, with its code of honour and its religious respect for womanhood. Feudalism might be out of date, but the feudal attitude, which viewed men as bound by reciprocal duties, remained the most desirable. They regretted the days when the rule of life had been *"Noblesse oblige.*" Perhaps it might still be possible to rekindle a dying flame.

In 1839 Lord Eglinton had organized a tournament in his grounds. The whole of the English nobility had come, wearing their ancestral armour. Lady Seymour, a friend of Dizzy's, had been the Queen of Beauty. Unfortunately a truly Mancastrian rain had drowned the enthusiasm; thousands of umbrellas opened over the mediaeval costumes. The Knight of the Lion, the Knight of the White Tower, the Knight of the Mirror, all became Knights of the Woeful Countenance. The gods had shown themselves to be Victorians. But youth defies the gods, and the movement took other shapes without perishing. At Oxford, it was a religious renaissance. The "marvellously tender" voice of Newman was beginning to ravish souls. Young clerics sought to bring the Church of England closer to the forms of Catholicism. For forty years the Church had shown a greater dread of faith than of indifference. The young men were weary of those cathedrals with closed doors and those icy services; some went as far as Rome, others struggled to introduce warmer rites into their own Church. At Cambridge, Disraeli's new friends, Lord John Manners, George Smythe and Cochrane, had assumed the task of learning the sufferings of the mass of the people and seeking the remedies.

Like all true friends, they had few points of resemblance. Lord John Manners, a serious and religious spirit, a pure soul, a Lancelot lost in a world of machinery, cherished a whole-hearted regret for the days when the monarch made obeisance before the Saint, when the people saw in their King the Lord's Anointed, in the nobleman, a chief and a protector. On those themes he wrote verses, rather bad but pleasantly naïve:

Let wealth and commerce, laws and learning die,
But leave us still our old nobility.

George Smythe was a remarkable and deceptive youth, profligate but a sentimentalist, cynical but romantical, quite as capable of sacrificing his ideas to mundane considerations as of making an abrupt renunciation of the world for some visionary caprice. A strange man, George Smythe, more disillusioned at twenty than an old sage, wilder at twenty-five than a child, a poet without a poet's asceticism, a dowry-hunter with no love for money, who wrote in his diary: "If you wish to taste life, you must sip it slowly"—and for his own part drank it at one gulp. Disraeli had a great admiration for George Smythe. He was the only man who never bored him. He liked Smythe's friendship for Manners, the confidence of Manners in Smythe's talents, the humility of Smythe, proud as he was, when he compared himself with Manners. Seeing them standing on the threshold of life, he thought of two knights-errant with their arms gleaming in the sunlight.

Peel had deceived this ardent band of youth. He lacked genius; his commonplaces bored them to extinction. The eloquence of Disraeli intoxicated them. In Dizzy Smythe found a spirit in perfect harmony with his own. Lord John was rather more reserved. After the first meeting he had said: "Disraeli spoke well, but a little too well." The moments of frankness alarmed him. He was amazed and shocked by the Dizzy who could come out from a sitting in which he had defended the Church and murmur: "It is curious, Walpole, that you and I have just been voting for a defunct mythology. . . ." He was a trifle taken aback when Dizzy declared to these young men that there is no English nobility: "We owe the English peerage to three sources: the spoliation of the Church; the open and flagrant sale of its honours by the early Stuarts; and the borough-mongering of our own times. When Henry IV. called his first Parliament, there were only twenty-nine temporal peers to be found. Of those twenty-nine only five remain." And then he explained to them that the only pedigree of long civilization was that of the House of Israel and that his family was far older than theirs. Smythe laughed; John Manners listened with angelic earnestness.

It is delightful to be surrounded by disciples, but time was flying, irrecoverable. Peel was in power, more solid than ever. Every road towards useful action remained closed. "I think," said Disraeli to his wife, "that this is the moment to imitate Talleyrand, who, when he could not see very clearly what ought to be done, took to his bed," and he decided to spend a winter in Paris. Before going off he went down to his constituents and explained his conduct to them. He would continue to vote for Peel out of party discipline, except however in the event of the Premier betraying the agriculturalists.

He installed himself with Mary Anne at the Hôtel de l'Europe in the Rue de Rivoli. He had an introduction from D'Orsay to his sister, the Duchesse de Gramont, who welcomed them, him and his wife, with great cordiality. She entertained three times a week in a small house in the Faubourg Saint-Honoré packed with old furniture and pictures. There one would meet Eugène Sue, "the only *littérateur*," Disraeli noted, "admitted into fashionable society." The Mesdemoiselles de Gramont, who were pretty, spent the early part of the evening with their guests, but at ten o'clock they kissed their mother and went to bed.

Immediately the Disraelis were invited by Mme. Baudrand, the wife of General Baudrand, aide-de-camp to the King, a lovely Englishwoman, and young enough to be her husband's daughter. There they met the Anglo-French couples of Paris, the Lamartines, the Odilon-Barrots, the Tocquevilles. General Baudrand undertook to inform the King that M. Disraeli, a member of Parliament, would be happy to set forth a few ideas to His Majesty on the state of parties in England, ideas which, if understood at their true value, might well exercise an important influence on the politics of both countries.

The King received him at Saint-Cloud, and his curiosity was aroused by this sad and clever face, shadowed by long black ringlets; Disraeli interested him and pleased him, and was invited to return. He became an accepted figure at the palace. The Queen, Mme. Adé-laïde, the Duchesse de Nemours, sat down round a table and worked. Ices were handed round; the King led Disraeli into a neighbouring room and talked with him, sometimes of politics, sometimes of his youth, his strange adventures, the hard life he had led. "Ah, Mr. Disraeli, mine has been a life of great vicissitudes!" he said in English, which he was very fond of speaking; he had a slight American accent. He told Disraeli that he alone knew the art of ruling the French: "The only way to manage these people is to give them their head, and then know when to pull up." This intimacy with a monarch of such perfect intelligence intoxicated Dis-raeli. One of his childhood's dreams had come to pass. All the more did he agree with General Baudrand, in finding the King somewhat deficient in dignity. At the great dinners in the Galerie de Diane, Louis-Philippe would order a ham to be brought, from which he would cut slices as thin as paper and send them to his favoured guests. He was very proud of this talent, and explained to Disraeli that he had learned the art when an exile, from the waiter of a London eating-house where he used to dine for ninepence. The kings in Disraeli's novels had a finer taste for background.

V

Young England

"And what were they going to do with the Grail when they found it, Mr. Rossetti?"

JOWETT TO ROSSETTI.

Manners and Smythe had made a long examination of the political position, and reached the opinion that the only way of remaining true to themselves was to form a party, however small. But they required a chief with experience. Why not Disraeli? He seemed to be available? Smythe and his friend Cochrane (familiarly known as "Kok") came to see Dizzy in Paris; there they found him in triumph, enjoying his success like a child, his anteroom packed with Ministers. Although close on his fortieth year, he kept intact the pleasing faculty of being dazzled by his own brilliance. "Closeted with Louis-Philippe at Saint-Cloud," wrote Smythe to Manners, "he already pictures himself the founder of some new dynasty with his Manfred love-locks stamped on the current coin of the realm."

He welcomed them enthusiastically. A secret understanding was come to between the members, so as to please the lover of conspiracies, engaging them always to vote together and to accept the decisions of the majority of the group. Straight away he saw the group expanded, a party of fifty members, sixty members; Peel beset, restless, humiliated.

They dined together in the country, at the Rocher de Cancale in the Plaine Monceau. They came down again into Paris, to a long discussion as they walked round and round the Place Vendôme, and an agreement was reached.

Kok was rather less satisfied with Dizzy than Smythe was. He considered him as being too calculating, too ambitious. He found fault with him for having too much cleverness and for a lack of humour, that is, of cleverness against himself. Manners also, when informed of the course of events, betrayed some apprehensions. Were they all in search of the same goal? Disraeli's foremost thought was to fight the Government; the disciples only wanted to unite friends by bonds of sympathy. Dizzy's vast schemes of combination they considered crazy. To overturn Peel? In the first place, it was impossible; the Premier had an immense majority at his back. And furthermore, was it desirable? As soon as their little group became a real party, obliged to sacrifice its ideals to the intrigues of politics, jealousy would intervene to separate them and the beautiful toy would be shattered. "If I could be sure," wrote John

Manners, "that Disraeli believes all that he says, I should feel happier. His historical views are my own, but does he believe in them?"

In matters of religion Manners was exacting because he was a believer, but after some talks with Disraeli he was convinced that the latter was strongly attached to a moderate Oxford position, that is to say, to a Church of England that should become more romantic without being Romanised. The cynical Smythe would listen with amusement to the religious discussions of his two friends. Their points of view were so divergent that neither of them so much as perceived the differences. To Dizzy the Church of England was a great historic force which had to be respected and maintained, but the idea that the slightest importance could be attached to the letter of its doctrines did not even faintly occur to him. To John Manners, faith was so obvious an essential that the very idea of a man being able to live without certainty on all points of doctrine, was all but inconceivable. Smythe, with perfect perspicuity, wrote: "Dizzy's attachment to moderate Oxfordism is something like Bonaparte's to moderate Mahomedanism."

With Dizzy's return to London, the group entered on its activities. The four initiates found seats together behind Peel, exchanged all their impressions of the sittings, and did not hesitate to vote against the Ministry when its attitude was contrary to the principles of Young England. Thus they voted with the Radicals for the bill for the protection of children (who then often worked in the factories for twelve hours a day), and refused to support repressive measures in Ireland. In those cases they solemnly disassociated themselves from the party, and one of them would expound the doctrine of popular conservatism.

Nothing could be calculated to annoy Peel more than this methodical rebellion based upon a doctrine. An authoritative man, accustomed to blind obedience, he had always led his supporters with impatient coldness. When one of them came and timidly said: "I think I ought to speak . . ." he would answer drily: "Do you think so?" Even at a Cabinet council, if one of his colleagues ventured to disagree with his opinion, he would pick up a newspaper and sulk. "But he would kick me out if I dared to speak to him," said one of his Ministers. This opposition of three boys and a novelist exasperated him. He attributed every intrigue to Disraeli as a matter of course, and began to treat the latter with contumely. In public session he replied to the most harmless questions with a crushing brevity which Disraeli underlined when he said: "The right honourable baronet, with all that courtesy which he reserves only for his supporters. . . ." The Tories, so often badly treated, lowered their eyes and smiled behind their hands.

One of the Ministers, Sir James Graham, wrote to Croker:

"With regard to Young England, the puppets are moved by Disraeli, who is the ablest man among them: I consider him unprincipled and disappointed, and in despair he has tried the effect of bullying. I think with you that they will return to the crib after prancing, capering, and snorting; but a crack or two of the whip may hasten and insure their return. Disraeli alone is mischievous; and with him I have no desire to keep terms. It would be better for the party if he were driven into the ranks of our open enemies."

The Queen herself, now profoundly attached to her dear Sir Robert, wrote with indignation to her uncle, the King of the Belgians, that through the fault of a band of young fools she had almost been deprived of her Minister. Peel fell in with Graham's and Croker's opinion, and decided to eliminate Disraeli from the party; once isolated, he would lose his seat at the next elections, and they would be rid of him. At the full meeting of the Conservative party, he was not summoned. He asked the Prime Minister whether this was an oversight or an act of exclusion. He was informed in reply that the omission was intentional and that his attitude for several months back was sufficient to explain it.

The public were beginning to be aware of the existence of Young England. This clique of young men of birth with their white waistcoats, who wrote bad verses, talked of knights and keeps and suzerain chiefs, and sought to win the working-classes by these feudal paraphernalia, greatly amused John Bull. *Punch* published some "Lines to a Judge," by a Young Englander, who asked to be tied to a cart-tail and flogged, in order to revive a good old English punishment. But not everybody laughed. The four friends went in company to Manchester, and a working-class audience gave them a good reception.

Manners and Smythe held long conversations with manufacturers, and recognized that, although flinty and
greedy men of business did exist, many of them were
humane men. There lay the elements for a new feudalism, if only it could recognize its duties. To declaim
against industry was dull and ill-contrived. The task
was to win over the youth of industrialism to the beliefs
of popular conservatism.

During the recesses they all met again in one or another of the great country houses. Disraeli enjoyed those
reunions. His sympathetic understanding with the young
men was more complete than ever. Between himself and
them there was a strong bond of union, a common love
for all that was romantic, an idea that life is not only
a rather base conflict of interests and needs, but that it
can find place for impassioned friendships, for noble
and absurd loyalties, and for the love of beauty. John
Manners, since recognizing those sentiments in Disraeli,
and proving their purity, was still more attracted to him
than the other two. All three wrote to him as "Dear Cid
and Captain." For his own part, he recovered his youth
in their company, but with a freedom due to social
standing which he had never known. The veneer of cynicism which the trials of life had imposed on him was
cracking. He was full of gratitude to his friends for
their likeness to his dreams.

Once again a strong emotion inspired him with a
desire to write. He meditated a romance with Smythe,
Manners and their friends as its heroes, a novel which
would be at the same time an act of political faith,

showing forth the mediocrity of the parties as they actually existed and the possible part waiting to be played by a truly conservative faith. In the leafy shadows of their great parks, he would talk of his projects with his allies. He succeeded in shadowing forth a trilogy of modern England: the Aristocracy, the People, the Church. Fiction was resuming its sway over him; political realism was retreating. He shut himself up at Bradenham and set to work. But familiar now with the oscillations of his character, he said: "I want to clear the deck if I can by the end of January for action and speculation will never blend."

In two successive strokes, in 1844 and 1845, Disraeli published the first two volumes of the Young England Trilogy, *Coningsby* and *Sybil*.

Coningsby, or The New Generation, was at once the romance of his friends, a satire of the political scene, and a means for Disraeli to make a clear picture for himself of his own doctrine through a medium of fiction. Smythe had been the model for the hero, Coningsby; Manners and Cochrane were depicted at his side. He showed them first at Eton and at Cambridge, disappointed by the platitude of the ideas of their time, with an equal scorn for Whig politicians and Tory politicians, Conservatives who have nothing they want to conserve, Liberals with a hatred of liberty. "A sound Conservative government? Oh yes, I understand: Tory men and Whig measures." Coningsby, in search of a doctrine, met with a mysterious personage named Sidonia, who at last explained the world for him.

Sidonia is a Jew of Spanish origins and kingly fortune,
a blend of Disraeli and Rothschild, or, to be more precise, just what Disraeli would have liked to be, or what
he would have liked Rothschild to be. His phrases are
short, his locution perfect. In a few words he resolves
the most difficult problems with an almost superhuman
calm. If there could be anything urged against him, it
was his lack of earnestness. His gravest speeches are
shot through with a light spirit of mockery. From the
most profound gravity he passes to a kind of poignant
sarcasm. But this apparent lack of seriousness is com-
pensated for by an extreme freedom of mind, which is
perhaps its consequence.

What Sidonia teaches Coningsby is faith in the individual man of genius. "But what is an individual?"
exclaimed Coningsby, "against a vast public opinion?"
—"Divine," said the stranger. "God made man in His
own image, but the Public is made by Newspapers,
Members of Parliament, Excise Officers, Poor Law
Guardians." And what end ought to be pursued by
youth? It must seek a form of government which can
be loved and not merely supported. It must understand
that men are led only by the power of the imagination.
It must possess heroic ambition, the sentiment without
which no State is stable, lacking which the political life
is a dish without salt, the Crown a bauble, the Church
an administration, the Constitution a dream.

The book ends with the entry of Coningsby to Parliament. It delighted Young England; it was their epic.

Sybil, or The Two Nations, was no less remarkable.
The two nations are the Rich and the Poor. The book

was to instruct the English in what the life of their poor really was. In it Disraeli painted the misery of the villages, the industrial towns, the mines. The plot was melodramatic, but the pictures of popular life were exact and moving without being exaggerated. One could feel that they were depicted sympathetically, but also honestly. In none of his books had Disraeli been more serious. To speak of the people, he dropped his irony, and it was with true ardour that he closed with a kind of act of faith, entrusting to the youthful elect the task of seeking the remedies for so many ills, the people being impotent unless they fought under their proper chiefs. "That we may live to see England once more possess a free Monarchy, and a privileged and prosperous People, is my prayer; that these great consequences can only be brought about by the energy and devotion of our Youth is my persuasion. We live in an age when to be young and to be indifferent can be no longer synonymous. We must prepare for the coming hour. The claims of the future are represented by suffering millions; and the Youth of a Nation are the Trustees of Posterity."

On the fly-leaf of *Sybil* there were these words:

"I would inscribe these volumes to one whose noble spirit and gentle nature ever prompt her to sympathise with the suffering; to one whose sweet voice has often encouraged, and whose taste and judgment have ever guided, their pages; the most severe of critics, but— a perfect wife!"

VI

The Oak and the Reed

It was a saying of Disraeli's that after the publication of a book his mind always took a bound forward. A novel was for him a means of analysis, the testing of an attitude, the rehearsal, as it were, of a political policy. "Poetry is the safety-valve of my passions, but I wish to act what I write." Having now expressed in *Coningsby* and *Sybil* the ideal side of politics, he returned with pleasure to the practical. Young England, unfortunately, was a sentiment and not a programme, and the portly, high-coloured gentlemen sitting around him could never have been led to take the whole doctrine seriously. Now he must take his bearings and sail forth into reality. Where did political England now stand?

The House of Commons was more than ever dominated by Sir Robert Peel, and Sir Robert Peel was anxious to have done with party government. Conscious of his strength, he believed himself capable of imposing respect on his adversaries no less than on his followers. Certain of his own moral worth, he had come to regard opposition as a sin. He was attacked by the gravest of political maladies, ambition with moral symptoms, and one that does not admit of pardon.

About this time Disraeli found pleasure in repeating a maxim of Cardinal de Retz: "Everything in the world has its decisive moment; the crowning achievement of a good conduct of life is to know and pick out that moment." From a close analysis of the parliamentary atmosphere he judged that the decisive moment had come. After long and patient observation his diagnosis of Peel's case was now clear. Like all intelligent men who are not in any way creative, Sir Robert was dangerously sympathetic towards the creations of others. Incapable of formulating a system, he threw himself voraciously on those he came across, and applied them more rigorously than would their inventors. He would defend a policy long after the time when it would have been wise to compromise, and then, with a sudden understanding of his adversaries' objections, would become an advocate for the Opposition policy. It was in this way that, after fighting Canning with an almost cruel doggedness for his anxiety to emancipate the Catholics in England, he himself, after Canning's death, became the Catholics' emancipator. And now too, elected by the county gentry to defend a custom-house policy, he was plunging head-long into the Free Trade camp. Thus it came about, that always at the instant when he was most sure of his good faith and intellectual courage, he seemed in other men's eyes to be a deserter. Disraeli fixed upon the most appropriate point to launch the attack, and drove it firmly home.

The opening skirmish was brought about by a retort of Peel's. Disraeli had just concluded some observations with an appeal to the Minister not to see in them an act of hostility but, on the contrary, one of amicable frankness. Peel rose, and turning towards Disraeli, quoted with cutting disdain some lines of his illustrious predecessor, Canning:

"Give me the avowed, the erect, the manly foe;
Bold I can meet, perhaps may turn, the blow;
But of all plagues, good Heaven, Thy wrath can send,
Save, save, O save me from the candid friend!"

A rash quotation to come from one who had played beside Canning just that same part of the dangerous friend, some would even say of the treacherous friend. Glances were exchanged; eyes were turned sidelong on Disraeli; he made no reply. A few days later he rose again, to protest against the system of appealing to the loyalty of the Tories in order to make them vote for Whig measures. "The right hon. gentleman caught the Whigs bathing, and walked away with their clothes. He has left them in the full enjoyment of their liberal position, and he is himself a strict conservative of their garments." The whole House laughed and cheered. With impassive seriousness, Disraeli went on:

"If the right hon. gentleman may find it sometimes convenient to reprove a supporter on his right flank, perhaps we deserve it. I for one am quite prepared to bow to the rod; but really, if the right hon. gentleman, instead of having recourse to obloquy, would only stick to quotation, he may rely on it it would be a safer weapon. It is one he always wields with the hand of a master; and when he does appeal to any authority, in prose or verse, he is sure to be successful, partly because he never quotes a passage that has not previously received the meed of Parliamentary approbation, and partly and principally because his quotations are so happy.

"The right hon. gentleman knows what the introduction of a great name does in debate—how important is its effects, and occasionally how electrical. He never refers to any author who is not great, and sometimes who is not loved—Canning for example. That is a name never to be mentioned, I am sure, in the House of Commons without emotion. We all admire his genius. We all, at least most of us, deplore his untimely end; and we all sympathise with him in his fierce struggle with supreme prejudice and sublime mediocrity—with inveterate foes and with candid friends. The right hon. gentleman may be sure that a quotation from such an authority will always tell. Some lines, for example, upon friendship, written by Mr. Canning, and quoted by the right hon. gentleman! The theme, the poet, the speaker —what a felicitous combination! Its effect in debate must be overwhelming; and I am sure, if it were addressed to me, all that would remain would be for me thus publicly to congratulate the right hon. gentleman, not only on his ready memory, but on his courageous conscience."

The winged and envenomed darts of these sentences had been shot with amazing skill. A feigned humility to begin with, a low and monotonous pitch of the voice, a slow preparation. Then suddenly the "Canning, for example . . ." giving all his listeners the pleasure of foreseeing the attack, and the attack coming all the more irresistibly in being veiled by the perfection of the form and the insinuating softness of the voice. The effect was prodigious, the enthusiasm so loud that a Minister who rose to reply had to stand a long time in silence. Peel sat with bowed head, very pale, breathing heavily. Disraeli alone remained indifferent, as if human passions had no hold on him. "The scene would have brought tears of pleasure to your eyes," wrote Smythe to Mary Anne. At Bradenham, the old blind father, seated at Sarah's side, kept repeating: "The theme, the poet, the speaker!"

Peel felt the storm over his head. He was a sensitive man, and accustomed to respect. He had great difficulty in restraining himself. What! Would the House tolerate this treatment of the greatest of parliamentarians at the hands of this insolent fellow? And how unjust! Canning? Of course he had loved Canning; circumstances were complicated . . . there were wrongs on both sides . . . as always. He tried to explain, but found his audience hostile. By some subtle shifting of humour, he was piqued into a violent hostility towards those agricultural interests which had put him into power. As the Budget showed a favourable balance, many Conservatives were asking that this surplus should be used towards helping the farmers. Peel refused, through one of his Ministers, without even troubling to answer in person. And now the House, with an impatience of mingled anxiety and enjoyment, was waiting for Disraeli to speak; it was painful to see Sir Robert's noble features turn pale and quiver, but the sight was none the less welcome. It was like the scene when some fine animal enters the arena to give battle, its coat gleaming with strength and fitness, and the gazing crowd feels the agony in advance, and rejoices in the *banderillos* provoking it to fury.

This time Disraeli addressed his Protectionist friends and scolded them ironically. Why these unreasonable complaints of the Premier's conduct? "There is no doubt a difference in the right hon. gentleman's demeanour as leader of the Opposition and as Minister of the Crown. But that's the old story; you must not contrast too strongly the hours of courtship with the years of possession. 'Tis very true that the right hon. gentleman's conduct is different. I remember him making his Protection speeches. They were the best speeches I ever heard. It was a great thing to hear the right hon. gentleman say: 'I would rather be the leader of the gentlemen of England than possess the confidence of sovereigns.'

That was a grand thing. We don't hear much of the 'gentlemen of England' now. But what of that? They have the pleasures of memory—the charms of reminiscence. They were his first love, and, though he may not kneel to them now as in the hour of passion, still they can recall the past; and nothing is more useless or unwise than these scenes of crimination and reproach, for we know that in all these cases, when the beloved object has ceased to charm, it is in vain to appeal to the feelings. You know that this is true. Every man almost has gone through it. My honourable friends reproach the right hon. gentleman. The right hon. gentleman does what he can to keep them quiet; he sometimes takes refuge in arrogant silence, and sometimes he treats them with haughty frigidity; and if they knew anything of human nature, they would take the hint and shut their mouths. But they won't. And what then happens? What happens under all such circumstances? The right hon. gentleman, being compelled to interfere, sends down his valet, who says in the genteelest manner: 'We can have no whining here.' And that, sir, is exactly the case of the great agricultural interest—that beauty which everybody wooed and one deluded."

It is impossible to convey an idea of the effect produced. The tone added greatly to it. The words all came forth in a low, monotonously pitched voice, which was silent when the cheers and laughter became too loud, and then resumed, still unchanged and with no apparent effort, like a continuous stream of humour and blame falling drop by drop on to the massive form of the Minister. The House was simultaneously delighted and

shamefaced; overawed by the power of the man whom
it thus dared to stand up to, it applauded without looking at him. Peel pulled his hat over his eyes and could
not conceal his nervous movements, and Lord John Russell murmured, "That is all true," and even the fierce
Ellice laughed and Macaulay seemed gleeful.

The parliamentary recess came in time to give Sir
Robert Peel a short but welcome respite. He found pleasure in rejoining his family in the country. For this stern
Minister was the fondest of husbands and fathers, and
no doubt Disraeli, himself a man keenly alive to domestic affections, would have felt some pity if he could have
read the letters which Lady Peel received:

"MY OWN DEAREST LOVE,—I cannot much longer bear
this separation from you, I get a sort of lassitude and
languor here which quite depresses me. The coming
home at 2 or 3 o'clock in the morning to a desolate
house, with the prospect of the same thing the next night,
the bedroom with your tables and glass, and all the outward marks of habitation, the lovely nursery and the
drawing-rooms all silent and unoccupied—are sometimes too much for me. . . . Tell little Julia that I have
got her watch at home, and that I will wind it up every
night and see how it goes."

But almost always the unmasked face of a man remains hidden from those who know him only in public
life. Peel and Disraeli stood facing each other, both of
them unjust, both estimable, both firmly barred to each
other. Two helmetted knights were giving battle; their

lances met nothing now but steel; and never again, for either of them, would the vizors be lifted.

With Parliament at a safe distance, Peel recovered his confidence. With his charming wife beside him, in his beautiful house at Drayton, he found once more a world of harmony wherein he was the unquestioned master, an atmosphere of trust and praise in which hope revived. All in all, the session had concluded without definite defeat and left him as powerful as ever. As the Whigs had not a majority to take over government themselves, their interest lay in supporting him; no doubt the country gentlemen hated him now, but they would go on fearing him and do his bidding like so many sheep. He had lost their hearts, but not their votes. Cobden was still saying that neither the Grand Turk nor the Emperor of Russia had greater power than Peel. Seen from the distance of solitude, little Disraeli seemed no more to this lion than a gnat.

The month of July, however, was rainy, and slowly the downpour that had drowned the Eglinton Tournament was forming the torrent which was to sweep Peel away.

Sarah, replying to Dizzy's request for news of the harvest, replied: "It rains here so much that I do not think a dove would find a dry spot to rest upon. It is a very bad harvest." During August Peel learned that a blight had attacked the potato crop. The fear of seeing England struck by famine fitted in so aptly with the Free Trade theories to which his feelings were drawing him closer and closer, that he now embraced them passionately. He immediately made use of that word "famine." No potatoes: therefore famine in Ireland. No corn in England: therefore no solution but the abolition of the Corn Duties and the authorization at last of free import of foodstuffs. Yes, the ports must be thrown open, these monstrous duties suppressed. What would the party say? Would it not still be shouting of betrayal? No matter: Peel had a thirst for martyrdom. Cobden and Bright would approve his action. Disraeli would make a sarcastic speech and amuse the House for an hour, but Peel would stand out to posterity as a benefactor who sacrificed the interests of a party to those of the country.

Soon London learned that four Cabinet meetings had been summoned in one week; that Peel, throwing overboard the doctrines which had meant power to him, wanted to abolish the Corn Duties; that Lord Stanley had threatened to resign; that the blight on the Government was worse even than that on the potatoes. Peel's panic was a surprise to every one. Lord Stanley said he could not understand; nothing could be known for certain about the harvest for two months yet; the importation of corn would not fill the stomachs of the Irish, who had not a penny to buy it with. What was more, Peel was talking of maintaining a moderate duty for three years, and in three years' time the famine would be a distant memory. The Premier replied that the crisis was world-wide, and that already all nations were laying an embargo on the shipping of foodstuffs abroad. "Then," said Stanley, "if there is nothing to export, why change the whole customs policy of the country?"

But he did not see that the decision was sentimental and not rational. In the general turmoil, people were asking "What does the Duke think?" The Duke did not care for this adventure. He said: "Rotten potatoes have done it all; they put Peel in his damned fright." And he grumbled: "Never saw a man in such a state of alarm." Old Melbourne, good Whig though he was, showed that he was scandalized: "Ma'am, it's a damned dishonest act." But the Duke, more and more encased in his flexible rigidity, made it a point of honour to obey orders whatever they were, and held himself in readiness to give the word of command once more: "My lords, about turn! March!" Disraeli learned the news when he was making another stay in Paris, and reflected: "These rotted potatoes are going to change the fate of the world." Thiers said to him: "If it be a *real* famine, Peel will be a great man. If it be a *false* famine, he is lost."

When the decision was final, Stanley resigned, and all the Ministry followed suit. The Queen summoned Lord John Russell, who immediately restored to Peel the poisoned cup which the latter had handed him. But Peel found an agreeable taste in the hemlock. He said to the Queen: "I shall be your Minister whatever may happen." And to a friend he wrote: "It is a strange dream; I feel like a man coming back to life." What others called betrayal was in his eyes a pious conversion. The Queen and Prince Albert, ardent Free Traders, kept assuring him that he was saving the country. He knew that he was invincible because no one was willing to take his place. All would yet be well. Like Ulysses, he was the one man who could bend this bow.

Parliament reassembled. In the Lords a Protectionist party directed by Stanley had been formed against Peel. Croker had gone over to examine the situation in Ireland and warned his chief that, as Thiers had said, the famine was not a real one. John Manners wrote to Disraeli: "The famine is wicked moonshine and the prospects of next year are glorious." But Ireland had no more connection with Peel's decision than Kamchatka. He was going through his intellectual crisis, and nothing could have stopped him.

At the first sitting he informed the party that all his economic ideas had altered. The country gentlemen listened with horror to his declarations, but they were uttered in such a tone of authority that not a single murmur was heard. Moreover, on this progress to martyrdom, the Prime Minister kept all his tactical mastery. Gladstone, on rising to speak one day, asked Sir Robert in a whisper: "Shall I be short and concise?" "No," the chief replied, "be long and diffuse." And it was this method which he himself applied in that difficult sitting. To an astonished House he spoke endlessly on the price of flax, the price of wool, interposed a dissertation on lard, and another on the salt-meats contracts for the Navy, and the whole affair was so commonplace, so dreary, that the audience, seeing the familiar figure of Sir Robert standing there before his scarlet box, and facing him Lord John's woebegone features, half-hidden as always beneath his wide-brimmed hat, wondered whether the whole drama might not be a dream. Such was the art of this master in parliamentary debate, who knew the importance in certain circumstances of investing it with an air of pettiness, and as Disraeli said, of going back from the steam-engine to the kettle.

In spite of everything, it seemed as if the curtain would fall on a Government success, when Disraeli rose. After a few sentences on the tone of the Prime Minister, a tone intolerable in a man who had just announced the complete reversal of his policy, he went on in his even voice, his thumbs in the armholes of his waistcoat:

"Sir, there is a difficulty in finding a parallel to the position of the right hon. gentleman in any part of history. The only parallel which I can find is an incident in the late war in the Levant, which was terminated by the policy of the noble lord opposite. I remember when that great struggle was taking place, when the existence of the Turkish Empire was at stake, the late Sultan, a man of great energy and fertile in resources, was determined to fit out an immense fleet to maintain his empire. Accordingly a vast armament was collected. The crews were picked men, the officers were the ablest that could be found, and both officers and men were rewarded before they fought. There was never an armament which left the Dardanelles similarly appointed since the days of Solyman the Great. The Sultan personally witnessed the departure of the fleet; all the muftis prayed for the expedition, as all the muftis here prayed for the success of the last general election. Away went the fleet, but what was the Sultan's consternation when the Lord High

Admiral steered at once into the enemy's port. Now, sir, the Lord High Admiral on that occasion was very much misrepresented. He, too, was called a traitor, and he, too, vindicated himself. 'True it is,' said he, 'I did place myself at the head of this great armada; true it is that my sovereign embraced me; true it is that all the muftis in the Empire offered up prayers for the expedition; but I have an objection to war. I see no use in prolonging the struggle, and the only reason I had for accepting the command was that I might terminate the contest by betraying my master.' (*Tremendous Tory cheering.*)"

Free Trade or Protection, Disraeli was ready to grant that a man could prefer one to the other, but what was intolerable was that a Parliament elected to carry out one of those policies should boast of carrying out the other, that a man designated to his Sovereign by the confidence of a party should now come forward and say that the confidence of that Sovereign permitted him to scorn that party, and that he cared little for the judgment passed by the House, because he was sure of that which would be passed by posterity.

The cheers lasted for several minutes, and were addressed not merely to the artist or the orator; the statesman now could feel himself on solid ground. At the close of the sitting Disraeli was surrounded by the country gentlemen, talking of the formation of a Protectionist party in the Commons, to oppose the Prime Minister.

For three years now Disraeli had been seeing much of a member of Parliament very different from himself,

Lord George Bentinck, the son of the Duke of Portland. Lord George Bentinck was chiefly known as the owner of one of the finest racing-stables in the kingdom. He was the dictator of the racing world and had cleared it of dishonest jockeys. There he was justly looked up to, and in spite of his great severity his grooms worshipped him. They appreciated his perfect frankness and the full force of his love for horses. Every horse bred from his stud, even to the second generation, was backed by Lord George's bets; no horse that once entered his stables ever left them again until death. He would have thought it an act of ingratitude to dispose of an old horse because it could not run.

For eight years he had been in Parliament, but he had never spoken. He treated the House as a club. Frequently when he dropped in of an evening, one could see the pink collar of a hunting-coat just showing beneath his great white overcoat. His influence derived in part from his being the intimate friend and companion of every member who was interested in horses (and they were numerous), still more from the esteem in which his personal character was held by the whole House. He was known to be violent, but to be as loyal in his friendships as he was tenacious in his enmities, and in spite of a mediocre standard of culture, to be possessed of clear and sane judgment.

From 1842 onwards Disraeli was assiduous in his cultivation of Lord George Bentinck's company. Between this open-air man who rarely opened a book, and the slightly effeminate writer whom a sense of duty occasionally forced to mount a horse, friendship would have seemed difficult. But, from the force of contrast no doubt, Disraeli was irresistibly attracted by all such magnificent and well-weathered beings. He himself was painfully conscious of the almost morbid currents of his own sensibility, and for that very reason admired this splendid lack of self-consciousness. His friendship for Lord George had even led him into taking a share with him in a thoroughbred filly, Kitty by name, the foal of a Derby winner. The trainer, John Kent, cast a doubting eye on this strange, pale man who walked through the stables with awkward precautions and talked of horses in a profane tongue. He fancied that he could see that this odd visitor was feigning an interest in matters of the Turf which he did not really feel, and that, so far from letting himself be converted by Lord George to the religion of racing, he was seeking to win his lordship over to that of politics. Sometimes in the evenings, when the trainer came to report on the day's gallops, he would find his master and his master's friend seated before the fire, turning over blue-books. Lord George would pass a hand wearily over his eyes, and John Kent would leave the room with a sense of gloomy foreboding.

On the day when Sir Robert Peel announced his change of front, Lord George Bentinck emerged from his silence like a lion from its lair. He had an inborn horror of disloyalty, and he showed himself most ardent of all in calling for the instant formation of a Protectionist party. Disraeli immediately asked him to act as leader of this in the Commons. Bentinck replied: "Virtually an uneducated man, never intended nor attracted by taste for political life, I am well aware of my own incapacity properly to fill the station I have been thrust into." They certainly had need of him; his rank and dignity reassured those who would have hesitated to follow Disraeli, and moreover he revealed himself in the struggle as a much more redoubtable figure than had been supposed. He had a curious small voice which he seemed to wrench with difficulty from his powerful frame, and queer gestures; when he had once begun to speak, he was unable to stop; but his will was unbreakable. By dint of patient toil he accumulated facts and figures, which he then quoted with unimaginable violence. The strength and sincerity of the feeling which impelled him may be gauged from the fact that, on the day he accepted the position as leader of the Protectionists, he gave orders for the sale of all his horses. The trainer's mournful presentiments had been all too true. Henceforward Bentinck was seen in assiduous attendance at every sitting, and as it was a family failing of his to fall asleep very easily after meals, he imposed a fast on himself every day until after he had left the House. This mode of life, coupled with the effects of brain-work on a man who was devoted to an open-air life, very seriously affected his health.

"Bentinck and Disraeli, a pretty pair!" said Peel's friends with a laugh. . . . But the division on the first reading of the Corn Bill showed that only 112 members of the party had voted for Peel, while 240 of them "upheld with Bentinck the integrity of their honour." The Ministry however had a majority, but one composed in great part of its Liberal adversaries; it was obvious that it would abandon the bill when passed, and that from that day Peel would stand condemned. Throughout all these readings of the bill, Disraeli and Bentinck gave him a hard time. Nowadays it seemed as if anything could be said to him. The more ruthless the epithets applied to him, the more satisfied did the House appear. Disraeli called him a burglar of others' intellect . . . declared that there was no statesman who had committed political petty larceny on so great a scale, spoke of this political speculator who bought a party in the cheapest market and sold it in the highest. Bentinck was less ingenious, but more brutal; his lack of tact was shocking to the gentle and chivalrous Lord John Manners. When Peel rose to reply and uttered the word "honour," the House greeted him with cries of derision and gestures of contempt. Several times the Speaker, moved and impotent, thought that the great Minister was on the verge of tears.

After these ruthless debates, lasting often until four or five o'clock in the morning, Disraeli would find on his return home that Mary Anne had got up from bed, and had a great wood fire burning in the hearth and all the lights blazing. "Lights, plenty of lights" was what Mary Anne asked for, anxious that her husband's impression on coming home should be one of comfort and gaiety. Sometimes she came down in the carriage to St. Stephen's and waited there at the door for part of the night with a cold supper ready on her knees. A story went round that such was her devotion to Dizzy that, when accompanying him down to the House on the day of a great debate, having had her hand crushed by a footman shutting a door too suddenly, she had been plucky enough to say nothing until her husband had left her, simply in case he should be worried at a time when he needed all his calm. Lady Peel likewise, from the country, supported her husband's courage with touching letters: "I read the papers till indeed *all my courage fails me*, when I know that in any event you only expect 'increased trouble and anxiety. . . .' I only honestly ask one thing. Will you assure me that at least you are confident of triumphantly *proving* (of course I know you can do so) your own high-mindedness and high principles? Will the justice, wisdom and uprightness of your intentions and of your conduct be manifest? . . . If all this, I may again be at ease . . . and though I am but a poor reed, rely upon me for the truest support and affection."

The Lords might have been able to block the bill, but the Duke of Wellington made them pass it. With an air of gloom, with his hat pulled down over his eyes, he was in the surliest of moods and answered those who opposed him: "I am quite of your opinion, sir, it's a damned mess, but I must look to the peace of the country and of the Queen." *Punch* published a little paragraph headed *Bigamy*: "A man named Peel was yesterday brought before the magistrate Mr. Bull, charged with having intermarried with a female named Free Trade, his first wife Agriculture being alive."

On the very evening of the day when the third reading of the Corn Bill was passed, Sir Robert was defeated by a coalition of Protectionists and Whigs. His neighbour whispered in his ear: "They say we're beaten by seventy-three votes." Sir Robert made no reply. He did not even turn his head; he looked very grave and thrust forward his chin, as was his habit when he was pained and did not wish to speak.

VII

Leader

The bitterness of victory. Men, in their long journey towards death, picture to themselves a variety of pleasant halts; a few steps more, the day's stage will be ended, and then will come the hour of repose round the fire. But in time's continuous flow there is neither repose nor halt. Every evening the past is a dream, the future a mystery.

The giant who had scorned David lay sorely stricken across the path. The Conservative forces, cut in two, were fleeing in opposite directions. Lord John Russell and his Liberals, unopposed, assumed power. And what was going to happen, in this mighty confusion, to Benjamin Disraeli?

Five years of campaigning had taught him many lessons. Manners and Bentinck, stern judges both, had found him a trusty comrade-in-arms. He had gained their confidence, and he knew that he deserved it. Superior though he felt himself to Bentinck, and notwithstanding his intense eagerness to become leader of the party, he had made up his mind to serve as lieutenant, with the utmost loyalty, so long as Bentinck should hold the command. Loyalty and courage, he had learned, do more for a man than dazzling clothes or dazzling speeches; a faked greatness does not last; fidelity to a party, however ungrateful, is a necessary virtue in politics. His work was greater, far greater, than that of the young dandy who had entered Parliament in 1837.

But his position was not stable. Peel's friends, Gladstone, Graham, all the intellectual elect, detested him and vowed never again to join hands with him. At Court, the Queen and Prince Albert, an austere and lofty-minded man, regarded him as a man of unprincipled ambitions who had tortured their excellent and beloved Sir Robert out of sheer spite. The country gentlemen had followed him blindly enough in the heat of battle, but now they drew in their horns. Although he dressed nowadays in black clothes, the mere cast of his face gave him in their midst the appearance of an ibis or a flamingo strayed into an English farmyard. When sunlight fell on the Conservative benches, all the faces became whiter, but his turned darker. His erudition alarmed them. To reassure them he tried to put his wit under a bushel. On leaving an interview with him, one powerful landed proprietor had declared that Mr. Disraeli was not a very intelligent man, but was certainly a very worthy man. A good impression, but all too rare.

At bottom the Conservatives were startled at having overturned Peel. They had seen the crash with their own eyes, but they did not believe it. How could a Hebrew conjuror with black ringlets have caused that great, imposing figure to disappear? Disraeli's person, in their eyes, was enveloped in something no longer comical, but in a sinister prestige. With the dandy's mask torn off, there was disclosed a potent but malign magician. And the most serious fact was that Lord Stanley, leader of the Protectionist party in the House of Lords, and his real chief, had never liked Disraeli. No doubt he would not now have said, as in the old days: "If that scum is in it, I shall resign." He admitted that during five years Disraeli's conduct had given him no reason to doubt his loyalty. But he felt an almost physical hostility towards him. Stanley was a great nobleman of the eighteenth century, heedless and mocking, of haughty disposition and gay bearing. He prided himself on doing everything well enough and doing nothing too well. He translated Homer into passable English verse. One of his horses had come in second in the Derby. But political programme he had none, and nothing would have been more tedious to him than to formulate one. He had a horror of going back to first principles and of explanations of conduct. He liked to be calm and negligent. The tuberous panic of Peel had annoyed him; Disraeli's sour ambition he found no less distasteful. A man of impulse, speedily worn out by the struggle, he was afraid of the active staying-power of plebeians. With the fullest acknowledgment of the talents and perhaps—who could tell?—the honesty of this fellow Disraeli, Stanley considered that he was entitled to refrain from inviting him to dinner, and so not to have him as colleague in the party leadership.

At this moment when it was important to reassure a distrustful Parliament, to dissipate the cloud of strangeness which clung to his name, Mr. Disraeli, M.P., did the most unreasonable thing that could be imagined: he published a mystical romance.

This novel, with *Tancred* as its title, was the story of a young Englishman of noble family who makes a pilgrimage to the Holy Sepulchre in an attempt to understand "the Asian mystery." It served mainly as a pretext for the author to develop his theories of Judaism and the Church. To Disraeli the mission of the Church was to defend, in a materialist society, certain Semitic principles expounded in the Old and New Testaments, the chief of which was the belief in the rôle of the Divine and the Spiritual in this world. It was a commonplace amongst summary judges to explain Disraeli by saying, "He is an Oriental." It was an inaccurate label, a judgment too scanty in light and shade. Brought up as an Englishman, shaped by English thought, surrounded by English friends, passionately attached to England, he was much further removed from a Jew of the East than from a man like George Bentinck. Yet he was very different too from his friends of English blood. In particular he shared with the Oriental that double sentiment of a desire for the good things of this world and a perception of their hollow emptiness.

Tancred was a strange book, courageous and rash. It shocked many people. Carlyle found Disraeli's Jewish jackasseries intolerable, and asked how long John Bull would allow this absurd monkey to dance on his chest. Fortunately for Disraeli, many of his party colleagues never read anything. But shortly after Peel's downfall, events led him to expound his doctrine openly in the House of Commons itself. Lionel de Rothschild had been elected to Parliament by the City of London but could not take his seat, as the law demanded the oath to be taken on the faith of a Christian. Lord John Russell, faithful to the Liberal doctrine that every Englishman born in England has a right to all the benefits of the Constitution, proposed to abolish the formula. The whole of the Protectionist party voted against Russell, except Disraeli and Bentinck, the latter only out of friendship for Disraeli, who delivered a great speech. In it he laid down to an astonished House that the most harmful mistake a conservative party can make is to persecute the Jews, a race who are essentially conservative, and yet are flung by this treatment into the camps of revolution and upheaval, to which they bring formidable powers of intellectual guidance. For his own part, it was as a Christian that he would vote for the Jews. "Has not the Church of Christ made the history of the Jews the most celebrated history in the world? On every sacred day you read to the people the exploits of Jewish heroes, the proofs of Jewish devotion, the brilliant annals of past Jewish magnificence. Every Sunday—every

Lord's Day—if you wish to express feelings of praise and thanksgiving to the Most High, or if you wish to find expression of solace in grief, you find both in the words of the Jewish poets." The House listened with impatience, and from different quarters there came cries of "Oh, oh!" But Disraeli concluded: "I cannot sit in this House with any misconception of my opinion on this subject. Whatever may be the consequences on the seat I hold, I cannot, for one, give a vote which is not in deference to what I believe to be the true principles of religion. Yes, it is as a Christian that I will not take upon me the awful responsibility of excluding from the legislature those who are of the religion in the bosom of which my Lord and Saviour was born."

He sat down amid profound silence. Not a single member of his own party cheered him. On the opposite benches Lord John Russell turned to a neighbour and said admiringly that "it needed great courage in a party leader thus to defend doctrines which his followers held in horror."

The party conveyed to Bentinck that his conduct in the Rothschild affair had not met with approval. He resigned his leadership. Shortly afterwards he was found lying face downwards in a field, dead; a heart attack, the doctors said. He was a man little used to mental toil; the change of habits he had imposed on himself, the divorce from his usual exercise, had ruined his health. Moreover, he had been overwhelmed by a terrible chagrin. His sole ambition in life had always been to win the Derby, and in that he had never succeeded. And now one of the horses which he had sold in order to devote himself to politics, Surplice, had just come in first in that race. It was a cruel disappointment, but Lord George never regretted having done what he considered his duty. During his last days, when his friends beseeched him to take some rest, he used to reply: "He who saves his life shall lose it." His death cast a deep gloom over Disraeli. He had become whole-heartedly attached to this bluff but honest friend of his, who more than once had said to those who had doubts concerning his lieutenant, "I make no claims to great knowledge, but I'm a good judge of horses and men."

With Bentinck gone from the scene, Disraeli lost his strongest prop. When the choice of a new leader was discussed, there was mention of several names; but not of his. Stanley wrote him a letter, polite in form but insolent in essence, suggesting that he should serve under the orders of a nominal chief, Disraeli doing the real work, but the other being the titular leader. Disraeli refused to shoulder all the risks without the honour. The secession of Peel and his friends had left the Protectionists without a single orator. In the old Conservative party, which could boast of Gladstone and several others, he would have had to wait a long time, a very long time; but now the schism, willy-nilly, was putting him at the head. Stanley held out as hard as he could. In the end he offered to have the party in the Commons led by a committee of three: Granby, Herries, Disraeli. "Sieyès, Roger Ducos, and Napoleon Bonaparte" commented an old Minister when he heard the news.

Three weeks later the other two were out of court, and in every one's eyes Disraeli stood forth as the official leader of the Opposition. Lord Melbourne, who was still alive, then remembered the ringleted young man who had answered him at Caroline Norton's: "I wish to be Prime Minister."

"By God," said he, "the fellow will do it yet!"

To be the acknowledged chief of a great party in the House of Commons—here certainly was one step forward on the road to power. But one idea became more and more obvious to Disraeli: that in England, and in a certain political society, a man who does not own land counts for nothing. He did not think the prejudice absurd. A landed proprietor, walking over his estates and talking with his farmers, learns the real state of feelings and needs, hears the complaints of the agriculturalist, can reckon for himself the effects of the laws on which he has voted. A London-dweller, spending his life in drawing-rooms and at the House, can be no more than a theorist. The mind has real need of contact, at close intervals, with the soil. After a spell of urban life the tumult of the brain is soothed by the calm and beauty of nature in the fields. Disraeli was passionately fond of trees and flowers; for long his dream had been to acquire a great house in that county of Bucks to which he had attached himself.

There was one for sale, not very far from Bradenham —the Manor of Hughenden. Disraeli and his brothers had often been there in boyhood, for games and flirtations. They were well acquainted with the splendid park, the stretching woods of beech and pine, the curving shoulders of grassland, the little stream in the valley where the trout lay hid, and the terrace sheltered by its flowery pergola. Over and over again they had heard the history of the demesne, given by William the Conqueror to Odo, Bishop of Bayeux; there Richard de Montfort had dwelt, and the famous Earl of Chesterfield; nothing could have given Disraeli livelier pleasure than to become the lord of the Manor of Hughenden. But he had no money. At the time of his marriage his youthful debts, swollen by the interest charged by the money-lenders and by the debts of friends for which he had gone surety, amounted in all to £20,000. His share in the paternal inheritance would come to £10,000, and Mr. Isaac D'Israeli was quite ready to devote this sum immediately to the acquisition of an estate, but the manor and woods were worth £35,000. Where was that to be found?

Whilst Lord George Bentinck was still alive, Disraeli had confided his desire to him, and Lord George, judging it certainly desirable that one of the leaders of the agricultural party should himself be a country gentleman, had offered to unite with his brothers in advancing this large sum. The agreement in principle being made, Isaac D'Israeli had bought Hughenden for his son. Not long afterwards he died, at the age of eighty-one, almost unawares, not having ceased, up to the last hour, to listen to Sarah reading aloud to him. In the same year, and before the manor had been paid for, Lord George Bentinck had died in his turn, but Disraeli had found in his friend's two brothers the same generosity. He explained to them with open and courageous frankness that his life would be no pleasure to himself and of no service to the party if he could not play high stakes. They were men capable of understanding how impossible life would be without playing high, and Dizzy was able to write to Mary Anne: "It is done, and you are now the lady of Hughenden."

The purchase might justly have been criticized by prudent people. But how could Disraeli let slip, for want of some paltry gold sovereigns, the chance of possessing a manor almost the image of those in his romances, a little church standing up in the very park itself, a vicarage, a stream, land, a long avenue of beeches, a natural palace with the leaves meeting in a great arch over a carpet of mossy grass . . . ? Already Mary Anne, the perfect mistress of the mansion, was plotting out footpaths in the pine-wood, which they called the German Forest, and settling on the sites for rustic benches. Disraeli took long walks on foot, his wife accompanying him in a little pony-trap.

October: the woods were putting on their autumn livery; the limes and larches still kept their yellowed leaves, the copper-burnished beeches were flaming in the sun; here and there still an oak or an elm was green as in midsummer. The lord and lady of Hughenden came quietly back towards their manor. He was forty-five, and she, fifty-nine; but he bent over towards her fondly, and she towards him with playfulness. On the terrace there were peacocks strutting, dazzling and majestic. "My dear lady, you cannot have a terrace without peacocks!"

VIII

Obstacles

"My God! The fellow will do it yet!" Lord Melbourne was an optimist; more so, indeed, than Disraeli, whose eye could see still, between him and power, a stiff course barred with difficult obstacles.

Barrier number one.—Although he was leader of the party in the Commons, he did not feel himself respected. Disraeli was the Mephistopheles to the Conservative party's Faust. "Strength and youth shall I give you, but on one condition: that I must ever be by your side." Faust put up with Mephisto, but he hardly liked him. It was admitted that the new leader carried out his duties well. When he was not in the House he was turning over blue-books, taking notes, preparing speeches. Only Mary Anne maintained contact with the solid world, and at last Dizzy could show openly that profound contempt for frivolity which the need of making a good impression had long forced him to conceal. Often enough, when with friends, he would pass the whole evening without uttering more than a word or two. So lost in thought did he appear that people hardly ventured to address him.

But the Whips sent Stanley reports on him rather like those which some colonial functionary might send to his governor on a native chief only lately brought to submission. "He strikes me as feeling himself completely embarked now with us, and I do trust that he is fully compromised and will remain true." During the parliamentary recesses, a controlling eye was kept on him, even on his face: "Disraeli, I hear, is figuring about with a fierce pair of moustaches. Now this is very sad, for he is not the person who ought to attract attention by *outré* dress and appearance, but by his talents. I trust that this style is only assumed while he is rusticating in the beech-woods of Buckinghamshire, and that he will appear in the world in a more humanized form in January."

Unjust fears: he was irreproachably turned out. Chains and rings had disappeared. Winter and summer alike, the clothes were dark. In his early days his hectic manner might have left an unpleasant taste, but now the House must be satisfied by his immobility. During the sittings he remained seated on his bench with his head stiffly held, his arms folded tightly over his chest, his eyes half-closed.

His aspect reminded one inevitably of the stone figures of ancient Egypt. When he was violently attacked, he affected sleep. If the attack touched him on the quick, he would slightly draw back the point of one foot, or pull slightly at the cuff of his shirt. It was the only sign of life that the most minute observation could detect in him. Even in the lobbies he glided noiselessly along like a ghost, without seeming to notice the presence of external objects. When he spoke, it was without gesture, without calling effects of the voice into play. There was only this: that on the point of uttering some particularly pleasing remark, he would pull his handkerchief from his left-hand pocket, transfer it to his right hand, cough slightly—*hem*—pass the handkerchief under his nose, throw out the remark, and then put the handkerchief back in his left hand. Further, the stiffening of the body had disciplined his spirit. Disraeli, once so nervous, had become perfectly calm in appearance. If he were contradicted, he would answer, "Perhaps . . ." and immediately change the subject.

Barrier number two.—The Protectionist party had no doctrine. "And what about Protection?" Stanley would have said. But Protection could not serve as a programme to a great party. A party must have a faith. The imaginations of men cannot be set afire with customs regulations. And men are led only by force of the imagination. What is more, events had shown Peel's crime to have been less serious than had been supposed. "What did we maintain against Peel?" said Disraeli.

"That Free Trade would ruin the farmers and would not bring down the cost of living." Well, the cost of living had fallen, and the farmers were as prosperous as in the days of the Corn Duties. It may have been mere chance; it depended on the weather, on the harvests; perhaps in the days to come a different spell of weather would bring the hour of Protection, but Disraeli, as a realist, bowed to the facts: agriculture was not ruined. To re-establish the duties on corn, then, would be folly; the country would be provoked, the party would be finished. Protection was not only dead, but damned.

This attitude annoyed everybody. The Liberals wanted to see their opponents chained for a century to this condemned policy. Lord Stanley asked, not without a semblance of reason, whether it had really been worth while pouring invective on Sir Robert Peel and then just imitating him.

Stanley had neither time nor inclination to reflect on the real merits of Free Trade. He had his billiards and his horses. He had bound himself up with a Protectionist policy, and a Protectionist policy he would carry on —and let consequences go to the devil! The faithful John Manners also felt that honour demanded that they should shout "Down with the Income Tax, and hurrah for the Customs!" The old legends of political infidelity began to go the rounds once more. *Punch* caricatured Disraeli, representing him now as the will-o'-the-wisp vainly pursued by the farmers, now as a chameleon whom John Bull has placed on his table and is examining with curiosity, now as the village seducer, whom a stern father, pointing to his daughter Agriculture, is asking, "What are your intentions?"

Barrier number three.—So long as Sir Robert Peel was alive, it was impossible to reconstitute a united Conservative party without him, and impossible to do so with him. At the outset Disraeli had found it very painful to take his seat on the same bench with the man whose life he had shattered, separated from him only by Gladstone. Since his defeat, Sir Robert had become a sympathetic figure in Disraeli's eyes. He only spoke of him to praise him. If Gladstone's absence meant a risk of placing them actually side by side, Disraeli would summon a friend to sit between them, so as to spare Sir Robert a distressing proximity. But Peel looked at him without anger and observed him gravely. The posthumous success of his policy had consoled his pride. Once again his face was tranquil, almost happy. One evening when Disraeli sat down after a fine speech, Gladstone, who was Peel's neighbour, heard him quietly expressing approval.

That night the sitting lasted until five o'clock in the morning. When he came home Disraeli found his house all lighted as usual, went to bed, slept well, rose very late, and was persuaded by his wife to take a carriage drive with her. As they were going through Regent's Park two strangers on horseback stopped their carriage.

"Mr. Disraeli," they said, "you will be interested to know that Sir Robert Peel has been thrown by his horse and carried home in a dangerous state."

"Dangerous?" said Disraeli. "I hope not. His loss would be a great misfortune for this country."

The two strangers seemed surprised, and moved away.

The news was true. Peel had gone out riding in the morning; he was tired after the all-night sitting; his horse had been restive and had thrown him. His suffering was such that the doctors could not make a full examination of his injuries; Lady Peel was so overcome that she was not allowed into the sick-room, for the sight of her grief would have put the injured man into a real convulsion. An anxious crowd surrounded the house, awaiting news.

In the afternoon the Londonderrys gave a great rustic fête in a rose-covered cottage on the banks of the Thames. Lady Londonderry served tea to her guests from teapots of massive gold. The master of the house shook Disraeli by the hand with affectionate anxiety, and then disappeared. When he came back, much later, he murmured: "No hope. . . ." He had galloped as far as Peel's house while his fiddlers played their music and his guests ate ices.

Next day at the Carlton Gladstone said: "Peel has died at peace with everybody, even with Disraeli." Rachel that evening was playing *Bajazet* in French, and all London met there. It was strange to think that never again would Sir Robert be on his bench. "He had done his work," said Bulwer to Disraeli. "No man lives who has done his work. There was nothing left for him to do." Why? Bulwer was becoming very sententious.

Very sincerely Disraeli regretted his neighbour. Nevertheless, with Peel dead, it seemed easier to rally the Peelites to the party. But the Peelites were refractory. They considered it unworthy of their devotion to Peel's

memory to join hands so promptly with his foes, and
they were unwilling to serve under Disraeli, to whom
they themselves were old foes. They were taken by surprise when they learned that Disraeli was ready to yield
the leadership of the Commons to a veteran Peelite. The
abnegation astonished them to a point of incredulity. It
did not fit in with the character they had imagined. They
soon had occasion to put his sincerity to the test. Left
in a minority on a Radical motion, Lord John Russell
proffered his resignation, and Lord Stanley was summoned by the Queen. It was not without apprehensions
that she saw him approach. The royal household were
Free Traders. Stanley told the Queen with his elegant
frankness that his party could muster very few men of
talent and that he could hardly see any way of finding
amongst them the elements of a Ministry. He conferred
with Disraeli. Could half a dozen more or less intelligent Conservatives, without the help of the Peelites, be
found in the House of Commons? Stanley did not think
so. Disraeli told him that if, by sacrificing himself, the
party could get the support of Gladstone and his friends,
he, as leader, was prepared for the sacrifice; and he
then suggested several names, a Mr. Henley for example. Lord Stanley shrugged his shoulders, but raised no
objections. That was his way.

Next day about noon Stanley was announced at the
Disraelis', at Grosvenor Gate. He was taken upstairs to
the first floor, into the Blue Room. His face was radiant,
his eyes gay, and he lifted a mocking eyebrow, as he
often did, when he said, "Well, we are launched!" Then
he became serious. "I have promised the Queen that I

would try to form a Government." She had asked to whom he intended to entrust the leadership of the House of Commons, and he had named Disraeli. Whereupon she had interrupted him: "I do not approve of Mr. Disraeli. I do not approve of his conduct to Sir Robert Peel, and Sir Robert's death does not tend to lessen that feeling."

"Madam," said Stanley, "Mr. Disraeli has had to make his position, and men who make their positions will say and do things which are not necessary to those for whom positions are provided."

"That is true," the Queen had said. "All I can now hope is that, having attained this great position, he will be temperate. I accept Mr. Disraeli on your guarantee."

"And now," said Lord Stanley to Disraeli, "I am going to write to Gladstone to call on me. Be with me late in the afternoon to know the result and consult."

The interview with Gladstone was a complete check. Before entering a Ministry, the Peelites insisted upon an official disavowal of the Protectionist policy, a kind of *amende honorable*. This was something to which the proud Stanley could never consent. In spite of everything he kept his good temper and summoned for the following day a meeting at his house of his friends in the House of Lords, and those members of the Commons who were indicated by Disraeli. But when the latter saw this pitiful assemblage gathered in his chief's superb dining-room, he lost confidence. This Mr. Henley whose praises he had sung was sitting on a chair, both hands leaning on a heavy cane, his black eyebrows knotted, his eyes devoid of all thought, looking like a prison warder awaiting a reprimand for brutality. The others were worth about as much; as soon as they began to speak, Lord Stanley exchanged a glance with Disraeli, who grasped what was passing in his chief's mind. This clever and fastidious man could not bear such a spectacle very long. He wanted to pack the whole lot off to the devil. Already Disraeli had begun forming a vast programme, imagining a long ministry and favourable elections. And now the adventure was over before it had begun! Ah, if only Disraeli had been the chief, how patiently he would have tried the slow shaping of his colleagues! But chief he was not, and he had to submit to the caprices of this aristocrat whose resistance was already overtaxed. The goal was almost within his fingers, but it receded, perhaps beyond all reaching.

Lord Stanley signed to Disraeli to rise and led him over to the end of the room.

"This will never do," he said.

"I am not sanguine. But don't be in a hurry."

Stanley returned to the table. He said that it was his duty to decline to form a Government, particularly by reason of the lack of suitable members from the House of Commons. One of the Whips, Beresford, leapt up and assured Stanley that there were several men of worth waiting at the Carlton to be summoned.

"Who is there at the Carlton?" asked Stanley impatiently.

"Deedes," said Beresford.

"Pshaw!" exclaimed Stanley. "These are not names I can put before the Queen. Well, my lords and gentlemen, I am obliged to you for your kind attendance here to-day: but the thing is finished."

And they all dispersed, much confused in mind. Henley stayed on, silent and grim. Beresford had the bearing of a man who has just lost his whole fortune at roulette, and kept on declaring that Deedes was a first-rate man.

When Stanley explained his refusal to form a Government to the House of Lords, he drew a brilliant parallel between the nullity of his own party and the brilliance of the small group of the Peelites. It was not always very easy to be the lieutenant of Lord Stanley.

IX

Mr. Gladstone's Cruel Duty

Just as in Rugby football a good half-back, still keen in spite of disappointments, will pass the ball a score of times to slack three-quarters who do not even try to charge, so did Disraeli divert power into the negligent grasp of Stanley. His great task was "the education of the Party"; he had to extricate it from Protection, to raise it from a caste feeling to a national feeling, to teach it to take heed of popular comfort and of the solidity of the Empire. He put forward a bold programme to take the place of Protection, in the shape of an Imperial reform of Parliament: to admit the Colonies to a share in the administration of the Empire, to balance with their vote the democratic vote of the towns, and thus to introduce fresh elements and put an end to the absurd rivalries of Town *versus* Country, Industry *versus* Agriculture. "Romantic imaginings," thought the noble Lord, and returned to his pleasures.

But once again the ball was passed to him and the Queen summoned him to Windsor. He was now Lord Derby, through the death of his father a few months earlier. Once again he came to Grosvenor Gate and was shown into the Blue Room. This time he said to Disraeli: "You will be Chancellor of the Exchequer."

"I know nothing of finance," said Disraeli.

"You know as much as Canning knew. . . . They will give you the figures."

And next day the Ministry was formed. Such was the party's poverty in men that only three of the members of the Cabinet had already been Ministers. The Queen considered that the Ministry was composed of Lord Derby alone. And he, when asked for his views, replied "I am very well and my babes too." The Duke of Wellington had the list of new Ministers read out to him; but as he was very old and very deaf, and all the names were new to him, he kept interrupting his informant with a repeated "Who? Who?" The newspapers seized on the saying, and the Ministry came to be known as the "Who? Who?" Cabinet. As for the selection of Disraeli as Chancellor of the Exchequer, that was regarded ridiculous.

But what mattered that to him? He was like a young girl on the day of her first ball. The great old man Lyndhurst recalled to him those youthful conversations when he had expressed his desires, boyish enough in those days, and now made real. Sarah, in the depths of her rustic solitude, found herself besieged by people of the district asking for favours. The postman wanted to be transferred to the town, and spoke to Miss D'Israeli in timid, trembling tones. Dizzy went to obtain his Chancellor's robe, a robe of black silk heavily broidered with gold braid; it descended in a straight line from the great Pitt.

"You will find it very heavy," said the judge who received him.

"Oh, I find it uncommonly light," he answered.

The beginnings were none too bad. The Queen herself was amused by the reports which it was the duty of the leader of the House of Commons to address to her every evening: "Mr. Disraeli (*alias* Dizzy) writes very curious reports, much in the style of his books." Derby was well enough pleased with his crew of beginners. The House was awaiting the election. But when this was over, and it took an unfavourable turn, the unhappy Chancellor knew very well that he would not be allowed a long taste of the duties in which he found so much pleasure. Gladstone in particular had a watching eye on him.

Although neither one nor the other would have desired it, political life was slowly assuming the form of a duel between these two. To all outward appearance they were good friends. Their wives exchanged visits. Sometimes, after a somewhat lively sitting, Gladstone would even come in to say good-evening to Mary Anne. In theory the two men were Conservatives. Gladstone, with his love for indefinable shades of difference, said that he preferred to be on the liberal side of the Conservative party rather than the conservative side of the Liberal party. But their temperaments clashed and the paths of their careers crossed. Without Disraeli, Gladstone would have been the natural heir to Peel. That was the latter's opinion: "Gladstone will be the Conservative Prime Minister," he said some time before his death; and when he was asked, "What of Disraeli?" he answered, "We shall make him Governor-General of India."

Each was stern in his judgment of the other. To Gladstone, Disraeli was a man without religion and without political faith. To Disraeli, Gladstone was a man of assumed piety, who cloaked his skill in manœvering with feigned scruples. Gladstone had all his days lived a model Sunday-school life. At Eton he said his prayers, morning and evening. At Oxford the young men drank less in 1840 because Gladstone had been up in 1830. In Parliament he had been straight away the studious pupil, and Peel's beloved disciple. Disraeli had lived a vagabond's life, in schools and politics alike. He had known the moneylenders' parlours before those of Ministers and Bishops. Disraeli's enemies said he was not an honest man. Gladstone's enemies said of him that he was an honest man in the worst sense of the word. Disraeli's foes said that he was not a Christian; Gladstone's said that he might be an excellent Christian but that he was assuredly a detestable pagan. Disraeli had learnt his reading from Molière and Voltaire; Gladstone regarded *Tartuffe* as a third-rate comedy. The cynical Disraeli whispered in the ear of the aged and austere Mr. Bright, as he helped him into his overcoat: "After all, Mr. Bright, we both know very well what brings you and me here: ambition." Gladstone unconsciously assured himself: "Well, I do not think I can tax myself with ever having been much moved by ambition." It was said of Gladstone that he could convince others of many things, and himself of anything at all. Disraeli could persuade others, but was powerless over himself. Gladstone liked to choose an abstract principle and from that to deduce his preferences. And his tendency was to believe that his desires were those of the Almighty. He was reproached, not so much for always having the ace of trumps up his sleeve as for claiming that God had put it there. Disraeli had a horror of abstract principles. He liked certain ideas because they appealed to his imagination. He left to action the care of putting them to the test. When Disraeli changed his views, as in the case of Protection, he admitted the change and was ready to appear changeable; Gladstone fastened his constancy to blades of straw and thought that they were planks. Disraeli was sure that Gladstone was no saint, but Gladstone was far from certain that Disraeli was not the Devil.

And each misread the other. Gladstone accepted as true all the cynical professions of faith which Disraeli made as a challenge; Disraeli put down as hypocritical the phrases by which Gladstone duped himself in all good faith. Disraeli, the doctrinaire, prided himself on being an opportunist; Gladstone, the opportunist, prided himself on being a doctrinaire. Disraeli affected to despise reason, but reasoned well; Gladstone, who believed himself a reasoner, acted only through passion. Gladstone with a great fortune still kept his account of daily expenses; Disraeli with his heavy debts spent his money without counting it. Both were fond of Dante, but Disraeli turned chiefly to the *Inferno*, Gladstone to the *Paradiso*. Disraeli had the name of being frivolous, but was taciturn in society; Gladstone, who was supposed to be grave, was so charming in company that to be able to go on hating him, one had to avoid meeting him. Gladstone was interested in two things only: religion and finance; Disraeli was interested in hundreds of things, religion and finance among them. Neither of the pair believed in the other's religious convictions, and there again they were both wrong. And finally, Disraeli would have been much surprised if he had known that Mr. Gladstone and his wife, when they had reason to be particularly merry, would stand in front of the fire, clasped together and swaying as they sang:

> "*A ragamuffin husband and a rantipoling wife,*
> *We'll fiddle it and scrape it through the ups*
> *and downs of life!*"

When the two rivals rose in succession on a very dark day in December 1852, for the Budget discussion, it seemed that two supernatural powers were opposing each other. Gladstone with his well-chiselled profile, his onyx eyes, his crest of black hair thrown backward with a powerful gesture, seemed like the Spirit of Ocean. Disraeli with his shining curls, his slightly stooping figure, his long supple hands, seemed rather a Spirit of Fire. As soon as they began to speak it was obvious that Disraeli had more genius, but Gladstone had assumed a tone of moral superiority which was more pleasing to the House.

Never had a Budget been attacked in Parliament as that of Disraeli was. For a whole week, night after night, it had been mocked at, made game of, scorned. All the brilliant economists in turn had demonstrated its ignorance and folly. All had ironically underlined its abandonment of Protection.

He had remained motionless, arms and legs crossed, his eyes half-closed, his pale face veiled with apathy. Were his thoughts perhaps turning to the ironical sentences he himself had hurled once against Peel? "We no longer hear much talk about the country gentlemen." Now it was to him that they were saying: "We no longer hear much talk about the famous Protection." He seemed neither to listen nor to feel. When at last he spoke, the smothered violence of his sarcasm showed that he had not been unscathed. He forced a calm, sustained tone upon himself, but from time to time there escaped a phrase of such bitter irony as to seem almost agonized. His opening—"I was not born and bred a Chancellor of the Exchequer; I am one of the Parliamentary rabble"—had strange reverberations of Rousseau, very unexpected in the leader of the Conservative party. A violent storm raged throughout the whole of his lengthy speech. The quick flashes of lightning, the roll of thunder, made a congruous setting for the diabolic figure whom his adversaries believed they were gazing upon. When Gladstone rose it was a relief. The storm had ceased. Solemn, moralizing sentences rocked the conscience very agreeably. The unctuous moderation of tone was restful.

The subtle poetry of a British Budget is perhaps the most recondite art for an unfortunate who, like Disraeli, has not been reared from infancy by the Muses of Westminster. Its mysterious but inexorable laws are such that a penny on sugar will suddenly set up a horrid dissonance (and all the old subscribers gnash their teeth and look pitifully on the new conductor of the orchestra), whereas a penny on beer would perhaps have made in their ears the most delectable harmony. The tax on malt and the naval reductions chase one another in difficult, but very strict, counterpoint, which is revealed no doubt by instinct to the born Chancellor of the Exchequer. Gladstone, a natural *maëstro* of this austere and sublime art, had no trouble in laying bare the faults of the prentice hand.

Disraeli listened, his arms still folded, his eyes very weary. From time to time he looked at the clock. In the gallery, Derby was awaiting the vote which should decide the fate of his Ministry. He listened to Gladstone attentively for a few minutes, and then let his head fall on his arm. "Dull!" he said simply.

At four o'clock in the morning the Ministry was overturned by 305 votes to 286. The taste of power had been brief. Nothing can convey the grace of Disraeli's farewells. He showed no trace of sadness, but asked pardon of the House for the unwonted warmth of his speech. Lord John congratulated him on the courage with which he had fought. And the curtain fell. That evening Gladstone noted in his journal that God knew how much he regretted having been the instrument chosen to bring about the fall of Disraeli. The man had, in all conscience, great talents. "I would only pray that they might be well used."

In the Liberal Ministry which was thereupon formed, Gladstone made the final break with his past, and took office with some of his Peelite friends. So brilliant was this Cabinet that, in distinction from "Who? Who?" it was styled that of "All the talents."

X

Shadows

Fifty . . . fifty-one . . . fifty-five. . . . The years were hollowing the features of that face. From beside the nostrils two furrows slanted downwards to meet the corners of the mouth. Under the eyes the skin was turning darker; the lower lip drooped heavily; he was aging, this transplanted Bedouin, he did not wear so well as the fair-skinned English. Young women, who had not known him in the days of the embroidered waistcoats and gold chains, in the days of the youthful ringlets, thought him ugly. But Mary Anne thought otherwise. "Mr. Disraeli," some one said to her, "spoke most eloquently in the House to-night. How splendid he is looking just now!"

"Ah, yes?" she said. "You think he looks splendid? People think that he is ugly, but he is not: he is very handsome. I should like them to see him when he is asleep."

The man had become more taciturn than ever, and there were not more than two people in London who could remember having seen him smile. He retained all his relish for high play, but was he ever to hold the winning hand? He began to doubt it. A hundred times over he had delivered speeches which were declared to be the finest that Parliament had ever listened to. Ten times over had he stormed the opposite benches, but either the chief would back out at the last obstacle, or the Ministry, once formed, would collapse after a few months. And then for a long time the Crimean War had imposed a kind of party truce in Lord Palmerston's favour. The breach left by the secession of the Peelites had never been repaired, and the party remained impotent.

Lord Derby had now become a friend, and when he was asked the old question—"Why does nobody trust Mr. Disraeli?"—he would answer: "I trust him." But Lord Derby was subject to attacks of the gout and did not like to be talked to about matters of State. When Disraeli visited him to discuss the question of electoral reform, he read his visitor a translation of a French poem, Millevoye's *La Chute des Feuilles*:

> *"Dear woods, farewell, your mournful hue*
> *Foretells the doom that waits on me. . . ."*

Lord Derby was not displeased with those lines. What did dear Dis think, who had been a poet himself in his day? And dear Dis sighed and tried to put a brave face on things. His air of pathetic and transparent resignation amused the old nobleman. What mattered the Ministry to him? Nothing could prevent him from being the fourteenth Earl of Derby—the first of them in Shakespeare, and the twelfth the founder of the Stakes. When his son Stanley came in after declining office, "Hullo, Stanley," was his greeting, "what good wind brings you here? Has Dizzy cut his throat, or are you going to be married?" But if any one suggested the supplanting of Dizzy by Stanley in the Commons, Derby would turn grave. The Captain was no less loyal than the Lieutenant.

For the prolonged clouding of Conservative fortunes, the Captain and the Lieutenant were held responsible by a whole clique of enemies. One section of the crew mutinied, dubbing them "the Jew and the Jockey." And Disraeli was feeling rather jaded. He knew that he had done his best, that he had acted honourably, that he had given his life to a party. Ambitious? Of course he had been ambitious, and he still believed that only by love of fame are men inspired to great deeds. And cynical? Without a doubt—but what romantic passion lay hidden still beneath that cynicism! Moreover, he had many a time subordinated to fidelity both ambition and cynicism. Even to Gladstone he had written a noble letter proposing a reconciliation, a gesture full of peril, for it might well have resulted in bringing his only possible rival into the party itself. But Gladstone sent a chilling reply, discovering reasons of morality for ceasing to be a Conservative. Soon, no doubt, they would be seeing him Liberal Prime Minister. And yet it was Gladstone who passed for a saint, and Disraeli for a monster. For Dizzy believed himself to be very unpopular, much more so than he really was. Wounded in his childhood, he still remained sensitive. "Ah! dear Dorothy," he wrote to Lady Dorothy Nevill, "it is not my politics they dislike! It is myself!"

The old friends had vanished. Lady Blessington died in Paris in 1851. She had been obliged to flee from London with D'Orsay, having dissipated the last penny they had. But still, before dying, she had been able to send a line of congratulation to the new leader, this old protégé of hers who had become a great man. D'Orsay did not survive her long, and side by side they lay at rest at Chambourcy, near Mantes, beneath one single pyramid of granite. Smythe was dead, the cynical and charming Smythe, who sat for the portrait of Coningsby and invented "Young England," and had died almost destitute. To Dizzy he left some verses:

What is life? A little strife where victories are vain,
Where those who conquer do not win, nor those receive
the gain.

Often did Dizzy repeat the distich: "What is life? . . ."

The Duke had died at last, that Man of Iron who had seemed immortal. Troops lined the street all the way to St. Paul's. Two thousand voices sang Handel, and when the choristers turned the pages of their music it seemed like a passing gust of wind. Disraeli made a speech. He made the mistake of copying it from Thiers, which was detected and shocked people's feelings. The aged Lyndhurst was still alive, eighty-eight years old, and blind, but as keen-witted as ever. Unable any longer to read, he learned his favourite poets and his prayer-book by heart. His granddaughter, only eight years old, would make him recite his lessons. Bulwer had greatly changed. He had become a Conservative, yes, he also, but he was none too sure a comrade. He lived in dread of the crazy Rosina, who pursued him with an insensate hatred. This fury made Bulwer a beaten man. He had but one dream left—a title, the House of Lords, a fortune, and repose.

Caroline Norton was beautiful still; the coils of hair that wreathed her forehead had a lovely blue-black sheen, but she had grown somewhat thin. Lady Seymour, she who had been the Queen of Beauty, had a son of thirty now, and was obliged to ask her neighbour's arm to rise from table. A serious loss was that of the faithful Sa, who died in 1859. Gone was the family fireside, the port of refuge, the centre of fond affection. Now it was Mary Anne who had to be wife, mother and sister, and who played all these parts to perfection. She always understood her Dizzy and she never bored him. She considered him the greatest genius of all time, and treasured up the tiniest scraps of paper on which he jotted a note. Sometimes, and even in public, she took his hand and kissed it with humility. She still continued to drop reprehensible remarks. At Windsor she said to a Princess of the blood: "But perhaps, my dear, you don't know what it is to have an affectionate husband!" One day the cold and daring George Smythe made bold to ask Disraeli whether his wife's conversation did not annoy him just a little.

"Oh, no! I'm never put out by that."—"Well, Diz, you must be a man of most extraordinary qualities."— "Not at all. I only possess one quality in which most men are deficient: gratitude." And to some one else he said: "She believed in me when men despised me." Every year, on the anniversary of their wedding, he wrote for her a short piece of verse.

A strange personage emerged into their life. For a long time back Disraeli had been receiving letters from an unknown admirer, Mrs. Brydges Willyams of Torquay, who declared herself, like him, to be of Jewish blood and Christian faith. "Do any of you know an old madwoman at Torquay . . . ?" he used to ask his friends. But one day Mrs. Brydges Willyams asked him to act as her testamentary executor and to accept an important legacy. He set off with Mary Anne to see her, and found a woman of seventy-five, enormous, ridiculous, and very pleasant. Friendship sprang up between the couple and the old lady. Hughenden sent violets to Torquay, Torquay roses to Hughenden. The daily letter to Mrs. Brydges Willyams took the place of the letter to Sarah. "My delight this year were the roses which you sent Mary Anne. They lived in my room, and on my table, for more than a week. I think I never met with roses so beautiful in form, so lustrous in colour, and with a perfume so exquisite—without which latter charm the rarest and the fairest flowers have little spell for me. I really

think your roses must have come from Cashmere."
"Where did you get the lobster which arrived for my
luncheon this morning? From the caves of Amphitrite?
It was so fresh! It tasted of the sweetness—not the salt
—of the Ocean, and almost as creamy as your picturesque cheese!"

Other feminine friendships lent graciousness to a life
that was all too morose. There was Lady Londonderry,
there was Lady Dorothy Nevill. "Dearest Dorothy, your
strawberries were as fresh and as delightful as yourself, and came to me at a welcome moment, when I was
spiritless and feverish." He still remembered the ball
at which he had first set eyes on her. "Pray," he had
said, "who is that young lady who looks as if she had
come out of a picture of George the Second's time?"
What grace and wit the women had in those days! Now,
in 1860, a young woman seemed to have no ambition
beyond being taken for a *Dame aux Camélias*. She
would walk out with her skirts up to the knee, showing
a pretty leg, and address men as Tom or John or Dick,
and discuss with the young men the latest scandalous
gossip born at White's.

Sovereigns were passing. Good King Louis-Philippe,
who used to send Disraeli such beautifully cut slices of
ham at the Tuileries, he had seen sitting in tears on his
bed, in an exile's bedroom. But as against that, he had
been received in that same palace of the Tuileries by
an Emperor who, in days gone by, had taken him out
in a rowing-boat on the Thames. Mary Anne, seated at
the right hand of Napoleon III., recalled how he had
run them aground and how he was always undertaking

things which he did not understand how to do. The Emperor laughed, and the Empress said, "Just like him!" Dizzy's taste for the Arabian Nights was satisfied by the Paris of the Second Empire: "Round her swanlike neck the Empress wore a necklace of emeralds and diamonds such as might have been found in the cave of Aladdin, and yet, though colossal gems, for her they were not too vast." His love for France remained unfaltering: and frequently, through secret emissaries, the Emperor was given his counsel; it was excellent, but alas, too often ignored.

The little Queen, upon whom Dizzy formerly waited in the company of his old friend Lyndhurst, had become an austere and powerful Sovereign. She was beginning, ever so little, to grow used to Disraeli, and treated them, himself and his wife, with kindness. Prince Albert had died the year before.

One thing gave Disraeli the feeling that he had not altogether bungled his life, and that was the admiration of the young. There was something in the imaginative flight of his policy that attracted them. A youthful and enthusiastic secretary, Montagu Corry, had attached himself to him, and showed a touching devotion. Derby's son, Stanley, was his pupil—too prudent a disciple, yet grateful. "But you have no imagination, you Derbys," Disraeli told him. One day the Greeks, looking round for a king, offered the throne to Stanley. But Stanley was no Byron, and declined. Ah, if only the throne of Greece had been offered to Dizzy!

In 1853 he went to Oxford to receive a doctor's degree, *honoris causa*. He arrived there not without apprehension, for he knew that undergraduates are given to raillery and that on occasion distinguished noblemen had been greeted with howls. But never since the Duke of Wellington had such enthusiasm been witnessed. Pale and impassive, he walked up towards the Chancellor, while the amphitheatre rang with applause. *"Placetne vobis, Domini?"* asked the Chancellor. *"Maxime placet! Immense placet!"* shouted the undergraduates. A trace of animation showed on his rigid features; with his monocle he scanned the ladies' gallery, and, discovering Mary Anne, he threw up to her with his fingers an almost imperceptible kiss.

Sixty . . . sixty-one. . . . Slow and short, the years were passing. The sessions, with their man-made rhythm, rolled on to the diviner rhythm of the seasons. Disraeli was growing old. Doubtless he was never now to be Prime Minister. Once again, or twice, he would serve under Derby, then Stanley's time would come: the great families have their privileges. It was a pity; he would have loved power. But the spirit must not be allowed to dwell too much on what was denied one: what one actually had was none too bad, bearing in mind the humble beginnings. *"Forti nihil difficile*—to the brave, nothing is difficult," he used to say in those days. A child's motto. Everything is difficult. And for some time now he had adopted another: "Never explain, never complain." Useless words must be avoided.

Mrs. Brydges Willyams had died, leaving nearly £30,000 to her old friends, and the sum enabled a part of the debts to be settled. The rest was not so burden-some, thanks to Andrew Montagu, a man of modesty and generosity, a large Yorkshire landowner, who out of admiration for Disraeli bought up all the money-lenders' bills (nearly £57,000) and fixed a uniform interest of three per cent. The old lady asked to be buried in the graveyard of Hughenden, and there she lay, close to the little church. Soon perhaps Disraeli would be joining her there; he had never been very strong and his life had been strenuous. The park was becoming an enchanting spot. Mary Anne had done mar-vels with it. On the terrace, in the white Florentine vases, pink geraniums alternated with blue African lilies. The house had been restored to its condition in the time of the Stuarts. In the terraced gardens, where statues of goddesses guarded the ends of the avenues, one could picture the Cavaliers strolling with their mistresses. Ex-cept for a few visits from friends, life was solitary and monotonous. On Sundays, the even tenour was broken by church.

Seated in the manorial pew of Hughenden, Disraeli dreamed. During the service the Rev. Mr. Clubbe glanced apprehensively at the great man who some day perhaps would have the naming of the Bishops in his power. Psalm 102:

"Hear my prayer, O Lord, and let my cry come unto thee . . . for my days are consumed like smoke, and my bones are burned as an hearth. . . . I am like a pelican of the wilderness: I am like an owl of the desert. I watch, and am as a sparrow alone on the house top. Mine enemies reproach me all the day; and they that are mad against me are sworn against me. My days are like a shadow that declineth; and I am withered like grass. But thou, O Lord, shalt endure for ever; and the remembrance unto all generations."

He would come back on foot, alongside Mary Anne's little trap. And while she drove her pony along she would grow animated as she pointed out her handiwork. She talked—and how she could talk, Mary Anne! On the little lake, she had just introduced a pair of splendid swans, and Dizzy named them Hero and Leander— though why, she could not exactly understand. In transforming the garden she had disturbed the owls that lodged in the old yew-trees, but Dizzy had said that the owl was the bird of Minerva, and took religious care of them. In the evenings they would come sometimes and tap their curving beaks against the window-panes, their great round eyes gleaming in the dark.

XI

The Top of the Greasy Pole

In 1859 *Punch* published a cartoon representing a sleeping lion, which Bright, Disraeli and Russell were trying to rouse by prodding it with red-hot iron bars. On each bar was the word "Reform." The image was exact. Ever since the partial reform of 1832, which had enfranchised so limited a class of electors, every party strove in turn to interest the British Lion in a new measure. But the well-fed Lion continued to snore, and the parliamentary Limbo was peopled with the ghosts of still-born reforms. Now a Tory Government would propose giving the vote to every elector paying more than £10 in rent, and the Whig Opposition would cry shame, and that £8 was the sane limit for the Rights of Man. Now a

Whig Government would propose £7, and Derby, through the mouth of his prophet Disraeli, declared that this was giving over England to all the dangers of demagogy. The real problem was to know which of the two great parties would be favoured by the new class of elector. But Gladstone held forth with indignation about the men who thus consulted electoral statistics and measured the forces of the people as those of invaders. "The persons to whom these remarks are applied are our fellow-subjects, our fellow-Christians, our own flesh and blood." Whereupon a Tory asked him why our flesh and blood stopped short at a £7 rental. A few even among the Whigs felt that this sentimental verbiage was not to their taste; they withdrew from the party, and Bright dubbed them the Adullamites, for when King David "escaped to the cave Adullam . . . every one that was in distress and that was in debt and every one that was discontented, gathered themselves unto him." And then Disraeli, aided by the Adullamites, overturned the woebegone Lord John and the fervent Gladstone; and then Lord Derby, having kissed the Queen's hand, assumed ministerial power along with Disraeli. Once again they were in power with a minority behind them and by the choice of a chance coalition, and this time again it looked as if their Ministry would be short-lived.

Suddenly, at the very outset of Derby's tenure of office, the British Lion quite inexplicably woke up in a bad temper, and burst the bars of his cage, as represented by the railings of Hyde Park. For three days on end crowds gathered loudly demanding Reform, and troops had to be brought up. The Home Secretary burst into tears. Watching the demonstrators from her window, Mary Anne saw that they had all the appearance of amusing themselves, and conceived a sympathy for them. The Queen summoned Derby to Balmoral. She told him that this question had now been agitating the country for thirty years, and that one day it must be ended by being settled, and that this had best be done by a Conservative Ministry. All of a sudden Disraeli saw a magnificent stroke to play.

In his heart of hearts he had always been friendly to the idea of a suffrage extended to the more responsible section of the working-classes. That union of the aristocracy and the people which he had preached in *Sybil* would thus find its expression, and the boldest step would perhaps be also the wisest. "Why not grant a domestic vote," he said to Derby, "one household, one vote, whatever the rental, with appropriate restrictions of time and residence?" It was at least a feasible principle, and a conservative principle; it could be argued that householders are always interested in the prosperity of the country, while these arbitrary lines drawn at £10 or £5 or £6, were absurd and impossible to justify. Moreover, the party which enfranchised these new electors would have some chance of rallying them to itself. Best of all, the Liberals would lose the most popular plank in their platform. Really, the risk was worth trying. But would the party accept it?

The party showed surprising intelligence. The Tories

had no reason for clinging to this electorate of 1832, which, called into being by their enemies, had kept them out of power now for thirty years. The idea of putting the ace of trumps on the Whigs' best card delighted them, and in spite of a few dissentients, the bulk of the rank-and-file accepted the plan of campaign. Immediately the dawn of a great victory was felt to be at hand. Many Liberals, taken aback, felt that if the Conservatives were thus carrying out a Liberal policy, they could not refuse to vote with that party. Gladstone saw himself routed. The only wise attitude for him would have been one of triumph, but he was speechless at seeing the Spirit of Evil thus waving aloft the banner of the angels. He fell with inconceivable violence on the machiavellian foe, who, for his part, was careful by his air of unconcern to accentuate the picture of wild rage which Gladstone had just displayed. "The right hon. gentleman," said Disraeli, "gets up and addresses me in a tone which, I must say, is very unusual in this House. Not that I at all care for the heat he displays, although really his manner is sometimes so very excited and so alarming, that one might almost feel thankful that gentlemen in this House, who sit on opposite sides of this table, are divided by a good broad piece of furniture."

The division gave the Ministry a majority of twenty-one. In a hostile Parliament, Disraeli had put through a bill which Whig Governments had vainly sought to pass for thirty years. It was a great parliamentary triumph. Gladstone felt as much, and noted in his diary: "A smash perhaps without example." He was deeply mortified. "I met Gladstone at breakfast," wrote one observer. "He seems quite awed by the diabolic cleverness of Dizzy." Derby was delighted; he recognized that the measure was "a leap in the dark," but he added, rubbing his hands, "Don't you see that we have *dished* the Whigs?"

After the division, the Conservative cheers on Dizzy's behalf were deafening and prolonged. Every one wanted to shake him by the hand. After leaving Westminster, many of them met at the Carlton and improvised a supper-party. Disraeli dropped in at the Club for a moment on his way home, and was once more welcomed with endless cheers. His friends beseeched him to sup with them, but he knew that Mary Anne was awaiting him, that she also had prepared a supper, and he did not wish to disappoint her. On the next day she said proudly to one of her friends, "Dizzy came straight home; I had got a pie ready and a bottle of champagne. He ate half of the pie and drank all the champagne, and he said to me, 'My dear, you are more of a mistress to me than a wife.' " She was then seventy-seven.

This success greatly altered Disraeli's position in Parliament. There was nothing in the defeat of Gladstone so pathetic as in that of Peel. It was slightly amusing, and also a little startling. Two party leaders, both of them among the greatest known to the House of Commons, had tried at twenty years' interval to engage this Dizzy in combat, and both had gone down. Here was the man who had so often talked of the Asian mysteries

—was he not himself a man of mystery? What was his goal? What were his designs? When he listened with that impassive mask of his to Gladstone's torrent of invective, what were his thoughts? A new character was taking shape in the popular imagination, that of the Sphinx. *Punch* published a drawing which showed an immense stone Sphinx being dragged towards the temple of Reform by a horde of naked slaves, Gladstone among them, flogged onwards by Lord Derby. It was entitled "D'ISRAEL-I IN TRIUMPH."

None who then met him could escape this complex impression of power and wizardry. The face had veritably acquired the immobility of stone, and there was a profound difference between him and the mortal men who surrounded him. "I would as soon have thoughts of sitting down at table with Hamlet, or Lear, or the Wandering Jew," wrote a contemporary after meeting him. And he added: "They say, and say truly enough, 'What an actor the man is!'—and yet the ultimate impression is of absolute sincerity and unreserve. Grant Duff will have it that he is an alien. What's England to him, or he to England? That is just where they are wrong. Whig or Radical or Tory don't matter much, perhaps; but this mightier Venice—this Imperial Republic on which the sun never sets—that vision fascinates him, or I am much mistaken. England is the Israel of his imagination, and he will be the Imperial Minister before he dies—if he gets the chance."

And this chance, contrary to all expectations, was close at hand. Derby's attacks of gout became so frequent, and so rarely was he able to fulfil the duties of his post, that he felt it his duty in the end to arrange for his retirement. Disraeli beseeched him to stay, pledging himself to do all the real work while Derby kept the titular leadership. But Derby replied that he was about to write to the Queen informing her of his resignation, and expressing his hope that Her Majesty would turn to Disraeli as his successor, and assuring her that he himself, from his retirement, would combine to support Disraeli with all the authority of his name. "And I cannot make this communication without gratefully acknowledging your cordial and loyal co-operation with me, in good times and bad, throughout this long period." Disraeli's merit in begging his chief to remain was all the greater because he then already knew that, in the event of Derby's retiral, it would be himself whom the Queen would summon. She had told him so herself. On the day of the chief's formal resignation, a messenger came to bid Disraeli have audience with Her Majesty at Osborne. The magician was not without belief in his sorcery, for it did not escape his notice that this messenger, General Grey, was none other than that Colonel Grey who had been his stammering and fortunate rival at Wycombe in his first battles at the hustings. The first note of congratulation came from Derby: "You have fairly and honourably won your way to the highest round of the political ladder, and long may you continue to retain your position!"

Next day Disraeli was received by the Queen at Osborne. She seemed radiant, and held out her hand, saying, "You must kiss hands." He fell on one knee, and very whole-heartedly he kissed that small plump hand.

He was profoundly happy. Outside a dazzling sun was shining. After all, life was worth living. One of the first members of Parliament whom he met was James Clay, who, as a young man, had discomfited him at Malta by his skill at billiards. "Well, Disraeli," said Clay, "when you and I travelled together, who would ever have thought that you would be Prime Minister?"

"Who, indeed! But, as we used to say in the East: God is great!—and now he is greater than ever."

On the whole his welcome was favourable. "A triumph of industry, courage and patience," even his adversaries admitted. When he entered the House of Commons for the first time as Prime Minister, the lobbies were thronged with men who had gathered to acclaim him. John Stuart Mill was speaking and had to break off for several minutes.

A month later Mary Anne, as the wife of the Prime Minister, gave a great reception at the Foreign Office, where Lord Stanley had been good enough to lend her the necessary rooms for the evening. The weather was wretched; London was swept by a hurricane of wind and rain. Nevertheless, everybody was there, the whole Conservative party, some Liberals too, the Gladstones among them, and many friends. Dizzy, in all his glory, escorted the Princess of Wales round the rooms; on the Prince's arm was Mrs. Dizzy, looking very old and very ill. For a month now she had had a cancer, and knew it, but she refused to tell her husband. This mixture of the glorious and the decrepit added a touch of melancholy to the evening of triumph. A wave of sympathy had enveloped this old couple after all their struggles. They had been accepted. In every drawing-room in London the wife of the Prime Minister was simply known as "Mary Anne." Disraeli himself bore in mind the astounding acrobatics which had brought about his elevation. "Yes," he replied to those who offered their congratulations, "I have climbed to the top of the greasy pole." His friend Sir Philip Rose said to him, "If only your sister had been alive now to witness your triumph, what happiness it would have given her!"

"Poor Sa," he said, "poor Sa! Yes, we have lost our audience."

PART III

Listen! the wind is rising,
    and the air is wild with leaves;
we have had our summer evenings;
    now for October eves!

The great beech trees lean forward,
    and strip like a diver. We
had better turn to the fire
    and shut our minds to the sea,

where the ships of youth are running
    close-hauled on the edge of the wind,
with all adventure before them,
    and only the old behind.

HUMBERT WOLFE.

I

The Queen

A new Chancellor of the Exchequer was chosen. The Prime Minister sent word of this to the Queen: "Mr. Disraeli ought to observe to Her Majesty that Mr. Ward Hunt's appearance is rather remarkable, but anything but displeasing. He is more than six feet four inches in stature, but doesn't look so tall from his proportionate breadth; like St. Peter's at Rome no one is at first aware of his dimensions. But he has the sagacity of the elephant as well as its form." For writing to a Sovereign, the tone was startlingly light, but she was delighted.

Disraeli had exasperated more men than one in the course of his life, but women he had found indulgent. His horror of abstract reasoning, his old-world courtesy,

the imperceptible undercurrent of cynicism, his con-
sciously flowery phrases—he had everything in him to
attract women. And they inspired him with a sentiment
which was not sensual love, but rather a tenderness both
humble and superior, a gentle and hidden fraternity of
spirit. He liked their obstinacy, their ignorance, their
ingenuousness. It was a woman, Mrs. Austen, who had
found a publisher for *Vivian Grey*; it was women, the
Sheridan sisters, then Lady Cork and Lady Londonderry, who had launched him into society; it was a
woman, Mary Anne, who had given him a seat in Parliament. At every turning of memory's pathway he
found one of those ministering faces leaning over his
own self-disgust and vexation of soul. He looked with
an expert eye on this august widow, with her white tulle
cap, waiting for him at the top of the state staircase,
and he felt delightfully at his ease.

Since the death of her dearly loved consort, the Queen
had lived in solitary grandeur. She had vowed to respect
every wish and every custom of Albert's. Swathed in
crape, she wandered from castle to castle, from Windsor
to Osborne, from Osborne to Balmoral. The public complained of her seclusion, and she suffered from the
knowledge of her unpopularity. No one understood her,
and no one had understood Albert either, and he had
suffered from that, he too. . . . No one except Mr. Disraeli. It was surprising, for she often remembered the
mistrust he had inspired in them, both in her husband
and herself, at the time of poor Sir Robert Peel's downfall. In those days Albert had declared that this Disraeli
had not the slightest trace of a gentleman in his make-up.

And yet, the Prince, towards the close of his life, had sometimes taken a hesitating pleasure in conversing with the leader of the Opposition. He had found that Disraeli was cultivated, and better read in English history than any other statesman, and he had realized that towards the Throne his attitude was irreproachable.

But particularly on Prince Albert's death had Mr. Disraeli revealed himself. Nobody had written the Queen such a beautiful letter; nobody had spoken more finely of the Prince in the House of Commons. The Queen had come to believe that he was the only person who had really appreciated the Prince. And he had been rewarded by the gift of Prince Albert's speeches, and a letter: "The Queen cannot resist from expressing, personally, to Mr. Disraeli her deep gratification at the tribute he paid to her adored, beloved, and great husband. The perusal of it made her shed many tears, but it was very soothing to her broken heart to see such true appreciation of that spotless and unequalled character."

So the shade of Albert approved. But there were other bonds than one of memory between the Queen and her Minister; their natures, superficially so different, had subtle affinities of their own. Both would think with simple-hearted pride of the vast Eastern Empire governed, from a hyperborean island, by this stout, self-willed little woman and her old, stooping Minister. People might think some of the Queen's foibles ridiculous, and many of Disraeli's artificial, but in both of them dwelt courage and greatness. Through him she could savour more fully the pleasure of being a Sovereign. He set her with such manifest happiness at the

head of the splendid procession of life. When he talked
to her of her realms, she could feel herself all-powerful.
With this Minister who described Cabinet meetings to
her as if they were scenes of fiction, for whom politics
was a tale of personal adventures, her public business
recovered the charm it had held in Albert's day. Disraeli knew that he was amusing to the Queen, and found
pleasure in addressing ironic and perfectly polished
epistles to Her Majesty. Did she always grasp them?
She grasped much more fully than her familiars supposed. She relished the diversion of a successful sleight-
of-hand, and then, with a sharp sense for reality, she
firmly led the magician back towards the desired course
of action.

If the Prime Minister, in order to pacify in some
small degree a disturbed Ireland, was anxious for the
Prince of Wales to pay a visit to that country, he wrote:
"Mr. Disraeli would venture to observe that during two
centuries the Sovereign has only passed twenty-one days
in Ireland. His Royal Highness might hunt. This would
in a certain degree combine the fulfilment of public
duty with pastime, a combination which befits a princely
life." The Queen approved: "but with this understanding, that the expenses of these royal visits should be
borne by the Government, who press them constantly
and most annoyingly on the Queen, and which are solely
for political purposes. For health and relaxation, no one
would go to Ireland."

Frequently the Minister defended himself. When he
was asked later what was the secret of his success with
the Queen, he replied, "I never refuse; I never contra-

dict; I sometimes forget." A sacrifice to the pleasure of epigram. Contradict, he often did. When the Archbishop of Canterbury died and the Queen insisted on making Tait, the Bishop of London, his successor, Mr. Disraeli raised grave objections:

"This is to be observed of the Bishop of London, that though apparently of a spirit somewhat austere, there is in his idiosyncrasy a strange fund of enthusiasm, a quality which ought never to be possessed by an Archbishop of Canterbury or a Prime Minister. The Bishop of London sympathises with everything that is earnest; but what is earnest is not always true; on the contrary, error is often more earnest than truth. . . .

"Mr. Disraeli wishes not to conceal the infinite pain with which he thus seems to differ on so great a question, from a sovereign to whom he is not only bound by every tie of personal devotion, but whose large and peculiarly experienced intelligence he acknowledges and appreciates, and whose judgment on many occasions would have more influence with him than that of all his colleagues.

"His idea of the perfect relation between the sovereign and her minister is that there should be on her part perfect confidence; on his, perfect devotion. In the blended influence of two such sentiments, so ennobling and so refined, he sees the best security for Your Majesty's happiness and the welfare of the realm."

The Queen insisted. For her own part, she knew quite well that Bishop Tait was innocent of all enthusiasm.

Could she have said as much of the Prime Minister of England?

One day Mary Anne received a box of fresh primroses from Windsor, with a letter from the Princess Christian. "Mamma desires me to send you the accompanying flowers in her name for Mr. Disraeli. She heard him say one day that he was so fond of May and of all those lovely spring flowers that she has ventured to send him these, as they will make his rooms look so bright. The flowers come from Windsor." Mary Anne replied with a sentence which Dizzy had obviously edited for her: "I performed the most pleasing office which I ever, had to fulfil in obeying Her Majesty's commands. Mr. Disraeli is passionately fond of flowers, and their lustre and perfume were enhanced by the condescending hand which had showered upon him all the treasures of spring."

The Minister sent all his novels to the Queen. The Queen presented the Minister with her *Journal of Our Life in the Highlands*. "We authors, Ma'am . . ." the Premier would often say thereafter, and a smile showed on the masterful little mouth. Every week the primroses from Windsor, the violets from Osborne, would arrive at Grosvenor Gate in their moss-lined boxes. The official correspondence became a curious blend of pastoral poetry and realist politics.

There was at least one man in England in whose eyes this elevation of Disraeli, and this intimacy of the Crown with a Hebrew mountebank, was an intolerable scandal:

that was Mr. Gladstone. In March 1868, *Punch* published a drawing which showed a theatre dressing-room.
In front of the mirror, Mr. Bendizzy, a gaunt comedian
in the dress of Hamlet, was complacently repeating,
"To be or not to be, that is the question. . . . Ahem!"
In the background stood Mr. Gladstone, the tragedian
in ordinary clothes, gazing with envy and scorn, and
muttering: " 'Leading business' forsooth! His line is
'general utility'! Is the manager mad? But no matter-rr
—a time will come——"

The feeling was more complex than a mere jealousy
between star performers. Gladstone would doubtless
have stomached, with resignation and modesty, the triumph of, say, Stanley. But passions, like gods, take
human form in order to act, and ambition, to tempt
him, had assumed the shape of a virtuous hatred. For
twenty years, whilst he rose higher and ever higher, in
a long murmur of admiration, amidst his respectful
peers, he saw climbing over against him a hostile and
bizarre figure; in that lofty and almost unpeopled zone
into which his talents had brought him, this was almost
the only figure he met with, and despite himself he took
it as the measure of his own success, and deemed himself outstripped by all if he were outstripped by Disraeli. "One of the most grievous and constant puzzles
of King David was the prosperity of the wicked and the
scornful. . . . That the writer of frivolous stories about
Vivian Grey and Coningsby should grasp the sceptre before the writer of beautiful and serious things about
Ecce Homo—the man who is epigrammatic, flashy,
arrogant, before the man who never perpetrated an

epigram in his life, is always fervid, and would as soon die as admit that he had a shade more brain than his footman—the Radical corrupted into a Tory before the Tory purified and elevated into a Radical—is not this enough to make an honest man rend his mantle and shave his head and sit down among the ashes inconsolable."

But Gladstone was never the man to sit down among ashes. He may indeed have sung, "How long wilt thou forget me, O Lord? How long shall mine enemy be exalted over me?" But like King David, he added, "Lighten mine eyes, lest I sleep the sleep of death, lest mine enemy say, 'I have prevailed against him.'"

So ill did he conceal his spite that, contrary to parliamentary usage, he picked a quarrel in the very first week of Disraeli's Government. In carrying out the electoral Reform, Disraeli had certainly stolen a weapon from the Liberal party's armoury, but happily there remained much else to be reformed. The House of Lords could be reformed, and the Church, and the Crown, and the Army, and Education. Gladstone was ready to reform the solar system rather than leave Disraeli peacefully enjoying an unjust fortune. But with a very exact sense of what was actual in politics, he selected the Church, and in particular the Irish Church. Certainly, it was contrary to religious liberty that the Catholics of Ireland should have to maintain a State Protestant Church. Ireland was then in the depths of trouble. Crimes and outrages were being committed by the hundred, and the criminals could not possibly be punished because the whole country was their accomplice. Glad-

stone maintained that by the separation of Church and
State in Ireland, by "disestablishing" the Protestant
Irish Church, one cause of discontent, and perhaps the
gravest, would be removed, and then Disraeli realized
that his rival had determined to fight the elections on
a religious issue.

Nowhere was the Disraelian doctrine more firm. Was
he himself a believer? He could not, like Gladstone,
have plunged with passion into theological controversies.
He thought that men's minds are periodically submerged
by floods of ecclesiastical thought, and that these storms
are of small import, because the subsiding waters never
fail to reveal once again the same Ark, motionless on
the mountaintop. That Ark was the semitic and Christian
revelation, the Bible made complete by the Gospels; it
is also the sense of mystery. Disraeli believed whole-
heartedly that the world is divine; the thought of existence (and his own especially) as of a miracle; the
biological sciences, at that time greatly emblazoned by
Darwin and Huxley, sought to transform the miracle
into an equation, but that only annoyed him. He was
ignorant of them, and his scorn matched his ignorance.
A few years earlier, in a famous speech at Oxford, he
had defended the Church against the innovators: "Why,
my Lord, man is a being born to believe. And if no
Church comes forward with its title-deeds of truth, sustained by the tradition of sacred ages and by the conviction of countless generations, to guide him, he will
find altars and idols in his own heart and his own
imagination. . . . The discoveries of science, we are
told, are not consistent with the teachings of the Church.

. . . What is the question now placed before society with a glib assurance the most astounding? The question is this—Is man an ape or an angel? My Lord, I am on the side of the angels."

A burst of laughter echoed round the amphitheatre. Really? Was Mr. Disraeli on the side of the angels? All England held its sides with merriment. *Punch* did not lose such a fine opportunity: a simian Dizzy, in white robes, with large wings. But never had Disraeli been more deeply in earnest. He believed that man is more than a machine, and that over and above the matter submitted to physical and chemical reactions, there exists a different essence, which can be called the soul, the divine, the genius, an essence altogether of the angels. As for the literal truth of one religion or another, he probably gave that hardly a thought. But on this subject, nevertheless, he had ideas to which he clung.

The first was the necessity of fixity of dogma, for the peace of minds no less than of the State. In ethical or aesthetic pseudo-religions he put no trust. "Every religion of the Beautiful ends in orgy." To Dean Stanley, a partisan of the Broad Church, that is to say, of the wide interpretation of the sacred texts, he had one day remarked ironically, "No dogma, no dean, Mr. Dean." From boyhood he had admired the changelessness of the Roman Church. In default of Rome, the Church of England seemed to him the sole safeguard of the country's spiritual security.

His second idea was the necessity of a bond between Government and Religion. In this regard the situation in England appeared to him as peculiarly fortunate. The Sovereign was the Head of the Church, and its dignitaries were appointed by the Sovereign in person. Thus the Church, far from being a State within the State, *imperium in imperio*, actually fortified the State's authority. It was a bond which must not be broken; the disestablishment of the Irish Church might be a just measure, but Disraeli considered it to be the first step in a dangerous direction, and a reversal of the Constitution. He made ready, therefore, to engage in the electoral battle on the ground chosen by Gladstone. There, against a paradoxical assailant, he would stand forth as the paradoxical champion of the Church.

II

Mourning

Although Mr. Gladstone had completed his sixtieth year, the extraordinary vigour of his temperament still called for giant toils. Whilst awaiting the election results in the country, at Hawarden, he would sometimes cover thirty-three miles on foot in his day, and come home in the evening thirsting for further activity. More frequently he would fell trees. This was his favourite pastime; he flung himself upon these venerable trunks as zealously as if they were old-established wrongs. On December 1st, 1868, he was in his shirt-sleeves, just raising his woodman's axe, when a message reached him by telegram. The Queen announced the visit of General Grey. "Very significant," said Mr. Gladstone to his companion, and went on with his task. After a few minutes the blows of the axe ceased, and he remarked with the deepest gravity, "My mission is to pacify Ireland." And in his journal he noted: "The almighty seems to sustain and spare me for some purpose of his own, deeply unworthy as I know myself to be. Glory be to his name!"

Thus upheld by divine forces, and supported in the Commons by a stout majority, conscious of an athlete's body and a temper of steel, he felt himself invincible. Under the blows of his legislative axe, some of the oldest oaks of the forest would no doubt fall, but then the light and air could pass more freely to reach even the smallest plants of the clearings. "Hawarden. Jan. 13th. Wrote out a paper on the plan of the measure respecting the Irish Church, intended perhaps for the Queen. Worked on Homer. We felled a lime. . . . Jan. 15th. We felled an ash. Three hours' conversation with the viceroy and the archdeacon on the Irish church. Worked on Homer at night." Sometimes he would note that day had been as restless as the sea. And meantime Disraeli, preyed upon by rheumatism and asthma, was sunning himself on the terrace at Hughenden, watching the birds and the flowers, and pondering a new novel.

When he had learned the full result of the elections and his defeat, his first thought had been to withdraw from political life. Custom entitled him to request a peerage and to find an honourable retirement in the House of Lords. But on reflection he did not like the idea of abandoning a defeated party and a frontline post in the Commons. When the Queen showed herself anxious to recognize his services, he asked that Mary Anne should be made a peeress, he himself remaining plain Mr. Disraeli. The Queen graciously approved this plan, and he chose for his wife the title of Beaconsfield, from the small Buckinghamshire town. Disraeli knew that the great Burke, had he lived longer, would have liked to become Lord Beaconsfield. He himself had created a lord of that name in *Vivian Grey*. He always found pleasure in transposing his novels into real life. So Mary Anne became Viscountess Beaconsfield, and Dizzy remained Dizzy.

Those of his friends who had anticipated flashing attacks against the Liberal Government were mistaken. They had supposed that his rival's accession to power would incite their leader to surpass himself, but never had he been calmer, more indolent, more dull. His speech on the Irish Church Bill was light and superficial, like "the skirt of Columbine, muslin and spangles." Once more the Conservative party asked in amazement whither the man of mystery was driving. Did it suffice him to taste supreme power once and once only? Was he about to desert his troops on the field of battle? But behind that melancholy and impenetrable mask, an alert spirit was watching with an amused eye. What! Fight against that brand-new majority? Against that superb war-horse of a Gladstone fuming at the nostrils! Madness! He knew what they were, these majorities. To a young colt the trainer allows plenty of rope. He will be broken in all the quicker. Had Gladstone forces? Let him use them. Let him try to pacify Ireland by legislation. Ireland herself used sharper methods. Let his axe strike at finance, at education, at the army. The time would come of resistance, of yielding, of blunted swords. And that would be the moment for overturning the god already tottering on his pedestal; but meanwhile, patience, patience! Let our calmness contrast, agreeably, with all this turmoil.

So great was the dramatic effect of the opposition of these characters, that the two heroes themselves seemed to delight in it. On some days the parliamentary comedy was pushed to the bounds of farce. One day Gladstone stood in his place on the Treasury Bench, imposing and thunderous, hurtling upon his rival epithets that became ever more violent. As each of these fell, Disraeli slowly lowered his head a little further. He seemed to be literally crushed by the terrific hammering of Gladstone's voice. At last he ended, with such a smashing blow on the broad table between them that pens and papers flew in disorder. He sat down. For a moment the House, silent and motionless, wondered whether Dizzy would be able to raise his head. Then the prostrated figure was seen slowly coming back to life, first the head, then the shoulders. At last Disraeli rose, and said, in a voice so low as could barely be heard: "The right hon. gentleman has spoken with much passion, much eloquence, and much—*ahem*—violence. (*A pause —a long pause.*) But the damage can be repaired." And painfully he bent over, gathered up one by one the objects scattered by the fiery Gladstone, methodically ranged them in their accustomed places on the sacred table, looked complacently at this restored orderliness, and then, in his finest voice, replied. The fragment of symbolic drama enjoyed the success it deserved.

But such scenes were rare. It was plain that for the moment Disraeli had no mind to overturn Gladstone. His epigrams remained courteous. Once when Gladstone stopped short in the middle of a sentence, he obligingly intervened: "Your last word?—Revolution." At a dinner-party he was asked by one of his rival's daughters for light on a certain foreign Minister, and answered: "He is the most dangerous man in Europe, myself excepted—as your father would say; your father excepted—*I* should prefer to say."

So free was his mind that once more he had turned from activity to literary creation and was working on a novel, *Lothair*.

Lothair was a young Englishman of noble birth, heir to a Disraelian, that is, unbounded, fortune, whose soul is disputed by three conflicting forces, personified in three different women—the Church of Rome, the International Revolution, and the British Tradition. The champion of the Anglican Church, Lady Corisande, was of course victorious. The theme was dangerous, the execution remarkable. The Roman prelates, revolutionaries, English politicians, were types drawn with astonishing exactness. The success of the book was immense. English booksellers had never had a novel by a former Premier to sell. *Lothair* was the sole topic of every drawing-room.

Horses, ships, children and perfumes received the names of Lothair and Corisande. The Lothair mania seized America. Only Parliament was hostile. The Conservatives felt very deeply the disgrace of having as their leader a novelist, and a witty one.

Meanwhile, Mary Anne was very ill. From 1866 she had had a cancer of the stomach; she knew it, but forced herself to hide the truth from Dizzy, whilst he, thinking that she was ignorant of it, affected to speak lightly of the disease. Courageously she continued to live a social life. In 1872 the young *chargé d'affaires* of the French Embassy saw, in one drawing-room, a strange being trapped out like a kind of pagoda, whom he took for some aged rajah. It was Mary Anne, and behind her was Dizzy, painted and sepulchral, his last ringlet dyed jet-black and fixed on his bald brow. On her heart Mary Anne wore, as one wears the badge of an order, a huge medallion which framed a portrait of her husband. She was eighty-one, and he, sixty-eight: a ridiculous and touching pair.

It became hard for them to take care of each other. Sometimes they were both laid up, and they corresponded from one room to the other. Dizzy to Mrs. Dizzy: "Being on my back, pardon the pencil. You have sent me the most amusing and charming letter I ever had. It beats Horace Walpole and Mme. de Sévigné. Grosvenor Gate has become a hospital, but a hospital with you is worth a palace with anybody else. Your own D."

She would say to her friends, "Thanks to his kindness, my life has been simply one long scene of happiness." "We have been married for thirty years," he countered, "and I have never been bored with her." Mary Anne could hardly take nourishment any longer. Visiting friends one evening, she was seized with a bout of pain so severe that she could not hide it, and thenceforward she gave up going out. Her husband was forced then to leave her sometimes, but he never did so, for however short a period, without sending her countless letters. Dizzy to Mrs. Dizzy: "I have nothing to tell you except that I love you, which, I fear, you will think rather dull."—Mrs. Dizzy to Dizzy: "My own dearest, I miss you sadly. I certainly feel better this evening. . . . Your own devoted Beaconsfield."

She did not think she could stand a journey, so they spent the summer together in London. They drove in the carriage, visiting unknown districts and trying to forget that the park stretching before their windows was called Hyde. Then, as she grew gradually worse, she tried to think that Hughenden would do her good. But she was past curing; her stomach refused all nourishment. Although she died literally of starvation, she still received a few friends with a very good grace, taking the air with them in her little trap drawn by the old pony. As soon as she had left the room, Disraeli would talk of his wife's sufferings, and for the first time his visitors would see that face, which they had always known as impassive, overwhelmed by emotion. When it was obvious that she was beyond recovery, he wired for Montagu Corry to come, feeling himself unable to bear the catastrophe alone. She died on September 15th, 1872, and amongst her papers was found the following letter:—

"*June* 6, 1856.

"MY OWN DEAR HUSBAND,—If I should depart this life before you, leave orders that we may be buried in the same grave at whatever distance you may die from England. And now God bless you, my kindest, dearest! You have been a perfect husband to me. Be put by my side in the same grave. And now, farewell, my dear Dizzy. Do not live alone, dearest. Some one I earnestly hope you may find as attached to you as your own devoted

"MARY ANNE."

The most indifferent souls, and perhaps even the hardest, can feel the human values of a genuine grief. The keenest sympathy was universally felt. Gladstone forgot all political rancour and wrote a deeply moved letter: "You and I were, as I believe, married in the same year. It has been permitted to both of us to enjoy a priceless boon through a third of a century. Spared myself the blow which has fallen on you, I can form some conception of what it must have been and be. . . ." And he assured him that in this hour of trial he felt deeply for him and with him. He was sincere, and for an instant, no doubt, each of the two rivals appeared to the other in his true light, no longer distorted by passion. Thus it happens that from time to time a madman may have a few minutes of relief, during which his phantoms flee away. But then the shapes are twisted again, the faces around him begin to grimace, and once more his attendant turns into a monster.

While she lived, his Mary Anne had been justly proud of the fact that she spared Dizzy all those vexatious cares which exhaust a man's mind. Since his marriage, house and servants had for him become perfect machines to which he need not give a moment's thought. "There was no care that she could not mitigate, and no difficulty which she could not face. She was the most cheerful and courageous woman I ever knew." But once gone, she could no longer protect her great man. Her fortune had only been a life-interest, even the house passed to heirs, and Dizzy had to move out and take refuge in an hotel. To leave Grosvenor Gate, where he had spent thirty-three happy years, was like a second parting from Mary Anne. Here was the house where she had waited for him, night after night, on his return from the Commons, the house always lit up, which he could see shining from afar in the fog when he came home after a trying sitting. Here was the domestic hearth, the cosy spot where body and soul are relaxed, where criticism becomes praise, and blame, a caress. Never again, no doubt, would he know the kindliness of a true shelter. The loneliness of the hotel, the worst loneliness of all, alive only with stupid furniture, dreary meals and unknown neighbours—such would be his London life henceforth. When he called to his coachman "Home," he remembered suddenly that he no longer had a home, and his eyes filled with tears. Without his secretary, Montagu

Corry, who watched over him like a son, without friends like the Manners or the Rothschilds to welcome him, he would have been a wreck. But no friendship, however fine, can replace the fondness of a woman. In the silence of his hotel room, he watched memory fleeing from a certain gay voice.

His political friends had fears that his bereavement might become the pretext for a complete retiral. The opposite happened. Finding nothing within himself but mournful thoughts, he sought activity, and to escape from thinking, resumed the battle.

The moment happened to be favourable. The tactics of waiting had produced good results. He had given Gladstone plenty of rope; Gladstone had rushed in here, there and everywhere; it only remained to profit by the errors which are inevitably born of all activity. "My mission is to pacify Ireland," said the woodman of Hawarden, leaning on his mighty axe. To fulfil that mission he had abolished the Protestant Irish Church as a State institution, and had passed a whole series of laws designed to protect the farmers against the great landowners. But Ireland was less pacified than ever. Officials were clubbed by masked men, policemen stabbed, houses blown up. For a long time the Pacifier had put up with these outrages, and then in despair he had had to have recourse to the military. "I remember," remarked Disraeli sarcastically, "I remember one of Her Majesty's Ministers saying, I think last year: 'Any one can govern Ireland with troops and artillery.' So it seems; even that right hon. gentleman."

In foreign politics, Gladstone had accepted the principle of arbitration in all questions where England found herself involved. But it seemed that arbitration always went against him. Popular pride was irritated. At one of the theatres Gladstone was represented receiving an embassy from China come to demand Scotland from him. The Prime Minister reflected, then discovered that these replies were possible: to yield Scotland at once, to wait a little and end by yielding it, or to name an arbitrator. The public found the likeness a close one. The Queen felt with the public. She did not grow used to Gladstone. The great trees falling all around alarmed her. She had liked the forest. Her simple and direct brain could not apprehend the byways of this complicated mind. In vain did she read, and read again, his projected bills, and when he accompanied them with explanatory letters, she found the explanations more bewildering than the proposals. After the supple Mr. Disraeli, who would repeat that, first and foremost, the desires of Her Majesty must be realized, she could not endure this hard Scotsman who, with infinite respectfulness, refused her all that she asked. She clung to the idea of England's prestige, and she considered that Gladstone was destroying that. She was a Protestant Queen and Gladstone was despoiling the Irish Protestants. She had too strong a reverence for the Constitution to stand up against the votes of Parliament, but she longed with all her heart for the fall of this Ministry.

From 1873 it was clear that this event could not be

far distant. All the by-elections went in favour of the Conservatives. Disraeli made minute preparations for the campaign. Long ahead each constituency had an official Conservative candidate adopted. A central Conservative office was set up in Whitehall, where a permanent director with a general staff kept up to date the lists of constituencies already provided for, and those for which arrangements must be made. In every town a Conservative association was to be kept in existence, in which all classes of society would be represented, and in particular the support of workingmen was to be sought. Disraeli himself saw to it that this work was carried out everywhere. But, tempering the impatience of his followers, he was anxious to avoid taking office until Gladstone's energy had been exhausted by fresh reverses. Experience had shown him only too well the fragility of Cabinets lacking the support of a strong majority. In a speech at Manchester he described the last moments of the Ministry's death-agony: "As time advanced it was not difficult to perceive that extravagance was being substituted for energy by the Government. The unnatural stimulus was subsiding. Their paroxysms ended in prostration. Some took refuge in melancholy, and their eminent chief alternated between a menace and a sigh. As I sat opposite the Treasury Bench, the Ministers reminded me of one of those marine landscapes not very unusual on the coasts of South America. You behold a range of exhausted volcanoes. Not a flame flickers on a single pallid crest. But the situation is still dangerous. There are occasional earthquakes, and ever and anon the dark rumbling of the sea."

III

A Cloud of Grandmothers

Notwithstanding a string of triumphs in public life, the winter after Mary Anne's death was one of terrible sorrow. It was not only that Dizzy had lost in her the being he loved best in all the world, it was as if a great hunger and thirst for tenderness could find no satisfying. To Mary Anne, the Sphinx had delivered up his secret: it was—timidity. A timidity born in childhood from school-boy persecutions, fostered, under the guise of superficial brazenness, by the hostility of his peers, soothed in riper years by unique friendships, and cured at last by power; but it had moulded his character and impregnated all its elements. In particular, it had prevented him from ever finding real pleasure in the society of men. To feel himself their equal, he required to be their chief. In solitude any other Englishman would have taken to club life. But of this he had a horror: "There are many dreadful things in life," he had declared, "and a dinner of men is the worst of all."

"My need," he had written long ago to Mary Anne, "is for my life to be one perpetual love." The figure of his years had doubled, but the need remained. "I require," he now wrote, "perfect solitude, or perfect sympathy." The exaction of a sorely wounded man.

For several months he only visited at the houses of a few very intimate friends, passing all the parliamentary recesses at Hughenden, where he classified his wife's papers, moved to tears at finding amongst them the smallest scrap on which he had scribbled three words, and alone, so that a letter of any tenderness seemed to him like the sight of a sail to a shipwrecked man on his desert isle. All his feminine correspondents were dead, and with them had gone the charm and gaiety of those countless tiny incidents whose sole value lies in their being shared, but which alone make bearable the long adventure of life. In the spring, however, a chance visit enabled him to recover two friends of his youth, two sisters, Lady Chesterfield and Lady Bradford. Anne, Countess of Chesterfield, was seventy, Selina, Countess of Bradford, was fifty-five, and both were grandmothers. Disraeli recalled to them their childhood, spent close to the scene of his own youthful days (they had lived near Bradenham), and that brilliant fancy-dress ball to which Lady Chesterfield had gone as a sultana, her beautiful sister, Mrs. Anson, as a Greek slave with flowing hair, and Lady Londonderry as Cleopatra, richly laden with rubies. Mrs. Anson was dead, Fanny Londonderry was dead, but Lady Chesterfield and Lady Bradford had kept many of their charms. The meeting was pleasant; promises were made to write to each other, to see each other; with the summer came an invitation for Disraeli to spend a few days with one of the sisters, then with the other. Winter came round, and he was living only for "the delightful society of the two persons I love most in the world."

They were very different. Lady Chesterfield, much the elder, was the graver and more tender; Lady Bradford, the more playful. Lady Chesterfield had read all Disraeli's novels; Lady Bradford had begun them yawning and mixed up all the characters. Lady Chesterfield, always even-tempered, was a better friend; Lady Bradford, more whimsical and less certain, was the better loved. To both of them Disraeli wrote in a tone of very fond intimacy. Lady Chesterfield, a widow and a septuagenarian, read his letters with a smile; Lady Bradford, who had a perfect husband and marriageable daughters, protested, and on several occasions threatened to break off the correspondence if its tone continued to be so ardent. Disraeli had never been able to bear separation, even for a few days, from those whom he loved, and to ensure himself the constant society of both sisters, he proposed marriage to Lady Chesterfield. She refused, firstly because she considered marriage at her age rather ridiculous, but especially because Disraeli loved her sister. She became the confidante.

Every day the leader of the Opposition found time to indite a tender note for one or other of the peerless sisters. "The most fascinating of women was never more delightful than this afternoon. I could have sat for ever watching every movement that was grace, and listening to her sparkling words—but alas! the horrid thought, ever and anon, came over me—'it is a farewell visit.' It seemed too cruel! I might have truly said,

'Pleased to the last, I cropped the flowery food,
And kissed the hand just raised to shed my blood.'

"Constant separations! Will they never cease? If anything could make me love your delightful sister more than I do, it is her plans for Easter, which realize a dream! I am certain there is no greater misfortune than to have a heart that will not grow old."

He was an old man, powerful and overburdened with tasks, responsible for the life of a great Empire, but he felt himself in no way different from the young man he had been. Nay, perhaps the old man was more romantic than ever. In the youth, ambition had often fought victoriously against love. "I have lived to know that the twilight of love has its splendour and its richness." Perhaps in the old too there is an even greater yearning for happiness. Quite amazed at his discovery that he could still be desirous of a presence, and find pleasure in watching a woman live, and conscious too of the beauty of days passed at her side and the small number of those that remained to him, he could not endure separation from his friend. "To see you, or at least to hear from you, every day, is absolutely necessary to my existence." "To see you in society is a pleasure peculiar to itself; but different from that of seeing you alone; both are enchanting, like moonlight and sunshine." He would have liked to visit her every day, but Lady Bradford had endless obligations and rationed his visits. "Three times a week is very little!" There was a masked ball to which the old Minister wanted to go in domino. When he asked Selina to choose a sign by which he could recognize her, she coldly advised him not to go. He sulked a little and complained of this to his dear Lady Chesterfield. They knew he was unhappy, and he received a letter in kindlier terms which "took a load off my heart, and I pressed it to my lips." Such was the play of this old Alcestis with his ripe and charming Célimène.

But he was far from forgetting Mary Anne. During all the rest of his life the note-paper of his letters, even of his love-letters, was edged with black. And the symbol was just. One day, some time later, Lady Bradford happened to receive a letter written on ordinary note-paper, which gave her pleasure. He answered: "You said you were glad to see 'white paper' the other day. It is strange, but I always used to think that the Queen, persisting in these emblems of woe, indulged in a morbid sentiment; and yet it has become my lot, and seemingly an irresistible one."

He completed the sorting of the Hughendon papers,

finding there the countless memories of that meticulous affection. Every fortnight for thirty-three years, Mary Anne had cut her husband's hair, and every time the harvest had been garnered in a small sealed packet. He found hundreds of them. He discovered also thousands of letters, all those of Bulwer, all those of Alfred d'Orsay, all those of poor George Smythe, and Lady Blessington's last note. How many ghosts were waiting for him now!

At last Gladstone held the elections. Public feeling had undergone such a change that Disraeli had hopes of a great tranference of votes, perhaps even of a Conservative majority. Throughout the period of the election he sent daily letters to Lady Bradford. Before long he was able to tell her that his party had won ten seats, then twenty, then thirty, and then that Gladstone was completely routed. The Conservatives secured a clear majority of fifty seats over all parties together, and of more than a hundred over the Liberals alone. At last it was proved that a popular electorate could, as Disraeli had always maintained, be a conservative electorate. All the old malcontents of the party forgot their former mistrust. The Carlton was filled with an excited crowd calling for the Chief, like hounds barking round the huntsman the morning after a thaw.

Gladstone decided to resign without waiting for Parliament to meet, and announced that he would not remain leader of the party. He wanted to be an ordinary member and no longer to be in constant attendance at the House. He was sixty-five—an age when the great politicians of the century had long since rounded off their careers. His dominant desire was to occupy himself henceforth with religious matters and prepare himself for a Christian death. He informed the Queen of his decision. Her Majesty approved, with scarcely tactful vigour, and summoned Mr. Disraeli. One of the new Minister's first cares was to obtain an important post in the Royal Household for his dear Selina.

When Parliament reassembled, Disraeli spoke a few words of sympathy regarding Gladstone. The latter recognized that the other's attitude was generous. The man was a good winner as well as a good loser. But still, whenever Gladstone thought of him, he was stirred by a movement of indignation and felt within him the surge of wrath, "the inappeasable wrath of Achilles."

IV

The Chief

"The Chief"—it was thus that the Conservatives henceforward styled Disraeli, and the word betokened a great change. The adventurer, his genius tolerated by some, his authority contested by others, referred to as "Dizzy" with a familiarity sometimes affectionate, sometimes scornful, had now become an object of respect. Age had helped him in this; in all countries old age is a virtue in a public man, but especially in England. No people are more sensitive than the English to the beauty wherewith time can adorn an object; they love old statesmen, worn and polished by the struggle, as they love old leather and old wood. The Conservatives had not always understood the politics of their Chief, but he had led them to the most astounding victory the party had ever achieved. The fact must be faced: his spells might not be intelligible, but they were potent.

Apart from a few old men, almost the whole body of the party now had always known him as at their head, first as Lord Derby's colleague, and then by himself. There were many who still associated with his name some confused notion of Oriental mystery, but not so as to take fright. Just as a beautiful Moorish doorway, brought back stone by stone by some colonist returned home, reconstructed on a trimly mown lawn, and gradually overgrown by ivy and climbing roses, will slowly acquire a grace that is altogether English and blend discreetly with the green harmony of its setting, so too the old Disraeli, laden with British virtues, British whims, British prejudices, had become a natural ornament of Parliament and Society. True, a close observer might occasionally detect beneath the dark foliage the rather startling curve of an arch or the exotic line of an arabesque, but the slight discord would only heighten the beauty of this noble ruin with a barely perceptible touch of poetry and power.

From this time too there was mingled with the respect of the party, a manifest affection. Avowed enemies had become few and far between. The loyalty and goodwill of the Chief was admitted by nearly all. Even amongst his adversaries it was realized that, while he could deal stern blows to an enemy worthy of his steel, he always spared a weaker swordsman in debate. The examples of Peel and of Gladstone had proved that he never struck a man who was down. During his short tenure of power in 1868 he granted a pension to the children of John Leech, the *Punch* draughtsman, who had mercilessly attacked him for thirty years. Now, in 1874, his first action was to offer the highest distinction within his power to Thomas Carlyle, who had formerly asked how much longer John Bull would suffer this absurd monkey to dance on his chest. When a partisan of a more vindictive turn expressed astonishment at his meekness, he replied: "I never trouble to be avenged. When a man injures me, I put his name on a slip of paper and lock it up in a drawer. It is marvellous to see how the men I have thus labelled have the knack of disappearing."

With a strong majority to lean upon, and the support of the Queen, who welcomed his return with unconcealed delight, he at last had in his hands what all his life he had longed for: Power. The memory of youthful wounds was effaced. To Lady Dorothy Nevill, formerly the confidante of his trials, he said: "All goes well now. I feel my position assured." The security of victory brought a kind of relaxation. Never had the man been so completely natural. At last he knew that he would be accepted for what he was. He loosened his grip on himself. His wit was less harsh, less sarcastic. He spoke with less reserve of the sorrows of his young days. He freely delivered up a past which now had been redeemed. Walking with Lady Derby among his beech-woods, and pointing out Bradenham, he suddenly said to her:

"It was there that I spent my miserable youth."

"Why 'miserable'? Surely you were happy here."

"Not in those days. I was devoured by irresistible ambition, and had no means of satisfying it."

Social ambition had no further object. When a Duke tried to intimidate him, he exclaimed, "Dukes! I don't care for Dukes!" And it was true. Far indeed were the days when Isaac D'Israeli would ask, "Dukes? What does Ben know of Dukes?" A princess of the blood was merely a young woman, and one for whom he refused to put himself out in the morning. The Queen was a familiar figure, an old friend, a little difficult, but well liked. Yes, this time he was indeed at the summit. No longer did he feel within him that restless need of climbing ever higher, of domination. At last he ought to be happy.

But to a friend's congratulations he replied: "For me, it is twenty years too late. Give me your age and your health!" And he was heard to murmur, "Power! It has come to me too late. There were days when, on waking, I felt I could move dynasties and governments; but that has passed away." He had always been so great an admirer of youth, and his own had been frittered away because his starting-point was set too low; he had needed forty years to reach the level from which a Peel, a Gladstone, a Manners, had started off. A misfortune of birth—the hardest maybe of all, because the most unjust. Now it had come "too late." Hardly was he in power before his aged body broke down in various ways; the gout attacked him, and he had to attend Parliament in slippers; he had asthma, and to speak meant exhaustion. No one was at his side to tend him, save the faithful Montagu Corry. Fame is worthless, except as an offering of homage to those whom one loves. What could he do with this importunate fame of his? "Perhaps, and probably, I ought to be pleased. I can only tell you the truth. . . . I am wearied to extinction and profoundly unhappy. . . . I do not think there is really any person much unhappier than I am, and not fantastically so. Fortune, fashion, fame, even power, may increase, and do heighten happiness, but they cannot create it. Happiness can only spring from the affections. I am alone, with nothing to sustain me, but, occasionally, a little sympathy on paper, and that grudgingly. It is a terrible lot, almost intolerable."

What possible pleasures can power bestow? One at least: the press of business which allows one to forget oneself. But what vexations also: railway journeys when every station brings its crowd of enthusiasts shouting, "Here he is!" small boys running after one and standing open-mouthed before the compartment; young ladies begging for autographs; town bands at the door of the hotel. Ah, how little suited Disraeli was for these popular familiarities! One day he was waiting for a train at Swindon, slowly pacing up and down the platform, when a bagman, a hearty, downright fellow, approached him. "I have always voted for you, Mr. Disraeli, for twenty years now . . . and I should like to shake you by the hand." Disraeli raised his tired eyes and shook his head. "I don't know you," he said, and resumed his pacing to and fro. Mr. Gladstone, on a similar encounter, would have given both hands to the man and noted the fact in his journal. But Mr. Gladstone had the enthusiasm of a vigorous woodman; and this old man was worn out. His *mots* were still repeated, but their tone was altered. Hardly did a faint savour of irony keep afloat still on this ocean of melancholy. "Are you quite well, Mr. Disraeli?"—"Nobody is quite well. . . ." And if the lady of a house asked him what should be done for his diversion, "Ah!" he would answer, "let me exist."

One passion survived in this beaten body, and that was the taste for the fantastic. When he was alone, forced by his sufferings into silence and immobility, unable even to read, he would reflect with all an artist's pleasure on his marvellous adventures. Was there any tale of the Thousand and One Nights, any story of a cobbler made sultan, that could match the picturesqueness of his own life? Had he not realized, even in detail, the dreams of that small boy who lay stretched under the trees in the Italian garden, listening to his grandpapa's mandoline? "At last I have made my dream real." He had kept his preference for the tales and manners of chivalry. In this old heart Young England lived on. Amid "all his grandmothers," in the Russian Ambassador's mocking phrase, he believed himself at the tribunal of the Queen of Beauty. He gathered his feminine acquaintance into an order, and gave to each newly-elected lady a brooch fashioned like a Bee. True enough, the order was mainly composed of grandmothers—Lady Chesterfield, Lady Bradford—but there were a few young women too, such as the Princess Beatrice, with the permission of the Queen. And no doubt its Grand-Mistress was the Queen herself, whom he styled no longer the Queen, but the Faery.

Osborne. The green shades were restful to the eye after the fervent glare of the voyage. From the house one could see the blue bay studded with white sails. Hardly had the old visitor time to sit down for a moment in his room, before the august mistress of the place was asking for him. Downstairs he would come, and she would receive him with such delight that for an instant he thought she was going to embrace him. So full of smiles was she that she looked younger, and almost pretty. She twittered and glided about the room like a bird. She was happy. She had recovered her Minister, the only Minister who gave her confidence in herself. For the Queen had had a difficult life. She had been unpopular, very unpopular. She had seen people in London turn their backs on her carriage in the streets. First it was because of Lord Melbourne; and then it had been poor Albert, whom the public would not pardon for being a German; and then the Queen had been reproached for her mourning, and not one of her Ministers had defended her. All those Whigs were jealous of the Throne. But Mr. Disraeli had the same ideas on the Monarchy as the Queen herself. Doubtless he did not desire the Queen ever to oppose the will of Parliament, but he believed that the wisdom and experience of a constant and impartial witness provided a valuable ballast for the ship of Empire. Mr. Disraeli gave such fine expression to those ideas which had always been in the Queen's mind! "To think of you having the gout all the time! How you must have suffered! And you ought not to stand now. You shall have a chair!"

Mr. Disraeli was overcome by this unprecedented favour. No one had ever been seated during an audience with the Queen. Lord Derby had once told him, in token of her great kindness, how the Queen, seeing him one day when he was very ill, had said, "I am very sorry that etiquette does not allow me to ask you to be seated." Mr. Disraeli remembered the incident, and sighed with contentment; but he declined. He could very well remain standing. The Queen was kinder and kinder; she opened her heart to him on all subjects; and as she knew his curiosity, she showed him her most secret correspondence. She talked, she talked without stopping. She talked like Mary Anne, talked as women can talk. But she had risen greatly in Mr. Disraeli's intellectual esteem. She really had good sense, and was a sound judge of character. For instance, she saw through Gladstone. How lucky it was for Disraeli that England had a Queen and not a King! At dinner the conversation was lively and pleasant. Mr. Disraeli had never felt less constrained. He said all he had to say, in the most surprising terms, and the Queen thought she had never seen any one so amusing. She was enchanted by the bold simplicity with which he asked her over the table: "Madame, did Lord Melbourne ever tell your Majesty that you were not to do this or that?" Sometimes when they were alone, the Minister's compliments became flowery and almost direct. But the Queen excused him when she recalled that he had Eastern blood. The Queen loved the East. She delighted to have an Indian servant standing behind her chair, and at the head of her Realms this ingenious and sentimental Grand Vizier.

She invited him everywhere. She asked him to come and see her at Balmoral, where life was simpler and more free. Unfortunately, the guest was often ill. The long journeys fatigued him. The Queen sent her physician, the famous Sir William Jenner, to Mr. Disraeli's sick-room. Sir William insisted on the Premier keeping his bed. In the morning the Queen came to see him. "What do you think," he wrote to Lady Chesterfield, "of receiving your Sovereign in slippers and a dressing-gown?" Seeing him so weak, she became maternal. Their relations became entirely human. She talked to him of Albert; he told her of Mary Anne. Minister and Sovereign had both found happiness in marriage, in the past, and here was one more bond between them. When he returned to London, he received a box of flowers. "Mr. Disraeli, with his humble duty to your Majesty. Yesterday eve, there appeared in Whitehall Gardens, a delicate-looking case, with a royal superscription, which, when he opened, he thought, at first, that your Majesty had graciously bestowed upon him the stars of your Majesty's principal orders. And, indeed, he was so much impressed with this graceful illusion, that, having a banquet, where there were many stars and ribbons, he could not resist the temptation, by placing some snowdrops on his breast, of showing that he, too, was decorated by a gracious Sovereign.

"Then, in the middle of the night, it occurred to him, that it might all be enchantment, and that, perhaps, it was a Faery gift and came from another monarch: Queen Titania, gathering flowers, with her Court, in a soft and sea-girt isle, and sending magic blossoms, which, they say, turn the heads of those who receive them."

V

Action

"Thinking is easy; action is difficult; to act in accordance with one's thought is the most difficult thing in the world."

GOETHE.

In a strongly organized country, of an ancient and untouched civilization, man does not so much take power, as he is taken by power. A Bonaparte, after a revolution, may find a clean sweep made, and can impose the mould of his mind on a nation for a century. A Disraeli, Prime Minister of England, can only move within circumscribed limits. Events impose daily acts, and acts not always desired. Day after day goes by in repairing the blunders of a fool, or battling against the obstinacy of a friend. To have any immense plan would be useless, and the man had lived too long not to know it.

From the first days of his Ministry, the Queen and the Bishops obliged him to push forward a Bill designed to put a stop to Ritualism, that is, Romanist practices within the Anglican Church. Clergymen were to be prosecuted if their sacerdotal vestments or the splendour of their altars were offensive to Protestant eyes. Disraeli had a profound dread of ecclesiastical legislation, knowing only too well what violent passions might be roused. Even in the parish of Hughenden, small as it was, a civil war raged between partisans of the offertory made in a plate, and those who would only admit of a closed alms-box. "My friend the vicar will take what I call a collection and he calls an offertory, and it will be placed on what he calls an altar or on what his parishioners call a table."

But the Bishops were resolute. The Queen intervened: "Her *earnest* wish is that Mr. Disraeli should *go as far as he can without embarrassment* to the Government, in *satisfying* the *Protestant* feeling of the country in relation to this matter." And the Prime Minister had to spend the first weeks of his reign in amending, and then defending, a measure which he considered inopportune. However, the measures of which he disapproved actually increased his popularity for a time. Life is a topsy-turvy business.

But indeed it was not with laws of repression that he wished his name to be linked. On the contrary, he was anxious that the Conservative party's advent to power should be marked by a policy of generosity. Now was the moment to put into action the ideas of *Coningsby* and *Sybil*. Law after law was passed: equality of obligations between employers and employed; enlargement of

Action

the rights of Trade Unions; reduction of the hours of work to fifty-six in the week; half-holidays on Saturday; and numerous sanitary laws. The party's watchword, said Disraeli, should be *"Sanitas sanitatum et omnia sanitas."* A plumber's policy, said his enemies.

Another idea cherished by the Prime Minister from his youth upwards and now installed in power with him, was the idea of the Empire, the idea that England nowadays could not be considered apart from the Colonies. Twenty years earlier, he had proposed to Derby to grant representation to the Colonies and to create an Imperial Parliament. Forty years earlier, he had sung in poesy of Federal Power as the Spirit of the Future. Every time that a utilitarian had risen in Parliament to prove that the Colonies, and India in particular, were over-costly jewels of the Crown, and that it was desirable to renounce them, Disraeli had risen to insist that England is nothing if not the metropolis of a vast colonial Empire, and that the anti-colonists, in looking only at financial balance-sheets, were neglecting the political considerations which alone make a nation's greatness. For the organization of this Empire he had a programme: colonial autonomy, accompanied by an Imperial customs tariff, a Crown right over unoccupied territory, a military *entente*, and, lastly, the creation of an Imperial Parliament in London. So new and so bold did this policy seem, that he could not yet apply it, but he seized every opportunity of a striking display of his sentiments, and the importance he attached to Imperial communications.

On November 15th, 1875, Frederick Greenwood, the editor of the *Pall Mall Gazette,* called upon Lord Derby[1] at the Foreign Office. He had dined on the previous evening with a financier well versed in Egyptian affairs, and had learned that the Khedive, being short of money, was desirous of pledging his 177,000 shares in the Suez Canal. There were in all 400,000 Suez shares, the majority in the hands of French capitalists. Greenwood considered that it was in England's interest to acquire the Khedive's holding, as the Canal was the highway to India. Derby showed no great enthusiasm; he had a horror of large projects. But Disraeli's imagination was fired. He telegraphed to the British Agent in Egypt and learned that the Khedive had given an option to a French syndicate for £3,680,000 up to the following Tuesday. The Khedive was glad enough to deal with England, but he required money at once. Parliament was not in session, and four millions was not a sum which could be taken on to the Budget without a vote of credit. "Scarcely breathing time! But the thing must be done," wrote Disraeli to the Queen. The French Government offered no obstacles; on the contrary, the Duc Decazes was very anxious for Disraeli's support against Bismarck, and discouraged the French banks, who renounced their option. But £4,000,000 had to be found. On the day of the Cabinet's deliberation, Montagu Corry was posted in the anteroom. The Chief put his head round the half-opened door, and said one word: "Yes." Ten minutes later Corry was in New Court at Rothschild's, whom he

[1] We refer to the fifteenth Lord Derby, who, as Lord Stanley, had been Disraeli's friend and disciple. The father was now dead.

found at table. He told him that Disraeli needed four millions on the following day. Rothschild was eating grapes. He took one, spat out the skin, and said: "What is your security?"

"The British Government."

"You shall have it."

"Mr. Disraeli, with his humble duty to your Majesty:

"It is just settled. You have it, Madam. . . . Four millions sterling! and almost immediately. There was only one firm that could do it—Rothschild's. They behaved admirably; advanced the money at a low rate, and the entire interest of the Khedive is now yours, Madam."

The Queen was overjoyed. Never had Disraeli seen her so smiling; she kept him to dinner, "nothing but smiles and infinite *agaceries*." What particularly delighted the Faery was the thought of Bismarck's fury, for only shortly before he had insolently declared that England had ceased to be a political force.

Under Gladstone, with England abstaining and France crushed by the war, the German Chancellor had acquired a habit of playing the master of Europe. With Disraeli, England once more had a foreign policy and desires which she meant to have respected. In 1875, when Bismarck menaced Belgium and then threatened France, Disraeli wrote to Lady Chesterfield that Bismarck was really another old Bonaparte, and had to be bridled. He spoke of it to the Queen, who approved and offered to write to the Emperor of Russia. England and Russia acted simultaneously at Berlin, and Bismarck beat a retreat. England's return into European politics had been triumphant, and the Queen was in ecstasies. How strong she felt, Disraeli being Consul!

All of a sudden she demanded the title of Empress of India. There had been some question of this in 1858, at the time when India, after the Mutiny, had been brought under the Crown, and Disraeli had supported it in principle. But in 1875 the moment was unfavourable. Disraeli knew that this rather un-English idea would be attributed to the Prime Minister's taste for Oriental tinsel. He made endless attempts to obtain a few years of patience from Her Majesty. But in vain. She was obstinate, and a Bill had to be brought forward.

The public outcry was great. The English do not like changes. The Queen had always been the Queen: why should she not continue so? "The title of Emperor," said the puritans, "evokes the images of conquest, of persecution, and even of debauchery." Pamphlets were published: "How Little Ben, the innkeeper, changed the Sign of the Queen's Inn to the Empress Hotel Limited and what was the Result," or "Dizzi-ben-Dizzi, the Orphan of Bagdad." The embassies found it a comical story. "It is the freak of an artist and a king-maker in Dizzy," wrote the French *chargé d'affaires*. "In the Queen, the freak of an upstart; she imagines that her standing will be raised and that her children find a better place for themselves in life with this Imperial title. It is my impression that it is a grave mistake thus to raise the veil which ought to cover the origins of Crowns; these things ought not to be played with. One is born emperor and king, but it is very dangerous to become one."

Dizzy was to reassure everybody. As regards the evil associations of the name of Emperor, he pointed out that the golden age of humanity had been the era of the Antonines. As for the title of Queen, that would be maintained in England, and in all documents relating to Europe; only in acts concerning India and in the commissions of officers (who might be called upon to serve in India), the title of "Empress of India" would follow that of "Defender of the Faith." The Queen was much grieved by the opposition showed to *her* law, and especially by the personal attacks which her wishes had loosed against her dear Mr. Disraeli, but she was all the more closely drawn to him. When at last she had her title, she wrote him a letter of thanks, signing it "Victoria, Regina et Imperatrix," with a childlike delight. Then the new Empress gave a dinner, at which she appeared, contrary to all her customs, covered with Oriental jewels presented to her by the Indian princes. At the end of the repast, Disraeli rose, in conscious violation of etiquette, and proposed the health of the Empress of India in a short speech as crowded with imagery as a Persian poem, and the Queen, far from being scandalized, responded with a smiling bow that was almost a curtsey.

Thus the political vessel, tossed on the waves of fortune and climate, of the favour of the House and the humour of the Sovereign, rode the seas pretty well. But the skipper was very ill. So poor did his health become that more than once he told the Queen that he wanted to leave political life. This was a prospect which she would not have at any price, and she suggested that it would be easy to elevate the Prime Minister to the House of Lords, "where the fatigue would be *far less* and where he would be able to *direct* everything." This time he accepted. He took the name which he had had bestowed on Mary Anne, that of Beaconsfield, but whereas she had been only a Viscountess, he became the Earl of Beaconsfield and Viscount Hughenden of Hughenden. "Earl!" said Gladstone ironically, when he learned of this new avatar of the Evil One, "I cannot forgive him for not having himself made a Duke."

To avoid a farewell scene, affecting but unwelcome to his taste, he spoke for the last time in the Commons on the eve before the decision was announced. The secret had been well kept, and members were far from supposing that they would never again hear their leader. When the House rose, he walked slowly down the floor, right to the end, at the bar of the House. There he turned, and for a moment or two looked round the long room, at its benches and galleries, at the seat from which he had made his first speech, the Treasury Bench where he had seen the massive figure and the fine features of Peel, at the Opposition bench which he himself had occupied for so long a time. Then he came back, passed in front of the Speaker's chair, and, wrapped in his long white overcoat, leaning on the arm of his secretary, went out. A young man who was passing noticed that there were tears in his eyes, but could not tell why.

When members learned the news at the meeting of the House next day, they gathered in groups, deeply moved. Voices were lowered on the benches, as if there were a coffin in the chamber. A supporter, Sir William Hart Dyke, said: "All the real chivalry and delight of party politics seem to have departed; nothing remains but routine." And that was the feeling of the whole House. The interest taken by this old man in the game of life had in the end communicated itself to all those about him. With him one never knew what the morrow might not bring, but one could be certain that at least it would be nothing dull. "He corrected an immense platitude." The presence of this great artist in living had succeeded in making debates into works of art. "He was not only brilliant in himself, but he made others brilliant." Since his conquest of a position of authority, he had used it to impose a universal courtesy and respect for forms. An interruption from one of his own followers would make him turn round and cast a displeased look in his direction. In a discussion on finance he contrived to see a veritable tournament, and he made others see the same. "Your departure," wrote Manners, "terminates for me all personal interest in House of Commons life"; and Sir William Harcourt, an opponent, wrote: "Henceforth the game will be like a chessboard when the queen is gone—a petty struggle of pawns." And he quoted in conclusion the words of Metternich on the death of Napoleon: "You will perhaps think that when I heard of his death I felt a satisfaction at the removal of the great adversary of my country and my policy. It was just the reverse. I experienced only a sense of regret at the thought that I should never again have converse with that great intelligence." "Alas! alas!" wrote another, "we shall never see your like again. The days of the giants are over. Ichabod! Ichabod!"

When shortly afterwards the Queen opened the session of Parliament, a strange, motionless figure was seen standing by her side, draped in scarlet and ermine. It was the new Lord Beaconsfield. The fairest peeresses had come to see him take his seat. Derby and Bradford were his sponsors. With perfect composure he came forward and bowed, shook hands, raised his hat, as the ritual demanded, and then, having become Leader of the House of Lords on the very day of his entering it, he had to speak at its very first sitting. At twenty-five he had written in *The Young Duke:* "One thing is quite clear—that a man may speak very well in the House of Commons, and fail very completely in the House of Lords. There are two distinct styles requisite: I intend, in the course of my career, to give a specimen of both. In the Lower House, *Don Juan* may perhaps be our model; in the Upper House, *Paradise Lost.*" In both cases he had been mistaken, but even if it had taken him some time in the House of Commons to abjure his Byronic manner, he never in the House of Lords adopted the Miltonic style. A shade of difference there was, but it was subtle, and more indefinable than his youthfulness had foreseen. He noted it with perfect artistry. "I am dead," he said on coming out from his first sitting, "dead, but in the Elysian Fields."

VI

Atrocities

*"You remind me of certain Englishmen;
the more their minds are emancipated, the
more they cling to morality."*

ANDRÉ GIDE.

In the month of July, 1875, some peasants of Bosnia and Herzegovina revolted against the Turks, who treated their Infidel subjects like dogs. The episode seemed trifling; but it grew. The impotence of the Porte was astounding; to collect a couple of thousand men and dispatch them into Bosnia seemed to require a military genius who could not be found; and money too was wanting. In every Balkan village secret committees, organized by the Russian Orthodox brotherhood of Cyril and Methodius, kept up an anti-Turkish agitation. The Russians were prompted by two forces. One was sentimental: they were racial brethren, and in great part religious brethren, of the Bulgars, Serbs, and Roumanians. The other, political: they had need of access to the Mediterranean and were anxious to reach there, either by obtaining the mastery of Constantinople and the Straits, or by emancipating the Bulgars and Serbs, who would then, under Russian protection, form vassal principalities.

There was nothing in the world which Disraeli dreaded more than to see the Russians in the Mediterranean. The first axiom of British policy for him had been the maintenance of free communications with India and Australia. Now, overland, these communications were possible only through a friendly Turkey; by sea, they had to be made through the Suez Canal, a highly vulnerable point if the Turkish Asiatic provinces were in the hands of a hostile nation. The part played by the Russians in this affair seemed highly suspect; their designs might well be widespreading and dangerous. It was important to keep one's eyes open from the start. Disraeli had very exact recollections of the outbreak of the Crimean War, on which occasion he had seen how a pacific man, as Lord Aberdeen was, had let himself be driven into war by his very dread of war. The true means of safeguarding peace seemed to be to draw the precise line beyond which one would not withdraw.

Bulgaria followed Bosnia in revolt, and when Russia, Germany, and Austria, having drawn up a stern memorandum to be addressed to Turkey, requested England to sign it along with themselves, the Prime Minister refused. Was it England's duty to collaborate in the destruction of a Power in whose preservation her own interest lay, and join hands in doing so with Gortchakoff, an avowed enemy, and Bismarck, a doubtful friend? An openly stated attitude was preferable. "Whatever happens," he wrote to Lady Bradford, "we shall certainly not drift into war, but go to war if we do, because we intend it and have a purpose we mean to accomplish. I hope, however, that Russia, at the bottom of the whole affair, will be sensible, and then we shall have peace."

The Government's firm policy was on the whole generally approved, and the Liberal opposition itself had been silent until the *Daily News*, a very well-informed newspaper, and devoted to Gladstone, published an article, filled with horrible details on the atrocities committed by the Turks in Bulgaria. Children massacred, women violated, young girls sold as slaves, ten thousand Christians imprisoned—such was the work of the friends and allies of the Prime Minister. Disraeli read this terrible recital with ironic mistrust. He had received no report from his ambassador, he saw what interest Gladstone and his friends had in magnifying facts, and, what is more, in principle, he did not readily believe in atrocities. Already during the Indian Mutiny, with great courage and against the tide of public feeling, he had appealed to the sense of proportion and refused to be angry without proper inquiry. A kindly man, with no powerful passions except ambition, he could not easily imagine voluntary cruelty or sadism. He had travelled in Turkey and dined with the pashas, smoking narghiles with them, and he could not see these amiable gentlemen butchering little children. Some bands of irregular troops might possibly have committed excesses, but no doubt the insurgents themselves had not been particularly gentle. He had a horror of "movements of opinion." It was enough for him to hear talk of oppressed populations: instantly he scented some hypocrisy and felt oppressed himself.

The question being raised in the House of Commons, he replied that he hoped, for the honour of human nature, that more exact information would show the exaggeration of this news. "I cannot doubt that atrocities have been committed in Bulgaria; but that girls were sold into slavery, or that more than ten thousand persons have been imprisoned, I doubt. In fact, I doubt whether there is prison accommodation for so many, or that torture has been practised on a great scale among an Oriental people who seldom, I believe, resort to torture, but generally terminate their connection with culprits in a more expeditious manner."

For once, unfortunately, Dizzy's experience was faulty, and the story was true. The ambassador, suddenly roused by the outcry in England, obtained information, was obliged to confirm the facts, and public opinion took flame. Could it allow the Prime Minister to brush aside these victims with a few light phrases? Disraeli cursed the Foreign Office for their defective information, and hoped that the storm would blow over. It was very regrettable that Bulgarian villages should have been fired and young girls violated, but was that a reason for renouncing a policy both reasonable and of old standing?

Gladstone at this time was at Hawarden. Since writing to his dear Granville that at the age of seventy, and after fifty years of public life, he had a right to retiral, "he had frequently returned from the Isle of Elba." At every turn on his path, Disraeli met him, rearing his head like a dragon breathing fire. Not that he was insincere in his wish for repose, but the fact of the Wicked One being in power drew him back in spite of all his vows. In vain did he strive to divert his thoughts from this intolerable scandal by theological and Homeric studies; the more he pondered, the more he felt that the great evil of these times was the loss of the sense of sin! "Ah!" he used slowly to say, "the sense of sin, there is the great want in modern life." Amongst the writers whom he was then reading through once more, was there a single one who had given a sufficiently forcible expression to the detestation of vice? Sir Walter Scott had actually been friendly with a Byron! A youthful visitor nervously pointed out that a professional novelist is obliged to have knowledge of everything, and reminded him of Mme. de Staël's saying, *"Tout comprendre, c'est tout pardonner,"* but Mr. Gladstone shook his head, saying, "Do not blunt your sense of sin."

His own was far from blunted. With the description of the Bulgarian atrocities before him, he felt, in the flood of anger mounting within him against the Turks, the janissaries, and the new Lord Beaconsfield, that here, ready to his hand, was an admirable theme for righteous indignation. What subject could be better contrived for his inspiration? Peoples enchained, Christians the victims of Infidels, and, in the depths of this darkling intrigue, the Great Infidel himself, the tragic comedian, the man who had demoralized public opinion and cynically excited the egotism of the nation for the satisfaction of his own. Parliament was in recess, lumbago kept Gladstone in his bed, his axe reposed in idleness in the courtyard: he turned to the composition of a pamphlet. The violence of its language was remarkable: fell satanic orgies . . . the Turks, the one great anti-human specimen of humanity . . . there was not a criminal in a European gaol, nor a cannibal in the South Sea Islands, whose indignation would not rise at the recital of what had been done. . . . The remedy was to force the Turks "to carry away their abuses in the only possible manner, namely by carrying away themselves. Their Zaptiehs and their Mudirs, their Bimbashis and their Yuzbashis, their Kaimakams and their Pashas, one and all, bag and baggage, shall, I hope, clear out from the province they have desolated and profaned."

The pamphlet had an immense success; forty thousand copies were sold in a few days. All up and down England meetings were held, clamouring for the expulsion of the Turks, and subscriptions were opened on behalf of the crusade. At Liverpool, *Othello* was being played, and at the phrase, "the Turks were drowned," the whole audience rose and cheered. A cyclone of virtue swept across England. Gladstone rode the storm everywhere, with speeches and with writings. He suspected the Government of wishing to annex Egypt: Dizzy, he said, was upholding Turkey because he thought that she would break down, and his fleet was at Besika Bay so as to be ready, without a doubt, to lay hold of Egypt at the first opportunity. Perhaps they might yet see Disraeli Duke of Memphis. He thought of nothing but the Bulgars. Numerous anti-Turk visitors made the pilgrimage to Hawarden; they found him in his shirt-sleeves and offered the gifts which they had brought, a rustic walking-stick or a carved axe-handle, and then Mr. Gladtone spoke to them of the Bulgars. They set off again stoked up with enthusiasm: no, England should not fight beside the miscreants! "No matter how the Prime Minister may finger the hilt of the sword, the nation will take care that it never leaves the scabbard."

Beaconsfield had read the pamphlet. He had judged it passionate, vindictive, and ill-written—"of course"— and of all Bulgarian atrocities, the worst. In his letters to Lady Bradford, Gladstone was often referred to as "the Tartuffe," and as the voluntary victim of every lie that could bring him into power. To Lord Derby he wrote: "Posterity will do justice to that unprincipled maniac Gladstone—extraordinary mixture of envy, vindictiveness, hypocrisy and superstition; and with one commanding characteristic—whether Prime Minister, or Leader of Opposition, whether preaching or praying, speechifying or scribbling—never a gentleman!"

Come what might, Lord Beaconsfield was fully decided not to yield to public opinion. When the country goes out of its mind, one must bide one's time. The crisis would pass, and men could talk reason again. And in

any case, what was this bellicose pacifist driving at?
Declaring war on the Turks? Avenging Bulgarian atrocities by a world-wide butchery? Hatred of crime was not
the monopoly of a party. To judge from the cries of the
malcontents, any one might have thought that Lord
Beaconsfield was the Sultan and Lord Derby the Grand
Vizier. In reality, he felt no responsibility on himself.
He held massacres in horror. He did not support the
Turks; he would gladly have seen them all at the bottom
of the Black Sea. What he feared losing was the unity
of the Empire and the future of England.

Never had Dizzy shown more clearly his detestation
of hypocrisy. He knew that a few sentimental phrases
would have made his task easier, but nevertheless he
wrote to Derby that he laid great emphasis on the Foreign Secretary taking no step which might make it appear that he was acting under pressure of public opinion.
And another day: "You can't be too firm. What the public meetings want is nonsense, not politics: something
quite shadowy, speculative, and not practical." And at
Guildhall on Lord Mayor's Day: "Although the policy
of England is peace, there is no country so well prepared for war as our own. If she enters into conflict in
a righteous cause—if the contest is one which concerns
her liberty, her independence, or her Empire, her resources, I feel, are inexhaustible. She is not a country
that, when she enters on a campaign, has to ask herself
whether she can support a second or a third campaign.
She enters into a campaign which she will not terminate
till right is done."

VII

War?

In *Punch*, Britannia was shown as being conducted by a guide with Disraelian features up to the edge of a precipice, at the bottom of which one read "War." "Just a *leetle* nearer the edge." "Not an inch further; I'm a good deal nearer than is pleasant already." It was true that Britannia was in terror of falling. Lord Beaconsfield's policy was to alarm Russia by the threat of a war which he had no wish to make, but it was legitimate to believe that, in walking too often on the verge of the abyss, there was grave danger from loose stones.

Such was the opinion of the young Lord Derby who ruled at the Foreign Office. Totally different from his father, he was an awkward and eminently reasonable man whose healthy apathy was useful in danger, but who was not built for this diplomatic skating on thin ice. He disliked anything romantic and all theatrical backgrounds. He saw no reason for threatening Russia. It was not that he was an anti-Turk like Gladstone; that was another piece of romantic nonsense for which he had no greater liking; but he could not admit that the British Empire was endangered because the Russians might be at Constantinople. In his heart of hearts, he did not admit that the British Empire could ever be in danger. "Lack of imagination," the Chief might say again. Well and good. He had no imagination. He did not want any. He would never resolve to set loose a present and certain evil to avoid one that was both future and uncertain. All the measures proposed by Beaconsfield met with his discontent and hostility, and as he had a great name and was justly reputed for his sound sense, he could carry a good number of his colleagues with him.

While the Cabinet applied the brake, the Sovereign pushed at the wheels. The Queen had always had scant love for Russia. Albert had always said that the danger would come from that quarter. She regarded herself as responsible for the integrity of the Empire and the security of the highway to India. She blamed both Gladstone and Lord Derby. She could not understand the weakness of so many men, while she, a woman, would have been ready to march on the foe. She bombarded her Premier with bellicose notes. The organizers of pro-Russian meetings ought to be prosecuted. Why the delay in taking arms? "The Queen is feeling terribly anxious lest delay should cause us to be too late and lose our prestige for ever! It worries her night and day."—"The Queen appeals to the feelings of patriotism which she knows animate her Government, and is certain that every member of it will feel the absolute necessity of showing a bold and united front to the enemy in the country as well as outside it. . . . It is not the question of upholding Turkey; it is the question of Russian or British supremacy in the world!"

Even the Princesses joined in. When the Prime Minister happened to be seated at table beside Princess Mary of Cambridge, she said to him, "I cannot imagine what you are waiting for!" "Potatoes, at this moment, Madam," said Lord Beaconsfield.

Hitherto he had been able to navigate without mishap the narrow channel betwixt the Queen and Lord Derby, but could he always do so? And he would also have to avoid that third reef of danger, the Liberals, exasperated by the phrase, "the interests of England." "An egoistic policy," they said. "As egoistic as patriotism," said the old cynic. And, very calmly measuring with his eye the depth of the precipice, he felt glad that he was not subject to giddiness.

Russia declared war on Turkey. The Tsar sent General Ignatiev on a special mission to England to secure a promise of neutrality. Fashionable London gave dinner-parties for the Ignatievs. His wife was fair, pretty, and drank no heel-taps. She made a great hit. The Marchioness of Londonderry and she had a contest of diamonds. The Englishwoman won. Lord Beaconsfield warned Russia that he would not remain neutral unless the Tsar respected the three points indispensable to the preserving of the Empire: the Suez Canal, the Dardanelles, Constantinople. Gortchakoff promised. What did he risk? His informants reassured him. Public opinion was far from being united behind Lord Beaconsfield. Many Englishmen laughed at his menaces. *Punch* showed "Benjamin the Bully," and the British Lion saying to the Sphinx: "Look here, I don't understand you, but it's right you should understand me! I don't fight to uphold what's going on yonder." Schouvaloff, an admirable ambassador, who had managed to become "Schou" to everybody who counted for anything in London, and had realized that the key to the political world is to be found in the world of fashion, was so well informed that he was able to telegraph to St. Petersburg the names of the English Ministers opposing the Premier's design. Gortchakoff was reassured and played a double game. To the English he declared, "We recognize that the question of Constantinople can only be settled by an agreement between the Powers." To the Grand Duke Nicholas, chief of the armies, he gave the order, "Objective—Constantinople." Victory would clear up everything. When the Russian armies occupied the city, who would dare to dislodge them?

The Grand Duke entered Bulgaria. The Queen grew more and more agitated. Albert had always foreseen what was now coming to pass. Was she to stand by, a powerless Cassandra, watching the ruin of the Empire? "The Faery writes every day and telegraphs every hour."

She at least did not believe in Russian promises. She wanted pledges to be taken, that *something* at any rate should be done. "The reports which the Queen saw yesterday are very alarming! Surely Lord Derby cannot be indifferent to the dangers expressed therein? Warning after warning arrives and he seems to take it all without saying a word! Such a Foreign Minister the Queen really never remembers!—The Russians will be before Constantinople in no time! Then the Government will be fearfully blamed and the Queen so humiliated that she thinks she would abdicate at once. Be bold!—But if this is not done and done quickly . . . the Opposition will be the first to turn round on you, and delay of weeks or days only may be—mark the Queen's words—fatal! *Pray act* quickly!—The Queen is distressed not to see anything acted upon which Lord Beaconsfield tells her is to be done. He told her on Tuesday that in three days 5000 men could be sent to increase the garrisons, and that every effort should be made to be prepared, even for Gallipoli if the Russians did not make a dash for Constantinople. But she hears of no troops moving or going, and becomes more and more alarmed. The Queen always feels hopeful and encouraged when she sees Lord Beaconsfield, but somehow or other, whether intentionally or through want of energy on the part of those under him or at the offices, nothing material is done! It alarms her seriously.—And the language—the insulting language—used by the Russians against us! It makes the Queen's blood boil! What has become of the feeling of many in this country!"

War?

Endlessly she threatened to lay down this crown of
thorns, and Derby on his side offered his resignation on
every occasion, and the old Premier, gouty and short of
breath, and sad too at not seeing the dear orange-tinted
eyes of Lady Bradford, wrote to her: "I am very ill.
If I could only face the scene which would occur at
headquarters if I resigned, I would do so at once. But
I never could bear scenes. . . ."

A brief stand on the part of the Turks gave some
hope. The army was good, and the Sultan had said to
his troops: "Your sabres, the sabres of believers, will
open for you the gates of Paradise." It was learned that
the Russian army, checked before Plevna, had 50,000
dead, and counted 30,000 wounded, who, ill-tended in
improvised hospitals, would probably all die. In the
month of August, the Russians were held to be as good
as beaten. Marshal Moltke believed it. England is fond
of strong peoples; public sentiment became pro-Turkish.
In the streets of London, the song was heard:

> *We don't want to fight,*
> *But, by Jingo! if we do,*
> *We've got the ships,*
> *We've got the men,*
> *We've got the money too!*

The fashion now was to go on Sundays and boo Gladstone at his house and fling stones at his windows. The
grandsires of these demonstrators had submitted the
Duke of Wellington's windows to the same treatment.

The Houses of Parliament rose for the recess. Beaconsfield went to rest at Hughenden. He had great difficulty with his breathing, and could no longer walk at
all. To go to church, he had to take Mary Anne's little
pony-trap. The peacocks annoyed him: he almost desired, he said, to commit a kind of atrocity there and
massacre the peacocks. Returning to London, he consulted Dr. Kidd, a homœopathic physician who had been
strongly recommended to him. Kidd examined this old
body, stripped as if for the examination of a recruit.
He found in it asthma, bronchitis, and Bright's disease—
fit for holding the rampart on the highway to India. . . .

The game of bluff only demands an impenetrable
coolness, and this was the Premier's ruling quality. But
how was he to bluff, with two partners, one of them calling the bluff at every round, and the other disliking the
game so much that he insisted on laying his cards on
the table. The Queen in particular was terrible. She was
too fond of her Prime Minister. She counted on none
but him. Like herself, although for different reasons, he
alone possessed that concentrated patriotism which
sweeps away all other feelings. She clung to him. She
would have liked to load him with honours. She offered
to make him a Knight of the Garter, but he declined,
judging the moment inopportune. She went to visit him
at Hughenden, a favour she had shown to nobody since
Lord Melbourne. She authorized him, in writing to her,
to drop the official formulas, and he could now begin
his letter with "Madam and Most Beloved Sovereign."

She herself replied, "My dear Lord Beaconsfield," and concluded, "Believe me, with sincerest regards, yours affectionately, Victoria, R.I."

And yet she really annoyed him by her unqualified tenacity. There was this difference between them, that Beaconsfield was resolved to avoid war, and almost certain of doing so, while the Queen, far more passionate, had reached the point of desiring war. When the Russians, having at last captured Plevna, reached the heights commanding Constantinople, she naïvely reminded him of the promises that had been made. Yes or no, had Lord Beaconsfield said that in such an event he would declare war? What was he waiting for? Already, without consulting Europe, the Russians were negotiating a secret treaty with the Turks. Soon one would be faced with a *fait accompli*. Ah! Lord Beaconsfield was no better than the rest of them. All men were cowards. She alone, poor woman, had to give life to everything. Lord Beaconsfield bent very low his stooping shoulders. He strove to find forgiveness for his disobedience by exaggerating the expression of his devotion. "Lord Beaconsfield hopes that Your Majesty remembers her gracious promise not to write at night, at least not so much. He lives only for Her, and works only for Her, and without Her, all is lost." However, he kept watch on the game.

There was another great player who up to that moment had only observed the moves, but was awaiting the moment to enter the contest. That was Prince von Bismarck. Abruptly, on February 19th, he slammed down his cards with a great speech in the Reichstag, a speech that was intentionally obscure, and so very clear. Obliged to choose between Austria and Russia, and full of rancour against Gortchakoff since the incidents of 1875, Bismarck sided against Russia. He avowed his disinterestedness. The Eastern question was of small import to Germany. Constantinople was not worth the bones of a single Pomeranian grenadier. What Germany desired was to avoid a conflict. Her rôle, amidst opposing interests, would be that of "the honest broker." Naturally the treaty in course of elaboration between Turks and Russians would have to be submitted to the approval of the other European Powers in a Conference, or Congress, which would be held, if they were so willing, at Berlin. This was all set out in a vein of the utmost courtesy and loftiness of thought, but in a couple of hours Bismarck had razed the whole edifice reared by Gortchakoff in as many years. Already threatened by England, Russia could not brave Germany too; she immediately accepted the principle of the Congress, but accepted it with formulas involving the communication, and not the submission, of the treaty to the powers.

At last this treaty was published. It was read by the English people with stupefaction. To all outward appearance, Gortchakoff respected the promise given: Constantinople, Suez, and the Dardanelles remained free, but all these positions were hemmed about. Turkey lost all her European provinces. The Russians set up a Bulgaria which would be their vassal and afford them access

to the Mediterranean. In Armenia they occupied Kars
and Batum, thus taking a stride towards India and closing in Asiatic Turkey from the rear. With one of those
fine sweeping movements of opinion which unite her in
the face of danger, England ranged herself behind the
Premier: she would not go to the Congress to discuss
such a document.

Lord Beaconsfield remained very cool. He considered
the treaty as impossible of acceptance, and informed
Schouvaloff that he would attend the Congress only after
a direct Anglo-Russian agreement on the gravest points.
His conditions were twofold: no Great Bulgaria, and no
Russian Armenia. The ambassador leapt up: "This was
depriving Russia of all the fruits of war. . . ." That
might be. In any case the Premier let him understand
that if England did not receive satisfaction, she would
compel Russia to leave the contested territories, even by
force. Schouvaloff went away, perturbed but sceptical.
Lord Beaconsfield was not England. A Cabinet meeting.
The Prime Minister was anxious to prepare for war.
"If we are firm and determined, we shall have peace
and we shall dictate its terms to Europe." But readiness
there must be. He proposed the calling-up of the reserve,
a vote of credit, the dispatch of the Fleet to Constantinople, and above all, since the question was that of
defending the route to India, he desired that the Empire
should participate in its own defence, and that troops of
the Indian Army should be sent into the Mediterranean
to occupy positions commanding the Russian communications, that is, Cyprus and Alexandretta. The Cabinet
approved its Chief, all except Lord Derby, who resigned.

He considered those measures only fit to bring on war, and declined the responsibility. Lord Beaconsfield was not without regrets in parting with an old friend, and a Derby, but accepted his resignation.

This time Schouvaloff took fright. Derby's departure was a sign. At no price did Russia want war with England. She was much enfeebled by her campaigns. She had no fleet. And further, she much preferred an understanding with Beaconsfield than with Bismarck. The ambassador returned with concessions. Gortchakoff yielded on the Great Bulgaria question, reducing it to half its size and dropping the access to the sea, but he stood firm for a Russian Armenia. Beaconsfield was inflexible. So it was war—unless a guarantee could be given to England in the shape of a Gibraltar in the Eastern Mediterranean. At that moment a bombshell fell, in the shape of news of the troops brought in secrecy from India having begun to disembark. That was the final blow. Russia accepted everything. A secret convention was signed with the Sultan, who agreed to cede the island of Cyprus to England, whilst in return England would assure him defensive alliance in the event of Russia in Armenia pushing beyond Kars and Batum. Gortchakoff consented to go to the Congress to approve the treaty as thus modified. Turkey remained a European Power. The Slav advance was checked. The game was won, completely won, and without the loss of a single man, without a single rifle-shot. The guide brought his sightseers back to the shore, unscathed and happy, but a little tired. "A good guide," thought Britannia, "but reckless."

War?

In Beaconsfield's eyes, the most enchanting point in the affair was the acquisition of Cyprus. Thirty years earlier, in *Tancred*, he had made clear announcement of this. It pleased him thus to pass his romances and his dreams into history. What's more, Cyprus was the Isle of Venus. Richard Cœur de Lion had given it to Lusignan, King of Jerusalem, he who had become Count of Paphos. And now the city of Aphrodite and the romantic kingdom of the Crusaders would be joined with Gibraltar and Malta to round off the English Mediterranean. It was a great day for the old artist who took pleasure in these secular games.

VIII

The Congress of Berlin

An international Congress: the greatest of all possible
Vanity Fairs. To begin with, in the interior of each
country, there is the eliminating of local vanities. Each
Prime Minister thinks that he alone is capable of representing his country's policy. Each Foreign Secretary
thinks that the Premier knows nothing of diplomacy.
Each professional ambassador thinks the same about his
Foreign Secretary. With the assembly collected, and
the great men face to face, it is an orchestra of first
violins.

Prince Bismarck had hoped that the great actors
would not turn up. From Russia he expected Schouvaloff, whom he liked and with whom he had arranged

part of the programme. But Gortchakoff considered that he could not delegate the task to any one, and succeeded in persuading his Emperor of this. Bismarck promised himself the pleasure of a revenge: "He shall not climb a second time on my shoulders to make a pedestal for himself." From England, too, the Premier was desirous of coming in person. Who else was there who understood the East? Lord Beaconsfield and Lord Salisbury were appointed as plenipotentiaries. The special trains rolled off. Bismarck was thinking: "The Congress? *I* am the Congress." And both Beaconsfield and Gortchakoff, feeble old men stretched out on the cushions of the carriages which converged from Brussels and St. Petersburg upon Berlin, were nursing that same thought.

To this Conference, intended for the free discussion of a treaty, every State came armed with secret conventions. England had the London agreement with Russia. Turkey knew that she had ceded Cyprus to England, but was ignorant of the Bulgarian agreement. Austria had promises from England and Germany which gave her, without striking a single blow, Bosnia and Herzegovina. France had obtained assurances that Egypt and Syria would be left outside the discussions. The English public, picturing with admiring terror Lord Beaconsfield sallying forth to face the Muscovite Bear, little thought how thoroughly the play had already been rehearsed.

On arriving at his hotel, the Kaiserhof, Lord Beaconsfield found the table of his drawing-room entirely hidden under an immense basket of flowers and a large box of delicious strawberries, decked with orange-flowers and roses. This was the gift of welcome from the Crown Princess, Queen Victoria's daughter. He wrote to the Queen: "The Crown Prince and Princess have showered kindnesses on Lord Beaconsfield during his visit to Berlin, and what makes them more delightful is, that he feels they must be, in no slight degree, owing to the inspiration of one to whom he owes everything." He received a visit from Bismarck's secretary: "The Chancellor would like to see Lord Beaconsfield as soon as possible."

The two men knew each other, and appreciated each other. They had met in London sixteen years before. Each had divined in the other an intelligence and a will. Beaconsfield found Bismarck greatly changed. The pale, wasp-waisted giant whom he had seen in 1862, had grown stout, and was letting a white beard sprout on his ruddy face. But he still found the tone he had liked, simple and blunt, rather surly, brutally frank, and still found those terrible things spoken in a gentle voice which astounded one as coming from this vast bodily frame. Bismarck told him that his intention was to keep the Congress short and sharp, but that he thought it necessary to devote the opening days, when minds were still fresh, to the larger questions, those capable of being causes of war. Accordingly, they would begin with Bulgaria.

Next day, at two o'clock, the Congress assembled for the first time, in a magnificent hall which was in perfect keeping with the gold-braided uniforms, stars, badges, and swords of the diplomats. Before the sitting, every one passed to a buffet to drink port and nibble biscuits. Beaconsfield had himself introduced to the international personnel: the Turk, Carathéodory Pasha, a young, black-bearded man with a too gentle expression; the tottering old Gortchakoff; the Italian Corti, with the face of a Japanese; the Frenchman Waddington, half-English; the Austrian Andrassy. . . . Yes, everything was all right: except for Bismarck and himself, there was no giant character here.

Bismarck proceeded with military directness. Forthwith, the division of Bulgaria into two parts separated by the line of the Balkans was agreed to without discussion. Then everything went wrong. The Russians had granted the Turks the frontier of the Balkans, and wanted to refuse them the right to defend it or to maintain troops in that part of Bulgaria which had been left to them. This meant, indirectly, the destruction of all the results of the London agreement. An unoccupied Bulgaria would once again be at the mercy of Russia, and Russia would have her access to the Mediterranean.

Beaconsfield thundered. St. Petersburg must renounce the illusion that the will of England could be circumvented. Gortchakoff was piqued, and grew obstinate. Lord Beaconsfield solemnly declared that the English terms constituted an ultimatum. In consternation the Russians sent an emissary to their Emperor. Beaconsfield wrote to the Queen: "I have no fear about the result, as I have intimated in the proper quarter that I shall break up the Congress if England's views are not adopted."

On the morning of the ultimatum's expiration, strolling out on Corry's arm, *unter den Linden,* he told him to order a special train to take the British delegation to Calais. Corry passed on the order to the German railway officials. The outcome was speedy. At a quarter to four, Prince Bismarck came to the Kaiserhof. "Take me to Lord Beaconsfield," he said to Corry, "and let me know when it is five minutes to four, as I have an appointment at four." He asked whether a compromise could be found. "Compromise was found at the moment of the London agreements, and it is impossible to go back on those."—"Am I to understand that this is an ultimatum?"—"You are."—"I am obliged to go to the Crown Prince now. We should talk over this matter. Where do you dine to-day?"—"At the English Embassy."—"I should like you to dine with me. I am alone at six o'clock."

"I accepted his invitation," wrote Beaconsfield to the Queen. "After dinner we retired to another room, where he smoked and I followed his example. I believe I gave the last blow to my shattered constitution but I felt it absolutely necessary. In such circumstances, the man who does not smoke has the appearance of spying upon the other's words. . . . I had an hour and a half of the most interesting conversation, entirely political; he was convinced that the ultimatum was not a sham, and, before I went to bed, I had the satisfaction of knowing that St. Petersburg had surrendered."

"Once again there is a Turkey-in-Europe," said Bismarck. "We have sacrificed a hundred thousand soldiers and a hundred millions of money for nothing," sighed Gortchakoff.

This episode gave Prince Bismarck a high opinion of Lord Beaconsfield. *"Der alte Jude, das ist der Mann,"* he used to say. "The old Jew, that is the man." They became very friendly, and took a curious pleasure in talking "shop" together. They enjoyed conversing about relations with princes, ministers, parliaments. It is so rare to find a fellow-workman when one is Prime Minister. One feels quite naturally in sympathy with him. But Bismarck judged himself the superior, as being still more detached, still more cynical. Lord Beaconsfield had his weak points; he had joints in his armour; as soon as he was assailed by certain romantic associations of ideas, he resisted poorly. Bismarck observed his vanities, delighted in opposing them, and exploited his failings. Beaconsfield, for his part, divined the distant goal of the Chancellor. They were standing in front of a large map of the world, discussing the question of colonization, to which Bismarck thought it politic to appear opposed. Beaconsfield's finger strayed over the Balkan provinces. "Don't you think," said he, "that there is a fine field for colonization here too?" Bismarck looked at him, and made no reply.

After this great day the Congress became a routine proceeding. A more exciting kind of parliamentary existence, it would have been highly pleasing to Beaconsfield if he had not had the gout. Not only was he fond

of Bismarck, but Gortchakoff also had become a friend.
"He is the most courteous gentleman, quite caressing,
and it is quite painful to me to occasion him so much
annoyance." The weather was that of the Midsummer
Night's Dream. One evening there would be an excursion
to Potsdam, the capital of the kingdom of Rococo. The
next, a dinner at the Turkish Embassy, the best of all
the dinners, with an amazing *pilaff* of which M. Waddington had two helpings. Then a dinner at Bleich-
roeder, the banker's, where nothing was played but
Wagner. In the streets everybody turned to look at Lord
Beaconsfield. The booksellers had to wire to England
for fresh copies of his novels; the circulating libraries
had bought up complete editions from Tauchnitz.

During the third week of the Congress a bombshell
exploded. The Schouvaloff agreement regarding Armenia
had been divulged by an English newspaper, the *Globe*,
to which it had been sold by a copying-clerk in the
Foreign Office. The effect on English feeling was great.
The acquisition of Cyprus was still secret, and no com-
pensation was in sight to balance the Russian conquests
in Asia. So much outcry was there in the press that the
English plenipotentiaries sought to take back their concessions. Bismarck started up incidents just for the
pleasure of settling them. To his positive, precise, and
perfectly informed mind, the solemn quarrels of these
outmoded personages seemed comical. Neither Gortchakoff nor Beaconsfield were geographers. Gortchakoff
liked, as he would say, to take a bird's-eye view of
events, that is to say, he was a phrase-maker, but in

front of a map he could not point to Batum. So Schouvaloff was terrified when his chief told him that he would
reserve for himself the question of the Asiatic frontiers,
and would treat that with Lord Beaconsfield direct.

"What?" said Lord Salisbury when Schouvaloff told
him this news; "no, no, my dear Count, Lord Beaconsfield cannot negotiate: Prince Gortchakoff has never seen
a map of Asia Minor."

A few hours later the Congress learned with delight
that perfect agreement had been reached. Prince Bismarck convoked a plenary session. Beaconsfield and
Gortchakoff were placed side by side to make exposition
of the terms of their agreement, and each produced a
map of the new frontier. But the two maps were different. Nobody ever knew what had happened. Schouvaloff claimed that Gortchakoff, having received from
the Russian General Staff the tracing of two frontiers,
the desired one, and the one marking the extreme limit
of concessions, had been careless enough to hand the
second to Lord Beaconsfield. Corry believed that the
Russian Chancellor, after the agreement, had tried to
trick the British delegation. However it may have been,
the two old men, both of them ill, began to bandy con-
tradictions so violent and ridiculous that Bismarck, in
ironic tones, proposed a suspension of the sitting for
half an hour. During this *entr'acte*, Schouvaloff, Salisbury, and Prince Hohenlohe could attempt a solution of
the question. This was done, and an understanding was
come to on an intermediary line.

Next day the English made public the agreement

regarding Cyprus. This time British opinion was enthusiastic. It was delighted by this parade-ground in the Levant, this English Mediterranean. Even abroad the altogether Disraelian boldness of this *coup* was extolled. "The traditions of England," wrote the *Journal des Débats*, "are not altogether dead; they survive in the hearts of a woman and an aged statesman."

A magnificent welcome was arranged for the return of the negotiators to London. Charing Cross Station had been decorated with the flags of all the nations of the Congress; palms and masses of geraniums adorned its platforms and approaches; garlands of roses were twined round all the pillars. An enormous crowd was waiting. When the Prime Minister stepped out of his carriage, he was greeted by the Dukes of Northumberland, Sutherland, Abercorn and Bedford, and by the Lord Mayor and Sheriffs of London. John Manners was there too, and Sir Robert Peel, the son of the great Minister. Leaning on Lord Salisbury's arm, the old man moved painfully along between a double line of peers and peeresses and members of Parliament.

On emerging from the station, the cheers were tremendous. Trafalgar Square was a carpet of faces. Hats and handkerchiefs were waved, and women threw flowers into the carriage. At Downing Street, all draped with red, Lord Beaconsfield found an immense sheaf of flowers sent by the Queen. As the cheering went on and on, he had to appear with Lord Salisbury on the balcony.

He said to the crowd: "We have brought you back, I think, Peace with Honour."

A few days later, at Osborne, kneeling before the enraptured Queen, he received from her hands the Insignia of the Order of the Garter. "High and low," she had written to him, "the whole country is delighted, except Mr. Gladstone, who is frantic."

IX

Afghans, Zulus, Floods

If Lord Beaconsfield had held a General Election on the morrow of the Congress of Berlin, he could have assured himself six more years of power. But Parliament had still two years of life; it was faithful; and the Cabinet resolved to let it die a natural death. This was showing too much trust in the favours of Destiny. A country soon tires of the glories it has wrought; it should be consulted at the hour when one is smiled upon.

A few weeks after their triumph, the distant sky grew somewhat overcast. The Russians had long been carrying on a flirtation with the Amir of Afghanistan, whose mountainous domains command the northern gateways of India. In full accord with the Amir, they had dis-

patched a mission to his capital, Kabul, a success which
roused the jealousy of Lord Lytton, the Viceroy of India.
For this post the Prime Minister had chosen the son of
his friend, Bulwer, as a man of imagination, ambition,
and strong will. Events showed that Bulwer had too
much of all these qualities. Against the advice of the
Chief, who strove hard to obtain by friendly negotiations
the withdrawal of the mission, he took it on his own
initiative to send an English mission up to Kabul. The
Amir stopped Lytton's envoys at the entry to Afghan territory, and Beaconsfield suddenly found himself forced
either to bow shamefacedly before a small barbarian
potentate, or to wage a dangerous war. He was very
much irritated: "When a viceroy or a commander-in-
chief disobey orders, they ought at least to be certain
of success." Once again Gladstone and his friends raised
the cry of an unjust war, protesting against the deliberately aggressive policy of Beaconsfield, and this time
astute observers warned the latter that the country was
echoing the cry. Would he have to disavow Lytton, and
prove the innocence of the Government at the expense
of a subordinate? It was contrary to all the Prime Minister's principles. Lytton was blamed, but upheld. General Roberts routed the Amir's troops. The opposition
vanished, as it always does in the hour of victory, and
the country recovered its confidence.

But when once the jealousy of the gods is roused,
it is not easily appeased. For some years industry had
been prosperous, but now a crisis suddenly arose.
These accidents are periodic. This one was caused by
a succession of bad harvests. But the Government, of

course, was bound to get the blame. The Opposition complained of the inertia of the Ministry. Ministers would have been hard put to it to alter the harvests or bring orders to industry. But they were Ministers and they had to do something. "You are right," wrote Lord Beaconsfield to Lady Bradford, "in supposing that the business, which now takes up so much of my time, is the general distress; but it is one most difficult to deal with. There are so many plans, so many schemes, and so many reasons why there should be neither plans nor schemes. What I fear is that the Opposition, who will stick at nothing, may take up the theme for party purposes. If we then don't support them, we shall be stigmatized as unpatriotic: if we do, they will carry all the glory." In moments of solitude, his thoughts turned to Peel and his potatoes.

In administering this immense Empire, the devil of the business was that at any moment serious annoyances might spring up in the furthest corners of the earth. Afghanistan was still smouldering when South Africa burst into flames. There, three hostile powers had long been living side by side: the English at the Cape, the Dutch Boers in the Transvaal, and the natives in Zululand. The Colonial Minister, Lord Carnarvon, who had succeeded in the federation of the rival provinces of Canada into a single Dominion, was convinced, like all men who have had a success, that his prescription was efficacious for all ills. He believed himself capable of federating the universe. With a view to the federation of

South Africa, he annexed the Transvaal. This action suppressed the favourite adversary of the Zulus, who now turned against the English. Lord Chelmsford, in command of the troops, erred through overconfidence, and suddenly there descended on a totally unprepared public opinion the news of a disaster: Lord Chelmsford's headquarters had been surrounded, and the Zulus had taken or killed nearly 1500 men. This time the country was indignant. So long as the Conservative Ministry had brought it "peace with honour," the country had applauded. But when John Bull found himself engaged in ridiculous and difficult wars in all the four corners of the globe, he began to think that Gladstone was perhaps right in his talk of the danger of the colonies and the insane policy of his rival.

To crown the catastrophe, the young Prince Imperial, son of Napoleon III., wanted to go off and fight in South Africa. Beaconsfield did all he could to prevent him, but the Queen and the Empress Eugénie were so insistent that he had to yield. "What is one to do against two obstinate women?" Early in June 1879, the Prince was killed by Zulus in an outpost skirmish. The Queen had been very fond of him and was profoundly grieved. Feeling herself in part responsible for his death, she wanted to soothe her conscience by giving the fallen Prince a solemn funeral. The Prime Minister protested. What would the Republican Government of France say if the honours due only to Sovereigns were paid to a Bonaparte? The Queen was annoyed. Ah! Everything was going wrong! Beaconsfield was annoyed, and cursed the Faery, Lord Chelmsford, and the Zulus.

"What a wonderful people!" he remarked bitterly: "they beat our generals, they convert our bishops, and they write 'finis' to a French dynasty." He tried to smile, but the Queen sulked: she received him now only with an official coldness. This pained him. "My nature demands perfect solitude, or perfect sympathy. . . ." He wrote to the Marchioness of Ely, a lady-in-waiting, a bold and sincere letter, which he knew would be shown to the Queen. "I am grieved, and greatly, that anything I should say, or do, should be displeasing to Her Majesty. I love the Queen—perhaps the only person in this world left to me that I do love; and therefore you can understand how much it worries and disquiets me, when there is a cloud between us."

A telegram bade him to Windsor. The Faery was gentle and gracious, and said no more of her grievances; she had evidently read the letter. It was not altogether useless to have been a novelist. . . . But it was true none the less—he did love the Queen.

At last, about the month of August 1879, everything seemed to be settling down. Not a single Russian trooper now remained in the dominions of the Sultan; in the East, an English mission had been received at Kabul; in South Africa, Wolseley had captured the chief of the Zulus. The sole danger for the Ministry now was bad weather, which neither Roberts nor Wolseley could vanquish. A fifth bad harvest was threatening. At Hughenden it rained, day in, day out. Beaconsfield walked out in the downpour, slipping about in thick mud, and asking his farmers whether the dove had left the Ark yet. The peacocks, almost swallowed up, had lost nearly all their plumage, and persisted in strutting vaingloriously up and down, proud of a vanished beauty.

There, suddenly, the Prime Minister received a terrible piece of news: the whole of the British mission at Kabul had been assassinated. The stars in their courses were indeed fighting against him.

Once again there was at least one man in England who did not regard these murders, these reverses, and this deluge, as inevitable troughs of the waves of time, but saw in them the chastisement sent of the Lord God of Hosts, because His people had kindled His wrath by offering up sacrifice to a strange god. In the eyes of Gladstone, Beaconsfieldism was a terrible heresy which had sullied the soul of the English people, led it to battle against all the nations of the earth, and drawn down upon that people a just retribution. And now the country was beginning to understand that it had been following a false prophet. Many signs and tokens gave grounds for hope that at the forthcoming elections it would show its regret. And would not Gladstone's duty then be to take over the helm again and 'bout ship? Countless correspondents were giving expression to the wish. A Scottish professor used to copy out maxims of Goethe for his benefit: "How may a man attain to self-knowledge? By Contemplation? Certainly not: but by Action. Try to do your Duty and you will find what you are fit for. But what is your Duty? The Demand of the Hour." Another wrote that his children called Mr. Gladstone "St. William." Yes, he had no doubt about it: his mission was to become Prime Minister once more. But how? He had declared in emphatic fashion that he was leaving the leadership of the party. He had been rash enough to say so, and repeat it, to the Queen, who without a doubt had taken careful note of it. He had left Hartington and Granville in occupation of the foremost places. How was he to turn them out in the moment of success without making fools of them? And in any case, did he really want all this? Had he not desired retirement in order to prepare for death? But already his restless and subtle mind was catching glimpses of devious yet certain paths.

To put forward his case, he had chosen a Scottish constituency, that of Midlothian; and in 1879, although no election had been proclaimed, he went there to make a tour. It was a triumphal procession. In stations where his train stopped, people came in their thousands from distant villages to have a glimpse of the Grand Old Man. On snow-covered hillsides, hosts of listeners were to be seen moving. In the towns, fifty thousand applications were received for halls that could hold only six thousand. Gladstone delivered three, four, five speeches every day. It seemed as if the continuous ribbon of his long, obscure, musical sentences unrolled ceaselessly from morning till night. The people listened entranced. He told them that the question now was not of approving this or that political measure, but of choosing between two moralities. For five years they had heard nothing but talk of the interest of the British Empire, of scientific frontiers, of new Gibraltars: and what was the result? Russia aggrandized and hostile, Europe troubled, India at war, in Africa, a broad stain of blood. And why? Because there are other things in the world than political necessities: there are moral necessities. "Remember that the sanctity of life in the hill villages of Afghanistan, among the winter snows, is as inviolable in the eye of Almighty God as can be your own."

The handsome features, the strong piercing eyes, the voice whose continued vigour seemed a miracle, the lofty and religious morality, combined to fill the Scottish villagers, godly men that they were, with an almost awe-struck admiration. It seemed as if they were hearkening to the divine Word and looking upon a Prophet.

The Midlothian campaign stirred the whole country. Gladstone's titanic speeches filled columns of the newspapers. The whole of the powerful puritan section of England followed this pilgrimage of passion. The issue seemed now and henceforth to lie between Midlothian and Machiavelli, between Gladstone and Satan. The Conservatives rallied. One of them calculated that Mr. Gladstone had already uttered eighty-five thousand eight hundred and forty words. As for the Lord of Darkness, he was in London painfully accomplishing his daily duties as Prime Minister. The fogs and frosts of December left him bent double with his troubles. All this noise Gladstone was making, this moral affectation, this impious and conceited claim to represent the Divine will was all very fatiguing to Beaconsfield. He was annoyed by the physical health of his rival, and the pitiless strength of that voice. When it was over, he wrote to one of his Ministers: "It certainly is a relief that this drenching rhetoric has at length ceased: but I have never read a word of it. *Satis eloquentiae, sapientiae parum.*"

When he himself had the opportunity of speaking, it was at the annual Lord Mayor's Banquet, where the City merchants have the right, consecrated by long tradition, of receiving, after turtle soup, the confidences of the Prime Minister. There he proudly maintained the excellence of his policy: "So long as the power and advice of England are felt in the councils of Europe, peace, I believe, will be maintained, and maintained for a long period. Without their presence, war, as has happened before, and too frequently of late, seems to me to be inevitable. I speak on this subject with confidence to the citizens of London, because I know that they are men who are not ashamed of the Empire which their ancestors created; because I know that they are not ashamed of the noblest of human sentiments, now descried by philosophers—the sentiment of patriotism; because I know they will not be beguiled into believing that in maintaining their Empire they may forfeit their liberties. One of the greatest of Romans, when asked what were his politics, replied, *Imperium et Libertas.* That would not make a bad programme for a British Ministry. It is one from which Her Majesty's advisors do not shrink."

X

The Outer World

"What is earnest is not always the truth," Beaconsfield had once written to the Queen, and willingly would he have added: "What appears to be moral is not always moral." But the Englishman is both earnest and moral, and the man who can lay a question of fact before him as a question of conscience will secure his vote, in the provinces at any rate.

The elections were no more than a duel between Beaconsfield and Gladstone. In London Beaconsfield was the more popular of the two. Not only Tories, but moderate Liberals too, declared their confidence in him and their horror of Gladstone. To the common folk of the capital he had become an institution. When he took a cab, the cabman said to him, "I know who you are, sir, and I've read all your books." He would come back from the House of Lords, leaning on the arm of his faithful Corry, his overcoat, with its astrakhan collar, floating loosely round his emaciated limbs; and slowly walking across the park, he would stop now and then for breath, the passers-by recognizing him and marvelling at the courage of this half-dead old man who still could pass his sad and kindly eyes over the scene of life. In almost all classes of society, women were for him. At a supper-party of "Gaiety girls" the question was asked, "Which would you like to marry, Gladstone or Disraeli?" All these pretty girls chose Disraeli; only one said "Gladstone," and the others booed her. "Wait a minute," she said, "I'd like to marry Gladstone and get Disraeli to run away with me, just to see Gladstone's face!" A young nobleman who was present at the supper reported the saying to Lord Beaconsfield, and congratulated him on the extent of his popularity. "You ought to be pleased," he said to him. "Yesterday I saw the Queen, who regards you as the greatest man in her kingdom, and the dancing-girls, who adore you." The immobile face lit up slightly. "Of course I am pleased," he replied. "You know my tender sentiments for all women." But when he told this story at the end of a Cabinet meeting, the Ministers were cold, and exchanged glances.

The party, on this eve of battle, found the Chief's detachment somewhat surprising. To a newly-elected young member he talked of the Wandering Jew, of Byron, whom he called his moral self, and Lady Bradford's dogs. To Lord Cromer, on his return from Egypt, he delivered a eulogy of the Jesuits, and asked him to describe the pelicans of the Nile. Even in his correspondence with the Queen he let himself drop towards art: "Lord Beaconsfield has been reading, for relaxation in the evening, some of Shakespeare's romantic plays: among them the 'Midsummer Night's Dream.' He had not read any of them for a quarter of a century. What struck him, and very strongly, was this: The whole of the plot of the 'Midsummer Night's Dream' is laid on Maynight, and all the schemes and preparations are for the ensuing morn, 'May Day'! Whence then this incongruous title? As your Majesty has much poetic taste and reading, you might, Madam, in the inspiring silence of the 'Glassalt Shiel,' muse over this, and explain the mystery."

But the Queen and the dancers were not electors. In the Scottish villages men did not hesitate an instant between the Prophet of Midlothian and the Magician of Downing Street. The first results made it clear that the Conservative defeat would be even more startling than the Liberal defeat of six years before. The country, passing at once through an agricultural and a financial crisis, was in distress; and like all invalids, it kept turning over, in the hope of feeling better on the other side.

The Conservatives were wiped out. "All our heads," wrote Mr. Gladstone, "are still in a whirl from the great events of the last fortnight, which have given joy, I am convinced, to the large majority of the civilized world." The woodman was now about to slash down all the exotic and unhealthy vegetation that had grown up in six years, spreading its deadly umbrage over the virtuous English meadows. Already he was rolling up his sleeves over his still vigorous arms.

Beaconsfield accepted defeat with equanimity. So he was going to have a little time of rest amongst his trees and his books before death should come. His sole regret was at abandoning to other hands, in a difficult hour, the conduct of Foreign Affairs, and, above all, at leaving the Queen.

The Faery was at Baden, and could not believe the news. As soon as the result of the General Election was certain, she telegraphed: "Nothing more than trouble and trial await me. I consider it a great public misfortune." Lord Beaconsfield replied that it went to his heart too to have to forego those conversations in the course of which Her Majesty had deigned to mingle domestic confidences with Imperial confidences, and which, for him, had had an inexpressible charm. She made him promise that he would not altogether desert her, that he would continue to advise her on private concerns, and even, unknown to any one, on public affairs, so that even in Opposition he might keep watch and ward over the destinies of England.

Both of them, Queen and Minister, had a somewhat disingenuous hope of avoiding Gladstone. After all, the official leaders of the Liberal party were Granville and

Hartington. It was only logical that the Queen should call upon one of the two, and preferably "Harty-Tarty," who had been perfect in Opposition. Disraeli had always liked Hartington from the day when he had seen him, a young member, yawn during his own maiden speech. But Gladstone upset these over-simple plans with inexorable humility. After an obscure, but only too enlightening, conversation with him, Granville and Hartington were brought to realize that he would oppose any Ministry of which he was not the head. And to this the Queen had to resign herself.

So here was the end of that gentle political intimacy. The farewell audience was a sad affair; the Queen presented her old friend with her statuette in bronze and a plaster-cast of her pony. Beaconsfield kissed the Queen's hand; she made him promise to write often and to come and see her. She would have liked to give him some enduring token of her gratitude, to make him at least a Duke, but he considered that in the face of his reverse at the hands of the nation, this would be a mistake. He asked only one favour: a peerage for Montagu Corry. And so the latter became Lord Rowton, an unprecedented honour for a private secretary. "There has been nothing like it," said the jealous, "since the Emperor Caligula made his horse a Consul!"

Beaconsfield kept his word and came from time to time to see the Queen. The first time that he dined at Windsor, a few weeks after quitting office, she said to him, "I feel so happy that I think what has happened is only a horrid dream." He found her animated, charming, and even pretty, and realized once again that he was very fond of her. She continued to write to him. Sometimes it was only to say a pleasant word to him: "I often think of you—indeed constantly—and rejoice to see you looking down from the *wall* after dinner." Sometimes, despite the Constitution, it was to talk to him of national affairs. Concerning these his discretion was perfect, and the Queen suffered no unpleasantness.

Throughout his whole life he had passed, in regular rhythm, from action to creation, and even now, in spite of old age, he felt the desire to create. "When I want to read a novel," he said, "I write one." Who, indeed, could have written for him the novels he loved? Once again an ambitious hero had to become Prime Minister on the last page, and mysterious and royal influences had to be able to exercise themselves in his favour. *Endymion* was the story of a young politician whose success was brought about by female friendships. In the opening pages there appeared a perfect sister, in whom was vaguely reborn the shade of poor Sa, and, from beginning to end of the book, a crew of fair conspiratresses pushed the feeble Endymion in the direction of Downing Street. The book was not without faults, but what was charming was to find in it, so strong and unspoilt, the zest of this old man for youth.

Lord Rowton shouldered the task of selling the author's rights, and got £10,000 for them. The sum allowed a new house in London to be furnished for Lord Beaconsfield, who took a lease for nine years. "It will see me out." The novel was greeted with curiosity, but had less success than *Lothair*. The publisher told Beaconsfield that he was losing money, and at once the author generously offered to annul the contract. But Longman refused, and a popular edition brought in the sum that was wanting.

Beaconsfield was seventy-seven years old. The pursuit of power had lost its attraction for him; he had no further thought of it: "I have known something of action in my life, it is a life of baffled hopes and wasted energies." If he let his spirit glean the field of memory, he could garner a rich harvest of lessons in modesty. He had seen the Whigs in a frenzy to pass a Reform Bill, the first effect of which had been to keep them out of power, and the Tories hailing as a triumph the extension of this detested Reform. He had seen Peel emancipate the Catholics after bringing Canning to ruin, Disraeli drop Protection after overturning Peel; and now he beheld Gladstone in the act of threatening Russia, after heaping maledictions upon Beaconsfield. He had seen the mob acclaim Wellington, and then boo him; acclaiming, booing, then again adoring Gladstone. He had seen the most pacific of Ministers adopt the most bellicose of politics, and the most Germanophile of Queens take delight in thwarting Bismarck. And what, in fifty years, would be the consequences of his own Berlin policy?

For his own part, he had remained astonishingly faithful to his ideas of youth, and his programme of 1880 might well have been signed by Coningsby. But whereas in Coningsby's day he believed in the almost boundless potency of an individual genius, he now recognized the

immense strength of the Outer World. Not that he was
discouraged, or discouraging either, but he was modest,
infinitely modest. Under the leafy shades of Deepdene,
Smythe and Manners and Dizzy had thought that a great
man, supported by the Church and the young nobility,
could refashion England. In old age Beaconsfield saw
in the Church first and foremost a body of jealous dignitaries, of seekers after bishoprics, of rival sects, and
if he had found amongst the young nobility friends,
he had never found there that great school of natural
leaders of the race, as he had so lovingly depicted them.
His desire had been to give to a whole nation an intellectual and romantic ideal; he had failed. And he had
failed precisely because he was an aristocrat of the
spirit, whereas the character of England is essentially
that of its middle-classes.

But the defeat was only relative. Nothing would have
been more distasteful to him than to find it interpreted
as a pathetic intellectual disaster. He had pieced together
the fragments of a great party. He had re-established
the balance between the historic forces and the forces
of transition and change. Thanks to him, England would
be able to know the healthy rhythm of alternation. His
life had not been wasted. There was only this, that more
and more he mistrusted words and sought far beneath
them for the real; and more and more did he find the
real in individuals only, and in a supreme degree in
nations, which are States so highly evolved as to attain
to individuality. Certain political philosophers claimed
that in this closing phase of his life he had become a
Whig, and the most liberal of them all. The truth was

that it was only loyalty that held him to any party. He would willingly have replied like Solon, to one who asked what is the best form of constitution: "For whom? and at what time?"

Otherwise he had lost nothing of his relish for the marvellous adventure of life. He had not ceased to believe in the efficaciousness of action, but he wanted that to be mapped and limited. It was only in designs on the grand scale that he had lost confidence. He was that "unique but pleasing phenomenon, an old romantic who is no longer duped by fanciful illusion but none the less can still delight in it, a cynic, but ardent." In certain respects his old age was even happier than his youth. "In youth everything appears grave and irremediable; in old age one knows that everything arranges itself, more or less ill." He remained inquisitive, loving to surround himself with new faces, and going to many pains to attract the young intellectuals towards the Conservative party. "A party is lost," he used to say, "if it has not a constant reinforcement of young and energetic men."

In 1881 Mr. Hyndman, one of the first English socialists, requested an interview with Lord Beaconsfield. Paradoxical as it may appear he had hopes of winning him over and obtaining through him Conservative support for certain projected industrial laws. He had read *Sybil*, and felt drawn towards the old Chief by reason of the latter's sympathy with the common people. He was received, and shown into a drawing-room with red and gold walls; and its chairs, too heavily gilt, upholstered in scarlet damask. For a moment Hyndman waited, and then the door opened and a strange figure was outlined against the light. An old man clad in a long red dressing-gown, with a red fez on his head, which drooped forward over his chest, one eye quite closed, the other only half open. From under the fez projected the gleaming, varnished curve of the last black ringlet. The impression of ruin and fatigue was such that the young man at first despaired. "Ah," he thought, "I have come too late. Shall I even manage to lift those eyelids? Will he answer me except with some weary and sarcastic epigram?"

The old man sat down and remained silent, in rigid immobility. He waited, but it is not easy to address one's words to a statue. "Lord Beaconsfield," said Hyndman shyly, "Peace with Honour was a dead formula. Peace with Comfort was what the people would have liked to hear." One eyelid rose. "Peace with Comfort is not a bad phrase." He opened both eyes and smiled.

"You have some ideas on this subject, I suppose, Mr. Hyndman? What do you mean by Comfort, eh?"

"Plenty to eat, enough to drink, good clothes, pleasant homes, a thorough education, and sufficient leisure for all."

"Utopia to order? A fine dream, yes . . . and you think you have some chance of realizing this policy? Not with the Conservative party, I assure you. The moment you wish to act, you will find yourself beset by a phalanx of great families, men and especially women, who will put you to rout every time. . . . This England, mark you, Mr. Hyndman, is a very difficult country to move . . . A country in which one must expect more disappointments than successes. . . . One can make it do this"—and Lord Beaconsfield's hands, at first pressed one against the other, were separated half an inch, very painfully, as if the old Minister, to force them apart, had had to lift a whole world—"and then this"—and he managed one more half inch, "but never this——"

And the fleshless hands of the mummy, after one last vain effort to open further apart, fell back upon his knees.

"His Favourite Flower"

Hughenden, solitude, books, memories. . . . "I have not spoken to a soul for a fortnight," he wrote to the Duchess of Rutland. He found there a deep repose. "I have not exchanged a word with a human being for three weeks, but the joys of living in the country in summer are always fresh to me. There are half a dozen peacocks now basking at full length on the lawn, motionless. They are silent as well as motionless, and that's something. In the morning they strut about, and scream, and make love or war." He too was fond of warming his old limbs in the sun and strolling in the evening under the stars, at the Shakespearean hour when the bats begin their grey and gliding dance. He continued to surround himself with flowers, from violets and primroses to the gardenia and the orchid. After flowers, his preference was for lovely faces, musical voices, and that unreal and untamed grace which children and women sometimes have. In youth he had desired life to be one long and glorious procession; and so it had been; but now, weary of the glittering file, he desired nothing more than motionless warmth. When a pressing debate had called him to the House of Lords, he took the evening train home once more. "I cannot resist the fascination of the sultry note of the cuckoo, the cooing of the wood-pigeons, and the blaze of the rosy may."

The Christmas of 1880 he spent alone at Hughenden. He brought a book to table and read for ten minutes after each course. Often it was the history of the Venetian Republic, a favourite subject for sixty years now, sometimes a classic, Lucian, Horace, Theocritus, Virgil, of whom he grew more and more fond. Opposite him in the oak-panelled dining-room was the portrait of the Queen by von Angeli. In it the Faery looked a little dry, a little hard. He went to sit down by the fire in his library, read a little more, closed his eyes, and dreamed. The cry of an owl in the old cypresses had evoked Mary Anne's drawn features, so tired, so dear. He fancied he could hear the gay chatter which she had bravely kept up to the very end. A log slipped down. The old man poked, and there was a shower of sparks: a brief, gleaming image of life. It was nearly fifty years since, in a tiny drawing-room with white muslin curtains, he had seen smiling around him those ravishing faces of the Sheridans . . . Caroline Norton . . . how lovely she had been, with her black tresses and her violet eyes. . . . She had been so to the end. "Yes, I shall be beautiful even in my coffin." In that coffin she had now been for three years, after a life of many trials. "Love," she used to say towards the end, "love in life. . . . It always reminds me of the old landlady at Brighton who used to say to me, 'You live in the house, you know, but everything else is an extra. . . .' Yes, love is an extra in life . . . and extras have to be paid for." Old ladies caught glimpses of truth. . . . The Queen herself said that the older she grew, the less she could understand the world . . . she could not understand its pettinesses. . . . The sight of all this frivolity made her think that we must all be a little mad. . . . We were all a little mad, eh? He himself, for example, had spent all his life in seeking—what? What was there that had given him true happiness? Some grateful glances of Mary Anne's, the fine friendships of Manners and Bentinck, the confidence of old Derby, and that of the Queen, and some smiles of Lady Bradford's. . . . A young secretary surprised him poking the fire, breathing with difficulty, and murmuring to himself under his breath, "Dreams . . . dreams. . . ."

He went up to his room. He had taken pleasure in decorating the hall and staircase with the portraits of all who had adorned his own life. The Gallery of Friendship, he called it. Climbing the stair, slowly and painfully, he could stop for a moment before each picture.

. . . Here were the long curls that framed Lady Bradford's tiny face. . . . Good-night, Selina, gay and lovable. . . . The dreamy eyes and heavy features of Louis Napoleon . . . Byron, whom Dizzy had not known but who nevertheless had formed Dizzy. . . . Here was Tita, with his long moustachios, like a Gaul's. . . . Lyndhurst's clear-cut features, painted by D'Orsay . . . and D'Orsay himself, with a fringe of black beard. . . . "Ha, ha, my friend!" Bradford . . . Mary Derby . . . the last step.

On the last day of December he returned to London. "I wish to see many people and to use myself to the human face divine. It is no easy thing to step out of the profound solitude in which I live—often not speaking to a human being the whole day—and walk into the House of Lords and make a speech on a falling Empire." His difficulty in speaking was the greater as he was now hardly ever free from asthma. Lord Granville, the Liberal leader, was surprised to find him, usually so patient, demanding to speak with almost violent insistence. Granville even snubbed him slightly. Beaconsfield accepted the rebuff in silence. But later Lord Rowton explained to Granville that the old invalid could now only secure the necessary respite for speaking by the use of a drug, the effect of which only lasted for an hour. "It would have been easy to explain," said Granville in embarrassment. But Lord Beaconsfield never explained.

Whenever he was a little better, he went into society.

There he charmed people by the melancholy turn of his old epigrams and the outmoded graces of his courtesy. The brevity of his phrases became as famous as had been their brilliance in his youth. To a young woman who held out a bare arm, he murmured one word only: "Canova!"

On other days he would remain silent throughout a whole meal, his body and face so completely motionless that one might have thought of a mummy, some Pharaoh embalmed by pious hands and buried among the objects he had loved, the crystal, the silver dishes, the flowers.

In spite of the electoral reverse, he maintained his prestige. At the Conservatives' club his portrait was to be seen in the place of honour, the monstrous fixity of its gaze compelling the eyes of all. On the frame was carved a line of Homer: "He alone is wise, the rest are fleeting shades." In his own heart there was no bitterness, nor any regret. Visiting the studio of Sir John Millais, he looked for a long time at a sketch of Gladstone. "Would you care to have it?" asked the painter. "I did not dare to offer it to you."—"Ah! I should be delighted to have it. Do not imagine that I have ever hated William Gladstone. No, my only difficulty with him has been that I have never been able to understand him."

That month of January, 1881 was icy. The cold plunged Lord Beaconsfield into a kind of stupor which forced him to remain for whole days stretched on a sofa. On such days a brief gleam of sunshine was far more precious to him than the collar of the Garter. He roused himself only to write to Lady Bradford and Lady Chesterfield. In February and at the beginning of March he managed to go out again a little, to speak at the House of Lords, to dine with the Prince of Wales or with Harcourt; he watched anxiously for the spring. Towards the end of March he caught a chill and had to take to his bed. His breathing was troublesome. When the Queen received letters from him painfully scrawled in pencil, she grew anxious and asked who was attending him. It was still Dr. Kidd, the homœopathist. The Queen suggested a consultation, but medical rules forebade any doctor to associate himself with a homœopathist. In the end the royal will overcame professional hatreds; the diagnosis was bronchitis, with spasmodic asthma.

At first the doctors had hopes, but the sick man said: "I shall never survive this attack. I feel it is quite impossible." In days gone by he had written that a man must go proudly up to face death. Insistently he asked to be told whether he was dying, and added: "I should prefer to live, but I am not afraid of dying." He watched his own agony with the detachment of an artist. Never had his patience been greater; it charmed all those who surrounded him. Lying stretched out there, he corrected with difficulty the proofs of his last speech: "I will not go down to posterity talking bad grammar." To the last he retained his hatred for prosaic comfort. A nurse wanted to give him support by putting an air cushion behind his back: "No, no," he murmured, "take away that emblem of mortality."

Anxiously the Queen followed the sickness of her

old friend. Several times she proposed to come and see him, but the doctors had fears that the visit would excite the patient overmuch. She wired from Windsor every day for news: "I send some Osborne primroses and I meant to pay you a little visit this week, but I thought it better you should be quite quiet and not speak. And I beg you will be very good and obey the doctors and commit no imprudence." She saw to it that the sickroom was always provided with primroses and violets. The invalid's eyes fell with pleasure on these lovely bunches with their pure tints. When Victoria was setting off for the Isle of Wight, she sent a messenger, again, with flowers, and a letter. Beaconsfield was too feeble to read this himself; he turned it over in his hands in embarrassment, reflected a moment, and said, "This letter ought to be read to me by Lord Barrington, a Privy Councillor." He had always liked traditions to be observed. The Privy Councillor was sent for: "Dearest Lord Beaconsfield, I send you a few of your favourite spring flowers. . . ." How apt it was, this blend of solemnity and pastoral poetry, to the bedside of the dying Disraeli!

In the street outside, the crowd waited for news. A gentleman had sent an offer of his blood. People could hardly bring themselves to believe that this strange wizard, who had become so curiously national, could disappear like a common mortal. The unforeseen was expected, even in death. Queer stories went the rounds. It was said that he had sent for a Jesuit confessor. But the truth was that Lord Beaconsfield "was now no more mysterious than any one else," and that he sank quietly into the final torpor. On April 19th, about two in the morning, Dr. Kidd saw that the end was drawing near. Lord Rowton was there, holding the right hand of the motionless body. Suddenly the dying man slowly straightened up his head and shoulders, throwing back the shoulders with a movement which the astonished bystanders recognized as that familiar to him when, rising in the House, he was about to speak. His lips moved. His friends leaned over him, but could catch no word. He fell back, and did not emerge again from his sleep.

Gladstone, in the name of the Government, offered a public funeral and a tomb in Westminster Abbey, but the testamentary executors considered that Lord Beaconsfield would have wished to rest at Hughenden, near to his wife, in the little graveyard beside the church. The burial accordingly took place with all simplicity, in the park, in the presence of the Prince of Wales and a few friends. On the coffin were two wreaths from the Queen: one, of fresh primroses, bore the inscription "His favourite flower"; and on the other the Queen had written in her own hand: "A token of true affection, friendship, and respect."

At that moment she was at Osborne, too far off to be able to attend the ceremony, but on her return she at once made a point of visiting the grave, following on foot the very path from the Manor down which the funeral procession had passed. In the church she caused a monument to be put up at her own expense; on it one saw, under the arms of the peer, the marble profile of Lord Beaconsfield, with the inscription underneath:

TO
THE DEAR AND HONOURED MEMORY
OF
BENJAMIN EARL OF BEACONSFIELD
THIS MEMORIAL IS PLACED BY
HIS GRATEFUL SOVEREIGN AND FRIEND
VICTORIA R. I.

"Kings love him that speaketh right."
PROVERBS, xvi. 13.

There was much discussion as to the royal inscription, "His favourite flower." Primroses ... the simplicity of such a choice was troublesome to certain over-constant adversaries. Gladstone, seated at table beside Lady Dorothy Nevill, told her that he had grave doubts of Beaconsfield's taste for these flowers: "Tell me, Lady Dorothy, on your honour now, did you ever hear Lord Beaconsfield express particular admiration for primroses? The glorious lily, I think, was much more to his taste."

But in the following year, as the anniversary of his death on April 19th drew near, many of his disciples and friends ordered "Beaconsfield buttonholes" to be prepared at the London florists, made up of a few fresh primroses. When the day came round, the pavements of the West End saw certain passersby wearing flowers. Year by year the custom spread. A great Conservative league was founded, with the title of the Primrose

League. In Parliament Square, every spring time, Disraeli's statue is visited by countless of the faithful, come to deck it with "his favourite flower."

Some years after Disraeli's death, Lord Eustace Cecil was accosted at the Carlton Club by Dr. Bell. "Do you remember," Bell asked him, "the conversations we used to have here in the library, in the days when we were indignant with our leaders and called them 'the Jew and the Jockey'? And now this very morning when I was passing up by Westminster, I saw the statue of Mr. Disraeli all covered with flowers. . . . What! They have canonized him as a saint!"

As a saint? No, Disraeli was very far from being a saint. But perhaps as some old Spirit of Spring, ever vanquished and ever alive, and as a symbol of what can be accomplished, in a cold and hostile universe, by a long youthfulness of heart.

NOTE

It did not seem advisable in this volume to indicate my references in footnotes on every page; but I give below a list of the principal works which I have made use of. I would emphasize my great debt to Mr. Buckle, whose *Life* contains most of the documents cited; to M. Elie Halévy, whose *Histoire du peuple anglais au XIXe siècle* provides so admirable an introduction to the study of English political life; to M. Gabriel Hanotaux, who helped me greatly in grasping the difficulties of the Congress of Berlin; and to Mr. Desmond MacCarthy, who put me on the track of valuable and revealing anecdotes.

I allowed myself, following the example of English historians, to regard as autobiographical the story of the schoolboy battle which figures both in *Vivian Grey* and in *Contarini Fleming*.

I have made every effort to be fair to Peel and to Gladstone, but I should advise any reader who may want a picture of the latter undistorted by the Disraelian lens to read Morley's *Life of Gladstone*, and the admirable portrait sketched by Lytton Strachey in his essay on General Gordon. He will find that critics and admirers alike, if their intentions are sincere, are at one in discovering the same traits in their subject.

BAGEHOT, W.:
Essays on Parliamentary Reform.   1883.

BARING, EVELYN (LORD CROMER):
Disraeli.   1912.

BARRY O'BRIEN, R.:
John Bright, with preface by Augustine Birrell.

BERKELEY, HON. G. C. GRANTLEY F.:
My Life and Recollections.

BRANDES, GEORG:
Beaconsfield.

BRYCE, RT. HON. JAMES:
Studies in Contemporary Biography (Macmillan).

BUCKLE, PETER:
The Eglinton Tournament.

BUCKLE, G. E., and MONYPENNY, W. F.:
Life of Disraeli.   6 vols.

BULWER, R.:
Unpublished Letters.

CAZAMIAN:
Le Roman social en Angleterre.   1903.

CLARKE, SIR EDWARD:
Benjamin Disraeli (John Murray).

CLAYDEN, P. W.:
England under Lord Beaconsfield.   1890.

CONTADES, G. DE:
Le Comte D'Orsay.   1892.

Croker Papers.   1884.

CUCHEVAL-CLARIGNY:
Lord Beaconsfield et son temps.   1879.

DEVEY, L.:
Life of Lady Lytton.   1887.

Dictionary of National Biography.

Bibliography

D'ISRAELI, ISAAC:
The Works, with a Memoir by His Son. 1858.

D'ISRAELI, ISAAC:
Commentaries. 1851.

DREW:
Catherine Gladstone (Nisbet).

Eglinton Castle (Tournament at). 1839.

ESCOTT, T. H. S.:
Edward Buller.

ESCOTT, T. H. S.:
Great Victorians. 1916.

FITZGERALD, PERCY H.:
Lives of the Sheridans.

FRANCIS, C. H.:
The Late Sir Robert Peel. 1852.

FROUDE, A.:
Life of Lord Beaconsfield.

GARNETT, R.:
Shelley and Lord Beaconsfield.

GREVILLE, C. C. F.:
Journals.

GRONOW, R. H.:
Reminiscences.

HALÉVY, ELIE:
Histoire du peuple anglais au XIXᵉ siècle.

HANOTAUX, GABRIEL:
Histoire de la France Contemporaine (le Congrès de Berlin).

HARDY, GATHORNE:
A Memoir (Longmans).

HECTOR, A. F.:
Mrs. Norton. 1897.

HYAMSON, A. M.:
History of the Jews in England. 1908.

HYNDMAN, H. M.:
The Record of an Adventurous Life.   1911.

JERROLD, WALTER B.:
A Day with Disraeli.   1872.

KEBBEL, T. E.:
Speeches of Lord Beaconsfield.   1881.

KEBBEL, T. E.:
Life of Lord Beaconsfield.   1888.

KENT, JOHN:
Racing Life of Lord George Bentinck (Blackwood).

LAKE, HENRY:
Personal Reminiscences of Lord Beaconsfield.   1891.

LEE, E.:
Wives of Prime Ministers.   1918.

LEGOUIS, E., and CAZAMIAN, L.:
Histoire de la littérature anglaise.

LOCKHART, J. G.:
Theodore Hook, a Sketch.   1875.

LYTTON, THE EARL OF:
The Life of E. Edward Bulwer, 1st Lord Lytton.

MACCARTHY, J. H.:
Sir Robert Peel (Prime Ministers of Queen Victoria).   1906.

MADDEN, R. R.:
Literary Life and Correspondence of the Countess Blessington.
1855.

MARTIN, SIR THEODORE:
Life of H. R. H. the Prince Consort.   1880.

MARTIN, SIR THEODORE:
A Life of Lord Lyndhurst.   1883.

MEYNELL, W.:
Benjamin Disraeli.   1903.

MONTEFIORE, JUDITH:
Diaries of Sir Moses Montefiore and Lady Montefiore.   1890.

Bibliography

MORLEY, LORD:
Life of W. E. Gladstone (Macmillan).

NEVILL, LADY DOROTHY:
Reminiscences (Arnold).

NEVILL, LADY DOROTHY:
Life and Letters.

NEVILL, R. H.:
The World of Fashion.

O'CONNOR, T. P.:
Life of Lord Beaconsfield.

PEEL, GEORGE:
Private Letters of Sir Robert Peel (Murray).

PERKINS, JANE G.:
The Life of Mrs Norton. 1909.

QUEEN VICTORIA:
Letters.

REYMOND, E. T.:
The Alien Patriot.

RUMBOLD, SIR HORACE:
Recollections of a Diplomatist.

SICHEL, WALTER:
Disraeli (Methuen).

SOMERVELL:
Disraeli and Gladstone.

SPEARE, MORRIS-EDMUND:
The Political Novel (Univ. of Maryland, Baltimore).

STRACHEY, LYTTON:
Queen Victoria.

STRACHEY, LYTTON:
Eminent Victorians.

TOLLEMACHE, HON. LIONEL:
Talks with Gladstone (Arnold).

TREVELYAN, SIR GEORGE:
Life and Letters of Lord Macaulay.

WEST:
A History of the Chartist Movement.

WHIBLEY, CHARLES:
Political Portraits (Macmillan).

WHIBLEY, CHARLES:
Life of John Manners. 1925.

ZANGWILL, ISRAEL:
Children of the Ghetto.

André Maurois

INDEX

Index

ABBOTSFORD, 30, 31
Abdul Medjid, Sultan of Turkey, 305, 310
Abercorn, 1st Duke of, 320
Aberdeen, 4th Earl of, 293
Adelaide, Madame, 160
Adullamites, 231
Afghanistan War, 322–323
Against Commerce ... (Isaac D'Israeli), 7
Albert, Prince Consort, 148, 180, 279, 301; death of, 226; Disraeli's letter on, to the Queen, 243–244
Alexander II, Czar, 302
Alexandretta, 309
Alhambra, 51
"All the Talents" Ministry, 218
Almack's, 73
Alroy (D'Israeli), 54
Alroy, David, 54
Amsterdam, and the Jews, 4
Andrassy, Count, 315
Angeli, Heinrich von, 343
Anglo-Russian Agreement, 309
Anson, Hon. Mrs. George, 85, 101, 266
Anti-ritualism, of Queen and Bishops, 281–282
Arbitration, 262
Armenia, 309–310, 318
Asian Mystery, 193
Athenæum Club, 124
Austen, Mrs., 37, 40, 79–80, 84, 85–86, 242
Austria, 313

BALKANS: frontiers of, 313, 315; revolts and atrocities in (1875), 292–293
Balzac, Honoré de, 90
Bank of England, 77–78
Barrington, Viscount, 348
Batum, 309, 310, 319
Baudrand, General, 159–160
Baudrand, Madame, 159
Beaconsfield, Earl of. *See* Disraeli, Benjamin (2)
"Beaconsfield buttonholes," 350
Beaconsfield, Viscountess. *See* Disraeli, Mrs. Benjamin (2)

Beatrice, Princess (Princess Henry of Battenberg), 276–277
Bedford, 9th Duke of, 320
Bee, Order of the, 276–277
Bell, Dr., 351
Bentinck, Lord George, 184–187, 191, 194–196, 198, 344
Berlin, Congress of, 308, 310, 312, 322; maps at, 319
Besika Bay, 298
Bishops: and the mob, 63; and ritualism, 281–282
Bismarck, Prince, 285, 294, 337; and Congress of Berlin, 307–308, 312–313, 314
Blackwood, Hon. Mrs. Price (later Lady Dufferin, and Countess of Gifford), 69, 70, 76, 92, 130, 344
Blessington, Countess of, 86–91, 101, 129–130, 269; death, 222
Blessington, Earl of, 86–88
Bolingbroke, Lord, 82, 145
Boroughs, 59–60
Bosnia and Herzegovina, 293, 313
Boyle, Lady Harriet, Countess D'Orsay, 88, 89
Bradenham, 41, 44, 55, 67, 85, 90, 104, 122, 142, 174, 265, 273–274
Bradford, Selina, Countess of, 265–266, 276, 294, 298, 305, 324, 333, 347
Bradford, 3rd Earl of, 266, 345
Bright, Rt. Hon. John, 153, 214, 230
Brighton, 71
British Empire, 283, 303
British Museum, 7, 8
Brummell, George, 24
Buckingham and Chandos, 2nd Duke of, 78, 149
Bulgaria: atrocities and revolt in, 293, 294, 295; treaty and Congress on, 308–310, 313, 314
Bulwer, Edward George Lytton (later 1st Lord Lytton), 44–46, 66–67, 75, 79, 82, 90,

107, 117, 124, 125, 129, 205, 269

Bulwer, Mrs. Edward Lytton, 44, 45–46, 67, 109–110, 129

Byron, Lord, 8, 24, 25, 42, 49, 52, 56, 86, 296, 332–333, 345

CAMBRIDGE graduates, as M.P.s, 154–155

Campbell, Sir John (Attorney-General), 123

Canada, 324

Canning, Rt. Hon. George, 30, 47, 171–174; and Catholic emancipation, 171–172, 337

Carathéodory Pasha, 315

Carlton Club, 97, 116, 119, 149, 351; ovations at, 234, 269

Carlyle, Thomas, 194, 273

Carnarvon, 4th Earl of, 324–325

Carrington, Earl of, 61, 72–73

Catholic emancipation, 171–172, 337

Cavagnari Mission to Kabul, assassination of, 327

Cecil, Lord Eustace, 351

Chambourcy, 222

Chandos, Marquis of, 78, 81, 107, 123, 131

Charing Cross Station, ovation at, 320–321

Charles II, and the Jews, 4

Chartists, 143–146

Chelmsford, General Lord, 325

Chesterfield, Anne, Countess of, 85, 265–267, 276, 285, 347

Chesterfield, 6th Earl of, 198

Church of England, 156, 163, 193, 250–251, 282, 338

Church of Rome, 156, 250

Chute, La, des Feuilles (Millevoye), 220

Clay, James, 51, 52, 237

Club life, 265

Clubbe, Rev. Mr., at Hughenden, 228

Cobden, Richard, 178, 179

Coblentz, 33

Cochrane, Alexander Baille, 156, 161

Cogan, Rev. Dr. Eli, and his school, 15, 107

Colburn, Henry (publisher), 37–38, 46

Coningsby, or the New Generation (Disraeli), 167, 170, 222, 247, 282, 337

Conservative Party, 94, 104, 191–192, 196, 263

Constantinople, Russian designs on, 303–304, 307

Contarini Fleming (Disraeli), 54–55

Conversation, stages of, social, 44–45

Cork, Countess of, 71–73, 242

Corn Duties, 203; repeal of, 146, 179, 186, 188–189

Corry, Montagu (later Lord Rowton), 226, 258, 260–261, 275, 284–285, 316, 319, 332, 335

Corti, Count Ludovico, 315

Country gentlemen, 78–79, 110

Crimean War, 220

Croker, John Wilson, 33–34, 151, 164–165, 181

Cromwell, Oliver, and the Jews, 4

Curiosities of Literature (Isaac D'Israeli), 7

Cyprus (Isle of Venus), acquisition of, 310, 313, 318, 319–320

DAILY NEWS, 294

Dardanelles, 303, 308

Decazes, Duc, 284

Decisive moment, Retz's maxim on, 171

Deedes, Mr., 208

Derby, Countess of, 345

Derby, 14th Earl of, 241, 235–236, 272, 290, 298–299, 301, 304. *See also* Stanley, Lord (1)

Derby, 15th Earl of. *See* Stanley, Lord (2)

Derby, 185, 192, 195–196

D'Israeli, Benjamin (1) wife, son and grandchildren, 4–7

Disraeli, Benjamin (2) (formerly D'Israeli, later Earl of

Index

Beaconsfield), parents, sister (*See also* D'Israeli, Sarah (2)), early days and education, 9–13, 15–16, 19–21; legal studies, 24–25; foreign trip, 26; speculation and debt, 27–29, 33–35, 43, 107–108, 198, 227–228; booklet by, 28; business affair concerning a newspaper, 29; failure and gloom, 34–35; first novel written and published, 35–40; travels in Italy, 40; retreat, second novel written during, 41, 46–47; on speaking in Parliament, 47–48, 290; Grand Tour, 50; and resultant novels, 55; political views, 1831, 57–58; London successes, 67–68; Parliamentary candidatures, 78; and election, 107; question of party, 94–95; quarrel with O'Connell, 97–99; maiden speech, 117–118, 126–127; marriage, 136–137, 140–142; visit to Paris, 158–160; passed over by Peel, 148–153; Young England Party and, 155–156, 161–162; trilogy of novels thereon, 167, 170; struggles with Peel, 171; friendship with Bentinck, 183–186; leadership in Commons, 191; publication of *Tancred*, 193; purchase of Hughenden, 197–199; difficulties in career, 200–204; Chancellor of Exchequer, 211–212; first budget of, 215–217; clash and political duel with Gladstone, 212–215, 246–249, 269–270, 297–298, 327, 333–335, 346; a friend and a legacy, 224–225, 227–228; Oxford degree, 226; Reform Bill of, 232–234; Prime Minister at last, 237–238;

on Darwinism and religious standpoint, 249–251; peerage accepted for Mrs. Disraeli, 254; *Lothair* published, 256–257; loss of wife, 259–261; Leader of Opposition, 267; again Prime Minister, 270; legislation by, 272; ill health, 275–276, 279, 288, 305, 332; purchase of Suez Canal shares, 284–285; Earl of Beaconsfield, 254, 290; farewell to Lower House, entry into Upper, 289–290; leadership of Lords, 290; attitude on Bulgarian atrocities, 293; and on war with Russia, 300; Garter declined, 306; Cyprus acquired, 310; at Congress of Berlin, 312–320; troubles in Afghanistan and Zululand, and agricultural troubles at home, 322–323; Garter conferred on, 321; Guildhall speech, 330; out of office, 334; last novel, 336–337; death and burial, 346–350

Dress and appearance, 20, 24, 37, 50–52, 68–69, 89, 98, 118, 119, 161–162, 191, 201–202, 219–220, 247, 257, 332, 340, 341

Female and other friendships, 36–37, 40, 67, 78, 85–86, 104, 115–116, 129–130, 222, 228, 265–266, 343–345. *See also* Bentinck, Cochrane, Manners, Smythe

Love of flowers, and flowers sent him by friends and the Queen, 67, 224–225, 246, 279–280, 320, 342–343, 348, 349–351

Relations with Queen Victoria, and letters to and from Her Majesty, 207, 236, 241, 262, 273, 274, 285, 287–288,

301–302, 304, 306–307,
325–326, 333; peerage and
Garter conferred by her,
288, 321
D'Israeli, Isaac (father), 6–8,
9–15, 19, 21, 26, 28, 50,
55–56, 63, 79, 90, 99, 104,
109, 126, 128, 142, 174, 198,
274
D'Israeli, James (brother), 50, 128
D'Israeli, Mrs. Benjamin (1)
(Sarah (1)), 5–6, 10, 14
Disraeli, Mrs. Benjamin (2),
formerly Mrs. Wyndham
Lewis, q.v. (later Vis-
countess Beaconsfield),
132–137, 140–143, 152, 174,
187, 199, 212–213, 224,
225–226, 227, 228, 229, 232,
237–238, 246, 257–259, 278,
279, 306, 343; created Viscountess Beaconsfield, 254,
288; illness, death and
grave of, 237–238, 257–259,
349; husband's lasting
grief, 259–261, 264–265,
268; husband's loyalty and
tributes, 169, 224, 254,
257–258, 265, 268; on
husband's looks, 219–220;
on his affection, 224
D'Israeli, Mrs. Isaac (mother),
7, 9, 19, 20, 50, 90
D'Israeli, Ralph (brother), 50
D'Israeli, Sarah (2) (sister), 9, 41,
43–44, 46–47, 50, 54, 56, 67,
72, 73, 82, 99, 106, 108, 110,
123–124, 126–127, 131, 133,
142, 174, 178, 212, 336;
death, 223, 238
"Dizzy," 71, 271
Domestic vote, Disraeli's bill for,
233–234
Don Juan (Byron), 24, 47, 290
D'Orsay, Count Alfred, 68, 87,
105, 110, 130, 132, 159, 222,
269, 345
Drayton, 178
Duff, Grant, 235
Dukes, and Disraeli, 274
Durham, 1st Earl of, 65, 93, 96

EASTERN question, 308
Ecce Homo, 247–248
Edward I, and the Jews, 3
Eglinton Tournament, 156, 178
Egypt, 54, 298
Election without representation,
103
Elections: bribery at, 58, 59; cost
of, 58–59, 104, 150. *See also*
Maidstone election
Eliot, Lord, M.P. (later 3rd Earl
of St. Germans), 74
Ellice, Rt. Hon. Edward, 177
Ely, Marchioness of, 326
Empress of India, title demanded
by Queen, 286
Endymion (Beaconsfield),
336–337
England: character of people in,
338, 340–341; Disraeli's
novel-trilogy of modern,
167; and the Jews, 3–6;
nobility in, 158
Eton College, 15, 119, 167
Eugénie, Empress, 226, 325
Evans (clerk), 27–28, 34, 43
Evans, Major, 109

FAERY, the, 277, 280, 326
Fairfax, Lord, and the Jews, 4
France, 6; and the Jews, 4;
revolutions and English
parties in, 62
Franchise extensions, 230;
Disraeli's bill on, 232–234
Frederick, Crown Prince, 314
Frederick's Place, Old Jewry, 24,
26, 27, 107
Free Trade policy, 146, 154, 172,
178–180, 203, 206

GALLIPOLI, 304
Germany, 308, 312–317
Gibraltar, 50–51, 310, 311
Gladstone, Mrs. W. E. (Catherine
Glynne), 137–139, 215, 237
Gladstone, Rt. Hon. William
Ewart, career of, and at-
titude toward Disraeli, 96,
119, 137–139, 153, 181, 196,
204–207, 212–218, 221–222,
231, 237, 246–249, 252–253,

Index

254–256, 259, 262–263,
269–270, 272–273, 274, 276,
278, 285, 288, 294, 297–298,
305, 321, 323, 325, 327–329,
331–335, 337, 346, 349, 350
Globe, 318
Glynne, Catherine. *See* Gladstone,
    Mrs.
Gortchakoff, Prince, 294, 303,
    308–310; at Congress of
    Berlin, 313, 315, 318–319
Graham, Sir James and Lady,
    131, 164–165
Gramont, Duchess de, 159
Granby, Marquis of, 196
Grandmothers, the, 276
Granville, 2nd Earl, 117, 296, 328,
    335, 345
Greek throne, offered to Stanley,
    226
Greenwood, Frederick, and Suez
    Canal shares, 284
Grey, Colonel (later General)
    Hon. Charles, 79–80, 82,
    252
Grosvenor Gate, Park Lane, house
    at, 106, 132, 140, 152, 206,
    211, 257, 260

Hamilton, Duchess of, 72
Harcourt, Rt. Hon. Sir William,
    289–290, 347
Hardinge, 1st Viscount, 142
Hartington, Marquis of, 328,
    334–335
Helena, Princess, of Schleswig-
    Holstein, 246
Henley, Mr., 206
Henrietta Temple (Disraeli), 86
Henry IV, and his peers, 158
Herries, Lord, 196
Holland, 6
Holy Sepulchre, 54
House of Commons, 47, 103–104,
    290
House of Lords, 47, 103, 290, 343
Hughenden Manor, 197–198, 228,
    258, 265, 268–269, 282, 306,
    326, 342
Hugo, Victor, 90
Hume, Joseph, 79
Hunt, Ward, 241

Hurrying to fame, Isaac D'Israeli
    on, 23, 42, 126
Hyndman, Henry M., interview
    with Beaconsfield, 339–341

Ignatiev, General and Mrs.,
    302–303
Income tax, introduction of, 154
India, Russian menace to, 309
Indian Mutiny, 294
Indian troops, in Mediterranean,
    309
Ireland: disestablishment of
    Church in, 248–249,
    261–262; famine in, 179;
    royal visit to, 244
Irish Church Bill, 254
Ismail Pasha, Khedive, 284

Jenner, Sir William, 279
Jersey, 5th Earl and Countess of,
    131
Jerusalem, 53
Jewish communities, London
    (17th and 18th centuries),
    4
Jewish disabilities, and Par-
    liamentary oath, 194–195
Jews: Polish and Lithuanian, 4;
    Portuguese and Spanish, in
    London, 4, 10; vicissitudes
    of, 3–4
Jingoism, 305
Josephine, Empress, 88
Journal des Débats, on British
    acquisition of Cyprus, 320
Judaism, mission of, 193

Kabul, 323, 326
Kars, 309
Kean, Edmund, 115
Kent, John (trainer), 185
Kidd, Dr. (homœopathist), 306,
    347, 349
Kitty (Bentinck's filly), 185

Lamartine family, 159
Landed gentry, 197
Lansdowne, 3rd Marquis of, on
    bribery, 59
Lara family, 4

La Rochefoucauld, François de, 43
Lawrence, Sir Thomas, 152
Leech, John, 273
Leopold I, King, 165
Lewis, Mrs. Wyndham (later Mrs. Benjamin Disraeli (2), *q.v.* and Viscountess Beaconsfield), 68, 106, 109, 130–137
Lewis, Wyndham, 115, 134
Liberalism, Liberal Ministry and Party, 143, 218, 294
Life of Charles Stuart (Isaac D'Israeli), 10
Lockhart, John Gibson, 29
London: Agreement, 308–309, 316; citizens of, 330; D'Israeli's conquest of, 66, 331–332. *See also* Jewish communities
Londonderry, Marchioness of, 131–132, 205, 225, 266, 302–303
Londonderry, 3rd Marquis of, 131–132, 205
Longley, Rt. Rev. C. T. (Archbishop of Canterbury), 245
Longmans, Messrs., 336–337
Lonsdale, Countess of, 72
Lord Mayor and Sheriffs of London, welcome by, 320
Lothair (Disraeli), 256–257, 336–337
Louis-Philippe, King, 78, 159–160, 225
Loyola, St. Ignatius, 25, 64
Lusignan, Guy de, 311
Lyndhurst, Lord (Lord Chancellor), 96, 101–102, 105, 107, 116, 131, 149, 151, 211, 223, 226, 345
Lytton, 1st Earl of (Governor-General of India), 323

Macaulay, Lord, 82, 177
Maidstone election, 105–106, 150
Malta, 51, 237, 311
Manchester, 64, 71, 165
Manners family, 261
Manners, Lord John (later 7th Duke of Rutland), 155,
156–157, 161–163, 166, 203, 274, 289, 320, 344
Manufacturers, 166, 282–283
Maples, Miss, 23, 26
Maples, Mr., 22–23
Marie-Amélie, Queen, 160
Marriage, Disraeli's views on, 46, 73–74
Mary of Cambridge, Princess (Duchess of Teck), 302
"Mary Anne." *See* Disraeli, Mrs. Benjamin (2)
Medina family, 4
Mediterranean Sea, 293, 309, 310
Mehmed Pasha, 52
Melbourne, Viscount, 65, 69, 91–93, 115, 129, 180, 197, 200, 277, 278, 306
Meredith, William, 50, 54
Metternich, Prince, 289–290
Midlothian election campaign, of Gladstone, 328
Midsummer Night's Dream, comment on, 333
Mill, John Stuart, 237
Millais, Sir John, 346
Mob, the, 62–63, 95, 305, 337
Moltke, Marshal von, 305
Montagu, Andrew, 228
Montfort, Richard de, 198
Moore, Thomas, 25
Mount of Olives, 53
Murray, John (publisher), 25, 28–31, 43, 49, 107

Napoleon I, 26, 64, 83–84, 290
Napoleon, Prince Imperial, death of, 325
Napoleon, Prince Louis (later Napoleon III), 142–143, 225–226, 325, 345
Napoleonic wars, and Tory Party, 62
Nemours, Duchesse de, 160
Nevill, Lady Dorothy, 222, 225, 273, 350
Nicholas, Grand-Duke, 303
Northumberland, 6th Duke of, 320
Norton, Hon. George, 69–70, 129
Norton, Hon. Mrs. George, 68–70,

76, 91, 101, 129, 197, 223, 344
Novels, Disraeli's sayings on, 170, 336
Novels, Disraeli's, a German "run" on, 318

O'CONNELL, Daniel, 79, 97–98, 117, 122
O'Connell, Morgan, 98–100
Odilon-Barrot family, 159
Odo, Bishop of Bayeux, 198
Oliver Twist (Dickens), 144
Opposition, the, 171–172, 323–324
Osborne, visit to, 277–278
Othello, and Turkish atrocities, 297–298
Our Life in the Highlands (Queen Victoria), 246
Outer World, power of, 337–338
Oxford, 156, 226–227

PALESTINE, 53–54
Palmerston, Viscount, 116–117, 220
Paradise Lost (Milton), 47, 290
Paris, 158–159, 180, 226
"Peace with Comfort," 340
"Peace with Honour," 321
Peel, Julia, 177
Peel, Lady, 131, 152, 177–178, 205
Peel, Sir Robert, 47, 65, 74–75, 94, 102, 116, 117, 122–123, 126, 131, 148–154, 157–159, 163–165, 171–172, 177–181, 188–189, 202–207, 213, 234, 242, 272–273, 288, 337
Peel, Sir Robert, junior, 320
Peelites, 206, 220
Pelham (Lytton-Bulwer), 44
Philip the Fair, and the Jews, 4
Pignatelli, Prince, 51
Pitt, Rt. Hon. William, 212
Plevna, siege of, 305, 307
Polignac, Marquis de, 62
Politics: in Disraeli's novels, 170. *See also Coningsby*, and *Sybil*; and fashion (1831), 65
Poor Law Bill, 144; new, 144, 146
Portland, 4th Duke of, 184
Potticany, Rev. John, 11

Powles, John Diston, 28–29, 30, 43
Primrose Day, 350
Primrose League, 350–351
Primroses: cult developed, 350–351; inscription on Queen's wreath of, 349–350; from Queen, 348
Protection, and Protectionist Party, 60, 181, 183, 188, 196, 202–203, 210, 337
Punch: cartoons and caricatures on Disraeli, 203–204, 230, 235, 247, 250, 273, 303; on Peel, 188; on Russell, 230; verses on Young England, 165
Puritans, and the Jews, 4

QUARTERLY REVIEW, 28, 33

RACHEL (actress), 205
Radical Party, and Radicalism, 78, 146, 206
Railways, 115
Reform: Bill of 1832, 77, 143, 232–233, 337; Disraeli's bill on, 232–233, 248–249; electoral, 60–63
Representative, 31
Retz, Cardinal de, 43, 64, 171
Revolution (1688), and two great parties, 61–62
Rhine River, 26
Richard Cœur de Lion, 311
Ritualism, measure against urged on Disraeli, 281–282
Roberts, F.-M. Earl, 323
Rogers, Samuel, 25
Roper, Miss, 11
Rose, Sir Philip, 238
Rothschild, Lionel de: loan for purchase of Suez Canal shares, 284–285; and Parliamentary oath, 194; and Sidonia, 168
Rothschild family, 261
Rousseau, J. J., 216–217
Rowton, Lord. *See* Corry, Montagu
Russell, Lord John, 63, 116, 145,

177, 180, 181, 190, 194, 206, 218, 230

Russia, and Eastern Question, 292–293, 301, 303, 308–310

Russian intrigues, Afghanistan, 322–323, 326

Russo-Turkish Agreement, 308–310, 318–319

Russo-Turkish War, 302–303. *See also* Congress of Berlin

Rutland, Duchess of, 342

St. Cloud, 159

St. James's Palace, 63

Salisbury, 3rd Marquis of, at Berlin Congress, 313, 319, 320

Sand, George (Madame Dudevant), 90

Schouvaloff, Count Paul, 303, 309, 312–313, 318–319

Scott, Anne, 32

Scott, Sir Walter, 29, 31–32, 296

Seymour, Lady Edward (*née* Georgina Sheridan, later Duchess of Somerset), 69–70, 76, 91–92, 156, 223, 344

Sheil, R. L., M.P., 124–125

Shelley, Percy Bysshe, 86

Sheridan, Mrs. Thomas, 69

Sheridan, Richard Brinsley, 59, 68

Sidonia, in *Coningsby*, 167–168

Smith, Rev. Sydney, 60–61

Smythe, Hon. George (later 7th Lord Strangford), 155, 156–157, 161–163, 222, 224, 269, 338

Socialist ideals, Hyndman on, 340

South African War (1879), 325

South American mines, 28, 33, 107

Spain, 50–51

Spectator, 99

Spottiswoode, Mr., 118

Staël, Madame de, 296

Stanley, Dean, 250

Stanley, Lord, (1) (later 14th Earl of Derby, *q.v.*), 77, 94, 117, 122, 131, 149, 152,

153, 179–180, 192, 196, 201, 203, 206–209, 247

Stanley, Lord (2) (later 15th Earl of Derby), 221, 226, 283

Stock Exchange, 5, 33, 43

Straw, Jack, 145

Sue, Eugène, 90, 159

Suez, 308

Suez Canal, 293

Suez Canal shares, Disraeli's purchase of, 284–285

Surplice (Derby winner), 195–196

Sutherland, 3rd Duke of, 320

Swift, Dean, 36, 132

Sybil, or the Two Nations (Disraeli), 170, 232, 282, 339; dedication of, 168–169

Sykes, Lady, 72

Syria, 53

Tait, Rt. Rev. Dr. A. C. (Archbishop of Canterbury), 245

Talleyrand, Prince de, 158–159

Tancred (Disraeli), 193–194, 311

Thiers, Louis Adolphe, 180, 223

Thompson, Colonel, 108

Times, London, 29

Tita (valet), 52, 345

Tocqueville family, 159

Torquay, 224

Tory Party, 60, 62–65, 144

Transvaal, annexation of, 324–325

Tricolour flag, shown in England, 62

Troy, 83

Tuileries, 225

Turkey, 50, 52–53, 293, 316–317

Turkish atrocities, in Bulgaria, 294, 299

Turner, Sharon, 14

Tyler, Wat, 145

Utilitarianism, 63–64

Venetia (Disraeli), 86

Venice, 4–5, 40; and the Jews, 4

Venus, Isle of. *See* Cyprus

Victoria, Crown Princess, 314

Victoria, Queen, 243–244, 277–280; accession and coronation, 105, 131; anti-

ritualism of, 281–282;
Eastern interests of,
278–279; Free Trade views
of, 180; marriage, 148,
242–243; mourning, 268;
on pettiness of life, 344;
relations with Ministers,
especially Disraeli, 115,
165, 180, 191, 206–207, 211,
212, 226, 236, 243–246, 253,
261–262, 270, 274, 277–280,
282, 301–302, 303–304, 306–
307, 321, 347–348, 349–350;
threatened abdication of,
304; title of Empress of
India assumed by, 286–287;
unpopularity of, 277; von
Angeli portrait of, 343
Villa Real family, 4
*Vindication of the English Con-
stitution* . . . (Disraeli),
103
Vivian Grey (Disraeli), 35–36,
38–40, 43, 70, 89, 107, 242,
247
Voltaire, 6, 22, 36

WADDINGTON, William, 315
Wales, Prince of (later King
Edward VII), 237, 244, 347
Wales, Princess of (later Queen
Alexandra), 237
Walpole, Spencer H., 158
War, Beaconsfield on prepared-
ness for, 309–310

Waterloo, Battle of, 62
"We authors," 246
Wellington, F.-M. 1st Duke of,
47, 62, 73, 95, 104, 131, 180,
188, 211, 305, 337; death
and funeral, 222–223
"What is life? . . . ," Smythe's
distich, 222
Whig Party, 60, 62–65, 93, 337
White's Club, 225
"Who? Who?" Ministry, 211, 218
Widows, D'Orsay on, 110
William the Conqueror, 198
William IV, death of, 105, 120
Willyams, Mrs. Brydges, 224,
227–228
Wolseley, General Sir Garnet
(later F.-M. Viscount
Wolseley), 326
Women, friends, supporters and
mistress, 37, 39, 45, 67–68,
80, 85–86, 106, 115, 129,
223–224, 227–228, 265,
343–344, 345
Workhouse, 144
Wycombe, candidatures for, 61,
78, 81–82, 107

YOUNG DUKE, THE (Disraeli),
46–47, 68, 70, 290
Young England Party, 162, 222,
276

ZULU War, 324–326

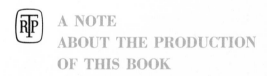

A NOTE
ABOUT THE PRODUCTION
OF THIS BOOK

The typeface for the text of this special edition of *Disraeli* is
Bodoni Book. It was set by Atlantic Linotype Co., Inc., Brooklyn,
New York, and was printed by W. R. Bean & Son, Inc., Atlanta,
Georgia. The binding was done by J. W. Clement Co., Buffalo,
New York. The cover was printed by Livermore and Knight Co.,
a division of Printing Corporation of America, in Providence,
Rhode Island.

ɪ

The paper, TIME Reading Text, is from The Mead Corporation,
Dayton, Ohio. The cover stock is from The Plastic Coating Corporation, Holyoke, Massachusetts.